THE BIRTH OF CHRIST
EXPLODING THE MYTH

P. A. H. Seymour PhD F.R.A.S.

First published in Great Britain in 1998 by
Virgin Publishing Limited
Thames Wharf Studios
Rainville Road
London W6 9HT

A catalogue record for this book is available from the British Library

ISBN 1 85227 796 3

Typeset by TW Typesetting, Plymouth, Devon

Printed and bound by Mackays of Chatham, Lordswood, Kent

CONTENTS

ACKNOWLEDGEMENTS

First I would like to thank my wife Dianna for her unstinting support and assistance, and our son Bruce for putting up with both his parents working on this project.

I first met Colin Wilson and his wife at an exhibition of work by the painter Robert Lenkiewicz. It was Colin who introduced me to Virgin Publishing, and I would like to thank him for his enthusiastic support of my ideas and for writing the foreword to this book.

Anna Cherrett of Virgin Publishing had faith in the book from the beginning, and she and Rod Green have been extremely helpful in bringing it to fruition.

I am most grateful to my former colleague, John Harvey, who very kindly translated two books about the Star of Bethlehem, by the Austrian astronomer Professor d'Occhieppo, and *Secret Messages in Paintings* by Erich von Beckerath. I would also like to thank Roderick Brown for helpful general editorial advice.

Robert Lenkiewicz gave permission for the reproduction of his painting in Plate 9, and I would like to thank Francis Reis for allowing me to use the photographs in Plates 9 and 10.

The following celestial maps were generated by SkyMap, written by Chris Marriot of 9 Severn Road, Culcheth, Cheshire WA3 5ED, and marketed by the Thompson Partnership: figures 1–5, 8, 10–12 and 17a.

The diagrams in figures 6, 7, 13a, 15, 17b and 17c were generated by Dance of the Planets, written by Thomas R. Ligon of ARC Science Simulations Software, PO Box 1955, Loveland CO 80539.

FOREWORD

In 1956, the bestseller of the year was a book called *The Bible as History* by Werner Keller. The author was a German journalist who had become fascinated by the results of recent archaeological digs in the Middle East – particularly those that seemed to confirm stories in the Bible. For example, evidence had come to light that in Ugarit the inhabitants of the land of Canaan really had worshipped a god called Baal. Other digs seemed to confirm the story of the Flood.

But the reason *The Bible as History* sold millions of copies all over the world was not because its readers were interested in archaeology. What excited them was that Keller's book pointed out that much of the Bible could be regarded as scientific fact. In the nineteenth century, a German professor named David Strauss had caused a scandal by speculating that the story of Jesus was partly mythological, and a whole new school of theologians followed his lead, some even suggesting that Jesus never existed. And now, a century later, German scholarship was declaring that many of the basic stories of the Bible were historical realities, and the response was a kind of universal sigh of relief.

The Bible as History was not only concerned with the Old Testament. A large section of the second part was entitled 'Jesus of Nazareth', and it had a chapter on the Star of Bethlehem. Keller discusses the idea that the star might, in fact, have been a comet, and the suggestion of the theologian Origen that it might have been a 'new star' – or, as we call them nowadays, a nova, or variable star. Then Keller mentions a 'star' seen by the astronomer Kepler during Christmas 1603 – in fact a 'conjunction' of Jupiter and Saturn in the constellation of Pisces. In conjunctions, Keller points out, planets sometimes move so close together that they look like a larger and more brilliant star. Could this, Kepler wondered, have been the Star of Bethlehem?

Kepler's idea failed to convince his contemporaries. But in 1925, a German scholar named Schnabel found some ancient Babylonian documents that noted the conjunction of Saturn and Jupiter in the year 7 BC. In fact, it had occurred three times – on 29 May, 3 October and 4 December.

For the Chaldeans, regarded by historians as the first astronomers (although this is disputable), Pisces was the astrological sign of the West. And for the Jews, it was the sign of Israel and of the Messiah. Moreover, Jerusalem was also linked with Pisces, for cities, like individuals, have their horoscopes, and the horoscope of Jerusalem showed it as being 'born' under Pisces. What is more likely, then, than that the Chaldean astronomers interpreted this treble event in Pisces as a sign of the birth of a Jewish Messiah, the founder of a new age, and set out for Jerusalem to pay their respects to the King of the Jews?

They no doubt expected that Herod the Great (37 BC–4 BC) would know all about it. But Herod had never heard of it. He called on his own wise men and asked them where the new Messiah might be born; they found a reference in the prophet Micah to Bethlehem as the birthplace of the ruler of Israel. And so the wise men set out for Bethlehem, able to see the 'star' (actually a conjunction) before their eyes all the time they went south.

They did not return to report to Herod. But the rumour of the birth of the new Messiah gave rise to a messianic movement in the following year, whose aim was to throw the Romans out of Palestine. This led, as everyone knows, to the great revolt in Judaea, which started in AD 66, and was ruthlessly suppressed by the Roman Emperor Vespasian, culminating in the destruction of the Temple.

So the appearance of the star of Bethlehem might be regarded, in some respects, as one of the most catastrophic events in Jewish history. Can we say, therefore, that this catastrophe was the result of an absurd superstition called astrology? After all, there is little doubt that the Three Wise Men *were* astrologers.

This is not, however, a view with which the author of this book would concur. For although Dr Percy Seymour is the Principal Lecturer in Astronomy at the University of Plymouth, and has worked at the Greenwich Observatory, his view of astrology is rather more flexible and interesting.

Let me say at once that I regard Percy Seymour as one of the boldest and most exciting scientific thinkers of our time. He is one of a small group of pioneers who have created a revolution, and which includes Michel Gauquelin, David Bohm, Frijhof Capra and Rupert Sheldrake. Yet although perhaps the least known, he is, in many ways, the most accessible of this group, and I regard one of his books, *The Paranormal*, as a masterpiece.

We might conveniently begin this story of the recent scientific revolution with the year 1979, when the eminent physicist John Wheeler, at a meeting of the American Association for the Advancement of Science, was met with a roar of approval when he demanded that the 'pseudos' should be driven out of the workshop of science. By 'pseudos' he meant all scientists engaged in the field of paranormal research – telepathy, precognition, out-of-the-body experience, and so on.

As far as Wheeler was concerned, this avalanche of obscurantism and superstition had started when Professor J. B. Rhine became director of the Parapsychology Laboratory at Duke University in 1935 (in fact, Rhine was to die in the year after Wheeler uttered his solemn curse on 'pseudos'). And as recently as 1975, the ranks of the dissenters had been swelled by the addition of the research physicist Fritjof Capra, whose immensely influential book *The Tao of Physics* had pointed out basic similarities between the world-picture of quantum physics and the mystical traditions of Hinduism, Taoism and Zen. Capra described later how he had experienced a kind of vision in which he saw the endless movement of universal energies as the dance of the Hindu goddess Shiva.

Another of Wheeler's *bêtes noires* was a statistician named Michel Gauquelin, who had set out in 1950 with an aim that Wheeler would have regarded as wholly laudable: to discredit astrology. He took the figures of a German astrologer named Krafft, who had tried to prove astrology by studying thousands of birthcharts of famous men, and put them through his computer; the result revealed that Krafft's statistics were little more than wishful thinking.

Flushed with success, Gauquelin tested some other basic assumptions of astrology, such as that a newborn baby is influenced by the planet that is rising over the horizon at the moment of birth, and that doctors tend to be born under Mars, actors under Jupiter, scientists under Saturn, and so on. But this time he met with a check. The statistics were overwhelmingly in favour of the truth of astrology. His results were repeated in four European countries. And when another well-known sceptic, the psychologist Professor Hans Eysenck, was asked to check the results, he was amazed to find that they seemed to be accurate. Eysenck was honest enough to write a book admitting this embarrassing result.

This was one reason why Wheeler uttered his battle cry in 1979; he felt that science was about to be engulfed by what Freud called 'the black tide of occultism'. In fact, the rebels were a very long way from winning, and a recently formed group called CSICOP – the Committee for the Scientific Investigation of Claims of the Paranormal – was baying for their blood. This committee actually had no intention of investigating claims of the paranormal; most of the time, they confined their activities to declaring vociferously and dogmatically that pure logic proved it to be an absurd superstition.

But in 1981, two books would reveal that the sceptics were far from getting it all their own way. One was called *A New Science of Life* by Rupert Sheldrake, which challenged the rigid Darwinian view of evolution that was being popularised by advocates like Stephen Jay Gould and Richard Dawkins, and suggested that heredity can be influenced by a factor Sheldrake called 'morphic resonance', which acts like a form of telepathy. The other was a physicist named David Bohm, who had been a close associate of Einstein. In *Wholeness and the Implicate Order*, Bohm suggested that our universe does not consist simply of a material reality spread out in space and time, but that it is a projection from some deeper, underlying reality. He used the parallel of a hologram – an image that appears in space, looking like a solid object, when a beam of laser light is shone through a photographic plate containing the holographic image. Our universe, Bohm implied, might be simply a hologram, while the 'reality' is more like the photographic plate. Bohm's critics suggested that he was simply trying to smuggle in religion by the back door, while a review of Sheldrake in *Nature* stated that, while the reviewer did not believe in book burning, perhaps an exception should be made in the present case.

Now in 1981, Percy Seymour still regarded himself as an orthodox astronomer; his speciality was magnetic fields, and some of his best-known work concerned the magnetic field of the Milky Way. He was also an educationalist, one of whose main concerns was to introduce more astronomy into the school curriculum.

He found himself working on a committee with the eminent astronomer Archie Roy, the Professor of Astronomy at Glasgow University, and the two became close friends. But there was one respect in which Archie Roy differed from any other astronomer Seymour had ever met. He was an active member of the Society for Psychical Research, and was interested in such bizarre matters as precognition, telepathy, apparitions and reincarnation. Like most scientists, Seymour was inclined to dismiss them as fantasy – or at least, as some kind of illusion of the mystically inclined. But Archie Roy was not in the least mystically inclined; he was a hard-headed, pragmatical Scot. And he nevertheless had no doubt whatever of the reality of the paranormal.

I should perhaps add here that I am also a friend of Archie Roy, and have even written an introduction to his remarkable book *The Archives of the Mind*. I came to share Archie's belief in the reality of the paranormal in the late 1960s, when I was asked to write a book about 'the occult'. I accepted the commission because I needed the money, but was half-convinced that it would all turn out to be nonsense and wishful thinking. As soon as I began to study the subject, I realised it was neither. Scientists have a perfect right to ignore the paranormal, because it seems quite irrelevant to the study of physics and cosmology. But they have no right whatever to dismiss it as moonshine. This attitude springs out of dogmatism and intellectual laziness, a failure to realise the immense mass of overwhelmingly convincing data.

Now Percy Seymour differed from most scientists in that he had a deep distrust of prejudice. He had been brought up in South Africa, the country that has finally had to be 'dragged kicking and screaming into the twentieth century'. He knew enough about ingrained prejudice to detest it, so he was perfectly willing to keep an open mind about what Archie Roy had to say.

In due course, Seymour met Michel Gauquelin, and once again listened with his customary open-mindedness. Now Archie Roy would have no truck with astrology, which seemed to him a pseudo-science. But when Percy Seymour read Gauquelin, then Eysenck, he recognised that his own discipline – the study of magnetism – seemed to suggest just how such phenomena as 'the Mars effect' might operate.

He expressed this in a book called *Astrology: The Evidence of Science*, which appeared in 1990. But his most comprehensive – and for me his most exciting – book is *The Paranormal: Beyond*

Sensory Science (1992). I would suggest that it is as important as *The Tao of Physics*, *A New Science of Life* or *Wholeness and the Implicate Order*.

He begins with a simple but brilliant account of modern physics, including the theory of relativity, quantum theory, and the latest speculations about quarks and superstrings. He also attaches particular importance to what has become known as Bell's Inequality Theorem. John Bell demonstrated that if two particles (such as photons) collide then fly apart at the speed of light, they can still influence one another; if one changes direction, so does the other – in spite of Einstein's assertion that the speed of light cannot be exceeded, and that communication should therefore be impossible. Bell's theorem has since been demonstrated in the laboratory and it seems to show that there is a sense in which all parts of the universe are connected. Separateness – as Bohm also thought – is a kind of illusion.

After explaining quark theory, superstring theory and the more recent bootstrap theory, Seymour suggests his own theory of elementary particles and their interaction – the plasma space theory. A plasma is a hot gas whose atoms have had the outer electrons stripped off through collisions. They are known as ions. The ions and the freed electrons react to magnetic fields – they will 'thread' along the lines of force like beads on a string. What Seymour is suggesting, is that in addition to 'ordinary space' there is another kind – 'plasma space', which is threaded with lines of force. Seymour believes the universe can only be understood in terms of what he calls cosmic magnetic fields.

In 1989, Seymour saw the Northern Lights near Plymouth. It is unusual to see them this far south, but he realised that the explanation was that three or more planets were in line with the sun, changing the direction of the 'solar wind' (made of plasma) which causes the Aurora Borealis.

It was this, and his theory of 'plasma space', that gave rise to the thought that the astrological observations of Gauquelin may be explained in terms of lines of magnetic force. And when these lines of force are 'plucked' by an encounter with another force, they vibrate – or resonate – like a plucked violin string. We could think of the solar system as a kind of cat's cradle of lines of force between the planets, all resonating like strings, which in turn produce an effect on the magnetic field of the earth. And Seymour suggests that newborn babies are suddenly subjected to this 'symphony' as they emerge from the womb, and that the 'tune' we hear affects us for the rest of our lives.

The Paranormal goes on to explore even more controversial aspects of his plasma space theory. He discusses the strange evidence that has accumulated from recent cases of twins. The 'Jim twins' from Ohio were separated at birth and met for the first time 39 years later. Both had been named Jim by their adoptive parents; both had dogs called Troy; both had worked as filling station attendants, then for the same hamburger chain; both had been married twice, first to girls called Linda, then to girls called Betty, and both drove Chevrolets and took their holidays at the same time of year on the same stretch of beach in Florida.

Several other pairs of twins had died at the same moment; when a girl called Peg was killed in a car crash, the steering column penetrating her chest, her twin Helen woke up with an agonising pain in her chest, and died on her way to hospital.

In Seymour's theory, the twins remain 'connected' – like Bell's particles – and the various 'coincidences' are due to this connection.

Seymour goes on to discuss telepathy, ghosts, doppelgangers ('psychic doubles') and precognition, and shows how all can be fitted neatly into his theory; regrettably, this Foreword is already becoming overlong, and there is no space to discuss all this. But it can be seen why I regard Percy Seymour as one of the most exciting minds in modern science. And also why, in my opinion, *The Birth of Christ* makes the ideal introduction to his ideas.

Colin Wilson

INTRODUCTION

A myth is, of course, not a fairy story.
It is the presentation of facts belonging to one category
in the idioms appropriate to another. To explode a
myth is accordingly not to deny the facts but to
re-allocate them.
(Gilbert Ryle, *Concept of Mind*)

I was born and raised on the African Veldt. My home town, Kimberley, was not a large place then, and views of the night sky were unhampered by the bright glow of city lights. My grandfather would tell me rambling stories about his life, and about the stars and planets, and I therefore grew up with an understanding of their movements. But not only that. South Africa is and was a multicultural society, and I also absorbed the myths and legends of the Bushmen, the Zulu, the Afrikaners and the other populations dwelling on the Veldt. I understood from an early age that the heavens were beautiful and inspiring, and also that they played a large part in people's feelings about the world and their place in it.

There is nothing to match the awesome vastness, stillness and beauty of a clear, moonless sky out in the country, away from city lights. Not everyone is lucky enough to see the full splendour of this, and many people therefore never really understand how deeply important celestial events have been to civilisations through the ages. However, we can go some way to recognising the feelings of splendour and awe created in the minds of those who do live closer to nature and who experience the reality of the night sky throughout the seasons.

The ability of a planetarium projector to simulate the night sky on the inner white surface of its dome can capture some of the feelings associated with the vision of stars and planets as seen on a clear night. From the outside the 26-feet-diameter dome of the William Day Planetarium at Plymouth University seems

1

unimpresssive, but once inside, as the lights are slowly dimmed and the stars begin to appear, the surface of the dome seems to dissolve and the stars look as if they are at very great distances from earth. As one of my adult visitors – a Dr Who fan – said, there is a TARDIS effect between the seemingly small outside size and the apparent vastness of the night sky inside. Also, like the TARDIS, the planetarium can go backward or forward in time, and the sky can be viewed from earth's surface from any position we please.

These facilities were what made the planetarium so useful to me in reconstructing the sky over Bethlehem about 2000 years ago. In December 1984 I used the William Day Planetarium to reconstruct the night sky over Bethlehem round about the time of the birth of Christ. As an astronomer I wanted to use the planetarium facilities to study the sky as seen from that region around that period to check out a suggestion that the real year of Christ's birth was 7 BC, and, more specifically, 15 September 7 BC.

Ever since the beginnings of the Christian Church 2000 years ago, there has been much debate about the Nativity, especially the Wise Men and their following of a star. Over the years many people have found difficulty with the notion that the 'Star' of Bethlehem was simply a miraculous occurrence, unconnected with normal celestial events and inexplicable in physical terms. For example, in December 1993, the Bishop of Durham questioned the whole Nativity story, including the Star of Bethlehem and the Wise Men. His comments invoked a storm of controversy and a supportive response from Ian Brady, lecturer in Church history at Aberdeen University:

> Once again the Bishop of Durham has managed to outrage traditionalist church members, and especially Conservative MPs, with remarks that will strike most theologians and biblical scholars as unexceptional and over-cautious.
>
> The sad fact is that most of the Christmas story is presented to us in carols, cards and Nativity plays has no foundation either in the Bible or in history.

Thus even today, with the benefit of modern education and improved scholarship, it is not easy for members of the Church to question established ideas.

However, churchmen and laypeople alike have come up with suggested birth dates for Christ and a variety of different ideas about what the Star of Bethlehem might actually have been.

So why should I consider the particular date of 15 September 7 BC to be so special? Because, quite simply, the night sky above Bethlehem on this date was unique in the history of the human race. It presented a planetary situation which could not fail to be of spectacular significance for a certain group of people: the astrologers of Jesus' time. The Magi were such astrologers and were among the most learned men of their day. For them, the celestial events of 7 BC heralded nothing less than the coming of a very special messiah.

I already knew of David Hughes' work, *The Star of Bethlehem Mystery*, a well-researched, academic study using the previous work of another astronomer, Professor K. F. d'Occhieppo. Hughes suggested that the Star was not one of the normal kind that fills the night sky – that was obvious anyway, since no star is close enough to earth to act as a guide to Bethlehem – but an unusual astronomical event, namely, the triple conjunction of Jupiter and Saturn during 7 BC. I knew from my studies of astrology that this series of events was of extraordinary significance from an astrological point of view, and therefore, in the context of the Magi's predictions and journey, much more convincing as a candidate for the Star than other celestial occurrences in or around that period.

I therefore wrote an article for a local paper, in which I explained the planetarium demonstration, supporting the date of 15 September 7 BC as the day on which Christ was born. Suddenly, and to my complete astonishment, this demonstration became world news. An item about it appeared on the front page of *The Times* on 16 December 1984, and then in many other newspapers. For the rest of that week I played host to reporters and television camera crews and gave telephone interviews to radio stations all over the world, from Canada to Australia, from the States to Singapore.

I am not the first person to claim a specific date for the birth of Christ, so why did my demonstration attract so much interest? In the first place, I actively supported a very specific set of circumstances and a very precise date. As I said, this idea that the Star of Bethlehem might refer to a specific set of circumstances in the night sky on that particular date was not new. The idea had been proposed by d'Occhieppo and was later developed by Hughes. But these astronomers confined themselves to a fairly scholastic presentation of the possibilities. It was in part my more accessible, visual demonstration of the most likely set of astronomical events that the Bible called 'the Star' which captured the imagination of the media. In particular we could see the projected images of Jupiter and Saturn rising in the constellation of Pisces, just as the sun was setting in Virgo.

I emphasised the importance of recognising the astrological interpretation of biblical references to the Star. As will be seen, these constellations and the planetary positions have enormous symbolic significance in relating to a Christian redeemer figure, symbolised by the Fish and called the Son of the Virgin. It would of course have to have been a rare and unusual event which would have held enough significance for the Magi-astrologers to cause them to set out on their journey to seek the new King of the Jews, the Messiah.

Yet acknowledgement of the necessary astrological significance of any 'signs' by which the Magi would predict events had been missed or ignored by most experts who were not well-versed in ancient traditions of cosmically based learning and religion. The proposal that the Star should be seen in astrological terms is not at all new. The great sixteenth-century astronomer, Johannes Kepler, who was also very interested in astrology, was one of the first to identify the triple conjunction of Jupiter and Saturn in 7 BC as a most likely candidate for the event which led the Magi first to Jerusalem and then on to Bethlehem. D'Occhieppo and Hughes also realised that it was necessary to give an astrological interpretation of the Star. But, although they acknowledged the cultural influence of astrology in ancient times, they, like others, believed there was no possible scientific basis to astrology.

However, I had formulated a theory which could account scientifically for certain tenets of astrology. This was the third reason why local journalists were interested. They knew I was working on a theory which could explain certain limited but important aspects of astrology. The theory gives scientific underpinning to the specific claim that Jesus Christ was born on 15 September 7 BC, and also to the claim that the Magi's astrological interpretation of astronomical events would have led them to predict this occurrence. The rising of Jupiter above the horizon was seen by the astrologers of the Magi's time as an indication of the birth of a king.

What made the sky unique on 15 September 7 BC was that in this year Jupiter was in conjunction with Saturn on three separate occasions. This is called a 'triple conjunction' and would have been considered of the highest significance to the Magi-astrologers. Yet that particular triple conjunction was of even greater significance in foretelling the birth of Christ, as we shall discover.

All this was twelve years ago, so why is there a need for a book about it now? For one thing, we are approaching the millennium which, amongst other things, is a celebration of 2000 years of Christianity. Our modern Western calendar uses the birth of Christ as the basis of our dating system (broadly speaking, although it was modified from older systems). Also, as I have already mentioned, there is perennial interest in the story of the Magi's journey in which they 'followed' the Star of Bethlehem, and since the beginnings of the Christian Church it has been debated and discussed intensely. People therefore continue to be interested in exactly what the Star was. Every year new or recycled theories appear in the press

In December 1987, for example, *The Times* carried a report based on an article by Dr Richard Stephenson, which had appeared in *Physics Bulletin*. Stephenson suggested that the Star was a supernova explosion, since two such supernovae had been recorded by Chinese astronomers in 4 BC and 5 BC. I wrote to *The Times* stating my objections, but my letter was not published. However, an expanded version of the letter was published a few months later in *Physics Bulletin*.

On 24 November 1996 *The Sunday Times* carried the story 'Wise men of the West find the Star of Bethlehem', which claimed that NASA scientists had used a new computer and improved software to show that the 'Jupiter–Venus conjunction of 17 June 2 BC was even closer than previously thought. This theory had been proposed by Roger Sinnott in December 1986, and in my book *Astrology: The Evidence of Science*, I have dealt with the main objections to this theory. The closeness of the conjunction is really totally irrelevant to its astrological associations.

In December 1997 newspapers reported a claim by Professor Barratta of Rome Observatory that Christ was born in 12 BC and that the Star of Bethlehem was Halley's comet, known to have been seen in that year. A similar claim had been made in 1985, and as long ago as the fourteenth century this idea had been incorporated by Giotto in his *Adoration of the Magi*.

One newer theory to emerge in recent years claims that the Star was an occultation of Jupiter by the moon, i.e. Jupiter was hidden for a short time as the moon passed in front of it. An article about this by Molnar appeared in the June 1995 issue of *The Quarterly Journal Of The Royal Astronomical Society*.

Objections to all these theories are dealt with in this book. Here I just want to mention two main problems about people's interpretations of what the Star of Bethlehem really was. Firstly, these ideas, and other theories mentioned later, do not take proper account of world-views, or cosmologies, which formed people's thinking around the time of Christ's birth. Yet it is absolutely essential to do this if we genuinely wish to understand the ideas within the context of their time. We must recognise how people saw themselves in relation to the cosmos.

Secondly, although some scholars who propose these theories do recognise that contemporary interpretations would inevitably be couched in astrological terms, they often do not themselves understand the use of astrology as it was practised by the Magi at that time.

Therefore, many of these theories fail to convince. They also leave unexplained why, for example, Pisces is a Christian symbol, or why the Magi went to Jerusalem and then to Bethlehem, or why people believed that Jesus was born the son of a virgin.

Most scientists, and astronomers in particular, accept without question that astrology was merely a body of pure superstition in the ancient world and that it has no basis whatsoever in science. In 1985 I first challenged this view publicly and started to work on the theory mentioned above which could explain certain scientific evidence relevant to some limited claims of astrologers. Over the last twelve years I have developed an improved mathematical framework for this theory.

I read a paper at the First International Conference on Geo-cosmic Relations, held in Amsterdam in April 1989. With the help of research students, I have since continued to work on the finer details. At the 1991 meeting of The British Association for the Advancement of Science we read a second paper, and a further paper appeared in May 1992 in *Vistas in Astronomy*, reprinted in *Cycles* in November 1992. Since then we have taken the theory even further. Although this is highly technical work, it has relevance to certain claims of astrology.

The theory uses evidence for interactions between tides of planets and the moon and the magnetic fields of the sun and earth.

But it also brings in biological evidence which establishes the influence of earth's own magnetic field, and its fluctuations, on a wide variety of living organisms, from bacteria to humans. Furthermore, it provides a causal basis for understanding the work of the French statistician and psychologist, Michel Gauquelin. He found statistical evidence for the astrological claim that great leaders have tended to be born with Jupiter just about to rise above the horizon, or at its highest point in the sky, at the moment of birth. Thus there is scientific underpinning for the ancient belief, held by the Magi, that Jupiter's position in the sky is of significance for the birth of kings.

A very special year

But why was the Star so significant for the Magi? Why should they depart from their own country and travel in search of the new King of the Jews? Whatever the identity of the Star referred to in the Bible, its significance was realised only by those learned enough to understand the meanings of the signs in the sky. Any such signs were certainly missed by Herod's advisors, and it was only after the arrival of the Magi that 'When Herod the king had heard these things, he was troubled and all Jerusalem with him.' (Matthew 2:3)

According to ancient astrology, the rising of Jupiter was seen as indicating the birth of a king or leader of people. Saturn, on the other hand, was considered to be the protector of the Jews, because it was supposed to rule over the first hour of Saturday (Saturn's Day) which is the Jewish sabbath. When two planets come together in the same part of the sky we say they are in conjunction. Just as cars drive along specific lanes of a motorway, so planets move in specific paths against the background of stars. Their paths seldom cross, but when one planet seems to 'overtake' another they are said to be in conjuction just as they draw level with one another.

Jupiter and Saturn are in conjunction every twenty years, so this, in itself, is not particularly unusual. However, in 7 BC the conjunction occurred three times. Such a conjunction is called a 'triple conjunction', and for these two planets it happens only once every 139 years. In 7 BC this was the very first time in recorded history that the triple conjunction had taken place in the constellation of Pisces, the Fishes, and ancient astrologers believed that the area around Jerusalem and Bethlehem was geographically under the influence of Pisces. Such a triple conjunction in Pisces takes place only once every 900 years. However, even more importantly, at this stage in history Pisces was in a particularly important phase in relation to the position of the sun.

We are talking about what astronomers call 'precession of the equinoxes'. The concept of precession is more fully explained further on, but to put it briefly in this context: the earth's axis wobbles slightly, which means that, over thousands of years, the sun has changed its position on the first day of spring (vernal equinox) against the background stars which formed the zodiac of astrology, and approximately every 2000 years it moves into a different constellation. Shortly before Christ's birth, the sun at the vernal equinox had moved into the constellation of Pisces. The astronomical period which began just around the time of Christ's birth is called the Age of Pisces. (In our own time the sun at the vernal equinox is moving into the constellation of Aquarius, hence the 'dawning of the Age of Aquarius'.)

According to some historians of science, precession was only discovered in the second century BC, and for them it is therefore impossible that the Magi should have regarded precession of the equinoxes as important. However, it is now generally accepted that the ancient Egyptians were not only aware of this precession about 4000 years before the birth of Christ, but that they also incorporated it into their religion. It is also clear that the systematic astrology of the Greeks and Romans was very different, indeed more comprehensive, than the earlier star-lore system of omens, which was much more widespread, and which did not appear to embrace a knowledge of precession. The Magi were among the most learned men of their age and would have been aware of Greek and Egyptian knowledge.

Since precession of the equinoxes from one constellation to another occurs over a timespan of about 2000 years, ancient sky watchers could not observe such a phenomenon, except over generations. But if knowledge of precession was handed down from ancient times – and there seems plenty of evidence that it was known about by the older civilisations – the Magi would certainly have been aware of it. Remember that, at the time of Christ's birth, astrology and all ancient learning were the means by which wise men made sense of their world.

This point about precession is important because it gives added significance to the sort of messiah whom the Wise Men were seeking. Later on we will look very briefly at the idea of the Great Year – that is, the time it takes the earth's axis to complete one single 'wobble', which is about 26,000 years at a rate of about 2000 years for each age. Before Christ, there had been the Age of Aries for approximately 2000 years, and before that the Age of Taurus. Today, roughly 2000 years after Christ's birth, we are entering the Age of Aquarius. Joseph Campbell has discussed the Great Year in his series *The Masks of God*, as have other writers interested in the foundations of Christianity.

If, for the purposes of our particular questions about the Star of Bethlehem, we accept that the Magi knew about the Great Year and the coming new Age of Pisces, and if, in common with the messianic expectations of the time, they therefore sought a messiah who would represent the new Piscean age, then the triple conjunction of 7 BC would be important, not only because of its astrological meanings and its particular significance for Judea and Bethlehem, but also because of the position of the sun at the vernal equinox in Pisces. Thus the Magi's search for the Messiah is put into the context of the age in which they lived. They were more than mere astrologers, though astrology was of high importance in their work. They also represented, and contributed to, the development of the religious ideas of their time. They foretold the coming of a new kind of messiah for a new age. This was none other than Jesus Christ, who became the foundation of a new religion, Christianity, whose (once secret) sign and symbol is the Fish.

Christianity began with, and has been, the religion of the Piscean age. The Magi could not 'know' this in advance, in any scientific sense of the word. They could, however, in terms of their own religious beliefs and ancient learning, anticipate what was coming, and they could use their learning and their art to make their journey to Bethlehem to find the new Saviour.

The triple conjunction of 7 BC was the first one to occur in Pisces, when the point of the vernal equinox was also in Pisces. All these circumstances taken together indicated, to the Magi, that a king of Jewish origin would be born in Bethlehem at the very beginning of the Age of Pisces.

Another advance that has taken place recently has been the ability to generate maps of the skies on the screen of an ordinary computer. These maps can show the skies as seen from any point on the earth's surface, at times ranging from 5000 BC to AD 4000.

Although these maps lack the three-dimensional impact of the planetarium sky, they can be used to check out details of the skies seen over Bethlehem 2000 years ago. It is also possible to print out these maps so that they can be reproduced in a book. Some of the diagrams in this book have been produced in this way.

A model of reality

Our perceptions of the world about us, and our relationships with it, are extremely complex. We are constantly bombarded with a vast amount of sensory information, which could be completely overwhelming. Nevertheless, we are able to live and work and have our being within this enormous field of information. Human beings have the capacity to rationalise the relatively small amount of information which is 'allowed' to filter through our senses in a way that is particularly useful at any given moment or in any given situation.

We therefore make a 'model' of reality. The model may seem extremely powerful and useful; it may seem to express exactly what we see and what we 'understand'. However, our understanding is not, and never could be, a complete understanding, a full picture of the world beyond our senses. Regardless of how much we feel we have understood a physical situation, a chemical process or another person, what we are using to formulate that understanding is some kind of model.

Models may be of many different kinds: a planetarium or a computer program is one kind of model; scientists construct more abstract, mathematical models to explain natural phenomena or the structure of the universe; artists and writers use yet another kind of model, such as a metaphor, to convey to us a stronger sense of their understanding of the world. Religious movements may use a model like that of the scientist, or a metaphor like that of the artist, or they may use the practice of myth-making which is as old as humanity and a very rich way of expressing the feelings and comprehensions which humans have about their surroundings. Mythologising may express feelings about every-thing: the spirit within the smoke from the home fire; the life energies in the trees, birds and animals; or the gods who inhabit the starry realms.

In the ancient world people made extensive use of myths to help them survive in a universe that must have seemed every bit as strange to them as it may do to us today. The practice of science

over the centuries has gradually replaced mythological explanation by very precise, self-consistent models. This has been an
astonishing development of human thought, and has given us
levels of understanding about our environment and the universe
as a whole which have changed the meaning of what it is to be
human. Yet, if we look honestly at the progress of human
knowledge and human development, we must admit that our
scientific understanding and technical explanations rest upon
notions which really are not very different from the myths used
by the ancients to explain our cosmos. This point was well made
by Giorgio de Santillana in the preface to *Hamlet's Mill*:

> If we come to think of it, we have been living in the age of
> Astronomical Myth until yesterday ... And shall we deny that
> Einstein's space–time is nothing more that a pure pan-
> mathematical myth, openly acknowledged at last as such.

An equally respected historian of science, Thomas S. Kuhn, said:

> If these out-of-date beliefs are to be called myths, then myths can
> be produced by the same sorts of methods and held for the same
> sorts of reason that now lead to scientific knowledge. If, on the
> other hand, they are to be called science, then science has included
> bodies of belief quite incompatible with the ones we hold to ...
> Out-of-date theories are not in principle unscientific because they
> have been discarded.

Today, we find ourselves at a point where we need to reassess the
very meaning of scientific explanation, to open our minds to the
possibility that other ways of expressing human truth may have
validity and usefulness, even for science and mathematics. And we
might have to acknowledge that the most rigorously formulated
scientific model may rest upon notions which originate with other
human disciplines, such as astrology.

CHAPTER

ONE

LIGHTS IN THE HEAVENS

*God said, 'Let there be lights in the vault of heaven to
separate day from night, and let them serve as signs
both for festivals and for seasons and years. Let them
also shine in the vault of heaven to give light on earth.'*
(Genesis, New English Bible)

For many people, ancient Egypt holds the key to all mysteries,
and, in terms of astronomy, its influence is felt to this day. The
civilisation of ancient Egypt was highly complex and, to modern
eyes, mysterious. We do, however, know that we inherited our
24-hour day/night period from this ancient civilisation.

The timekeeping and calendar systems of the ancient
Babylonian and Egyptian civilisations are of great importance to
our investigation into the story which surrounds the birth of
Christ. Many features of these systems were incorporated into the
Christian calendar and consequently affect certain statements
made about Christ's birth. These methods of timekeeping also
played an important role in the Magi's search for the new
Messiah. But, before we can look into exactly what the ancients
knew and how this knowledge contributed to the work of the
Magi, it is important to have a grasp of some basic astronomical
features.

Plate 1 shows a picture of the solar system as it is known today.
As will become clear, the Magi had a very different view of the
universe.

The Milky Way

Look upward on a very clear night somewhere far away from the
city lights, and you will see a beautiful, hazy band of light
stretching across the sky – this is the Milky Way. Telescopes in
the twentieth century have found that it consists of one hundred
billion (100,000,000,000) stars; some of these stars are to be
found within large clouds of gas, but gas and dust clouds also
exist between them.

The Milky Way galaxy is like a city of stars, the centre of which is called the 'nucleus', with spiral lanes of bright young stars radiating from its centre (see plate 2). Our sun is one of the many stars along one of these highways, about two-thirds out towards the edge of the city. All the bright stars which human imagination has framed into constellations are the nearby stars of this galaxy, while the light from the more distant ones combines to form what is traditionally known as 'the Milky Way'.

The Milky Way has attracted myths and legends from civilisations all over the world in their attempts to describe or explain its existence. Each group of people had their own beliefs about this silvery band of light: the Bushmen of South Africa saw it as the dying embers of the campfires spread across the Kalahari Desert reflected in the sky; the Arabs thought of it as a great river; the Incas saw it as gold dust; and to the Eskimos, it was a band of snow. The early Egyptians identified this band of stars as the celestial equivalent of the River Nile; for the Christian pilgrims of the Middle Ages, it was the road leading to Rome; while people as far apart as the Hindus in India and the North American Indians believed it to be a sacred way.

The night sky

As we know today, the earth spins on its own axis, and as a result the sun appears to rise above the eastern horizon and set below the western horizon, creating the cycle which we recognise as day and night. At night the stars also appear to rise in the east, move across the sky and set in the west. However, Polaris – the pole star – does not cross the sky. Instead, it seems to remain fixed at a point somewhere between the north point and the zenith (the top) of the sky.

Figure 1 shows a map of the sky as seen from Greenwich on 15 September 1998. It is possible to use maps like this to illustrate changes which take place in the sky at any given location over a night, over one cycle of seasons, or even over thousands of years.

The Wise Men of Jesus' time did not know that earth spins on its own axis. Neither did they know that the moon is a satellite of earth, nor that earth and the other planets orbit the sun, the centre of the solar system. Plate 1 shows the solar system as we know it today, an understanding which had to await the scientific revolution of the sixteenth century AD. Today, astronomical knowledge is based on the work of Copernicus, Galileo and their

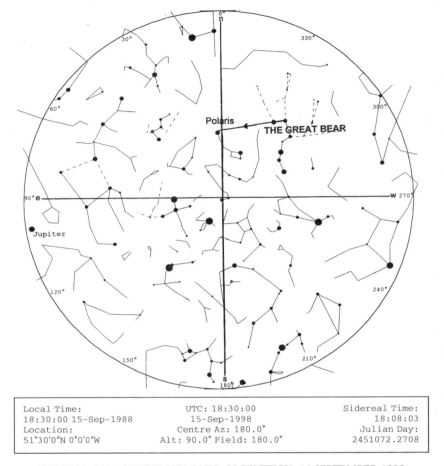

Local Time:	UTC: 18:30:00	Sidereal Time:
18:30:00 15-Sep-1988	15-Sep-1998	18:08:03
Location:	Centre Az: 180.0°	Julian Day:
51°30'0"N 0°0'0"W	Alt: 90.0° Field: 180.0°	2451072.2708

FIGURE 1. MAP OF THE SKY OVER GREENWICH, 15 SEPTEMBER 1998

successors, whereas the astronomical knowledge of the Magi was based on the Aristotelian concept of the cosmos (see plate 3), where the earth was at the centre of the universe, a concept which will be looked at more fully in chapter two. The difference between these two concepts of the cosmos is important because it affects the way in which the Magi would have studied the sky and interpreted what they saw. However, whether we follow an Aristotelian or a modern scientific view of cosmology does not for the most part affect our observations of celestial events in the night sky.

Observation of the stars shows that they appear to be grouped into shapes, known as 'constellations', which move in a regular

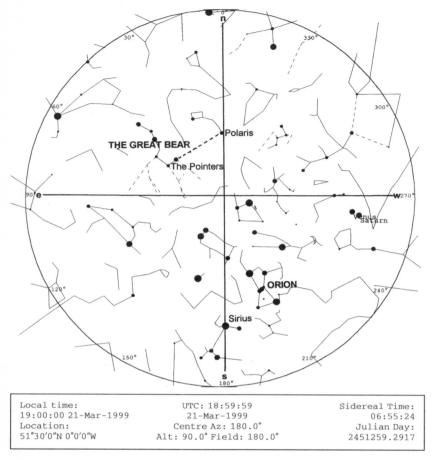

Local time:	UTC: 18:59:59	Sidereal Time:
19:00:00 21-Mar-1999	21-Mar-1999	06:55:24
Location:	Centre Az: 180.0°	Julian Day:
51°30'0"N 0°0'0"W	Alt: 90.0° Field: 180.0°	2451259.2917

FIGURE 2. MAP OF THE SKY OVER GREENWICH, 21 MARCH 1999, 1900 HOURS

band, night after night. It also shows that the constellations which rise in the east just after sunset will change as the year goes by.

Nightly changes in the sky

One well-known constellation, the Great Bear (Ursa Major), appears not to move across the sky with the other constellations, but instead circles about the stationary star Polaris as the year progresses. The seven brightest stars in the Great Bear are sometimes given the separate name of 'the Plough'. Polaris does in fact make a tiny apparent circle in the sky because it is not exactly at the north point. The reasons for this are explained later on in chapter two, but the movement is so small that for

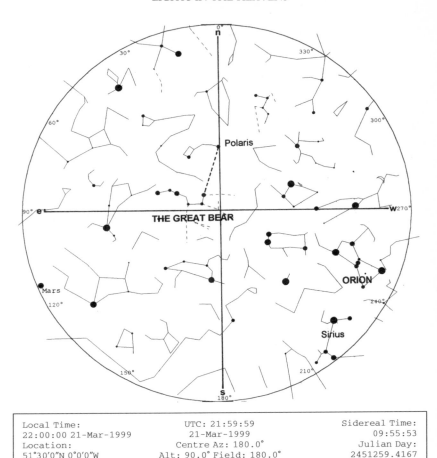

Local Time: 22:00:00 21-Mar-1999 Location: 51°30'0"N 0°0'0"W	UTC: 21:59:59 21-Mar-1999 Centre Az: 180.0° Alt: 90.0° Field: 180.0°	Sidereal Time: 09:55:53 Julian Day: 2451259.4167

FIGURE 3. MAP OF THE SKY OVER GREENWICH, 21 MARCH 1999, 2200 HOURS

most purposes Polaris can be regarded as stationary, indicating north.

Figures 2, 3, 4 and 5 show the sky at Greenwich, UK, at 1900 hours and 2200 hours on 21 March 1999, and also at 0100 hours and 0400 hours the following morning. These figures (explained below) show the movement of the stars across the sky from east to west, and the constant position of Polaris. Being aware of the movements of these stars is important in the understanding of the ancient Egyptian and Babylonian calendars and methods of timekeeping, all of which will be discussed later in this chapter.

At 1900 hours on 21 March, the sun will be just below the horizon, having set exactly in the west on this day; Ursa Major is

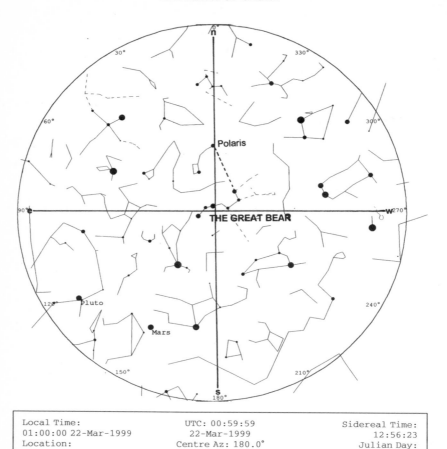

Local Time: 01:00:00 22-Mar-1999	UTC: 00:59:59 22-Mar-1999	Sidereal Time: 12:56:23
Location: 51°30'0"N 0°0'0"W	Centre Az: 180.0° Alt: 90.0° Field: 180.0°	Julian Day: 2451259.5417

FIGURE 4. MAP OF THE SKY OVER GREENWICH, 22 MARCH 1999, 0100 HOURS

high up in E-NE sector and its two brightest stars, 'the pointers', are pointing to Polaris; Orion, 'the hunter', is halfway up in the S-SW sector; and Sirius, 'the dog-star', is also due south somewhat lower in the sky.

By 2200 hours, Orion has moved to the W-SW sector; Sirius is slightly lower in the sky in the south-west; and Ursa Major, including the Plough, is about to move from the E-NE sector to the NE-N sector. Polaris is in virtually the same point of the sky, due north and about halfway up towards the zenith.

By 0100 hours the following morning, Ursa Major is mainly in the W-NW sector, although its tail is very close to the zenith, and Orion has now set.

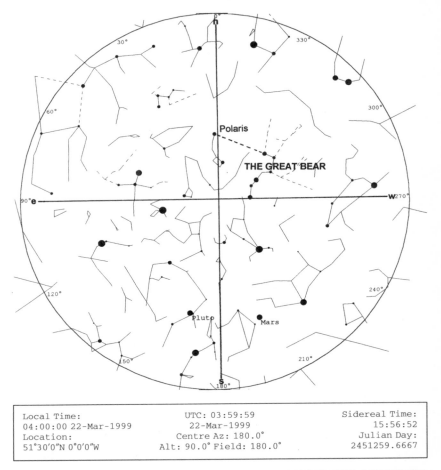

Local Time: 04:00:00 22-Mar-1999 Location: 51°30′0″N 0°0′0″W	UTC: 03:59:59 22-Mar-1999 Centre Az: 180.0° Alt: 90.0° Field: 180.0°	Sidereal Time: 15:56:52 Julian Day: 2451259.6667

FIGURE 5. MAP OF THE SKY OVER GREENWICH, 22 MARCH 1999, 0400 HOURS

Certain conclusions can be drawn from these nightly changes in the sky. Firstly, Polaris appears to be directly north when you look up, and as the earth spins on its own axis, so the whole sky seems to spin about a point very close to the pole star. Indeed, if you were standing at the North Pole when looking upward, Polaris would be almost directly overhead.

Secondly, the stars clustered around Polaris appear to circle it, but never dip below the horizon. These stars are known as 'the circumpolar stars', because they go around the pole of the sky in circles. Although they are always above the horizon, it is not possible to see them in the daytime. This is because of the bright glow in the sky whenever our nearest star, the sun, is above the horizon.

Thirdly, all other stars and groups of stars appear to make wider circles around the north point. They appear to rise in the east, if they are not already above the horizon at sunset, and then seem to cross the night sky, eventually setting in the west.

Movements of the planets

The word 'planet' means 'wanderer', and since ancient times people have realised that the planets differ in their movements from other objects in the night sky. In the course of a night the planets, like the stars and the moon, appear to rise in the east and set in the west, but very little change can be detected in the actual movements of most of the planets from one night to the next. However, over several days, a couple of weeks, or even a month, it becomes apparent that planets change their positions in relation to the background stars. Their speed is inconsistent and sometimes they even appear to move backwards against the background stars.

It is now known that this motion can be easily explained as a combination of the movement of earth and the other planets around the sun. However, the views of the world that existed in antiquity were not the same as ours. The wise men of the time inhabited a cosmos which was earth-centred. They did not have the scientific knowledge of the solar system, in which the earth and planets orbit the sun. Neither did they have Newton's law of gravity to explain gravitational pull. Nor did they realise that the displacement of planetary orbits is a consequence of the gravitational effects of both the planets and the sun. But whether the apparent planetary movements in the night sky are given in terms of an earth- or sun-centred point of view, the *observations* from the earth's surface show that visually, over thousands of years, there is no substantial change in the cyclical movements of the planets against the background stars.

The changes in the position of Venus against the background stars for the first eight months of 1996 are shown in figure 6. Venus was not visible during the whole of this period, because during June it was in the same part of the sky as the sun. Consequently, the stars and planets were obscured by the daylight. Before June Venus was seen as an evening object, and after June as a morning object. Figure 7 shows Jupiter for most of 1996 as seen from earth.

The changes which take place in the sky over time, as described

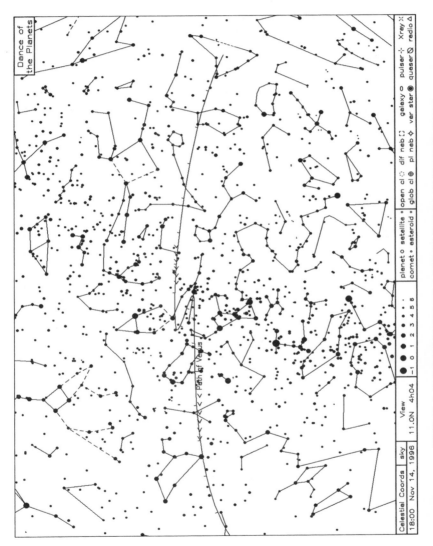

FIGURE 6. MOTION OF VENUS AGAINST THE BACKGROUND STARS

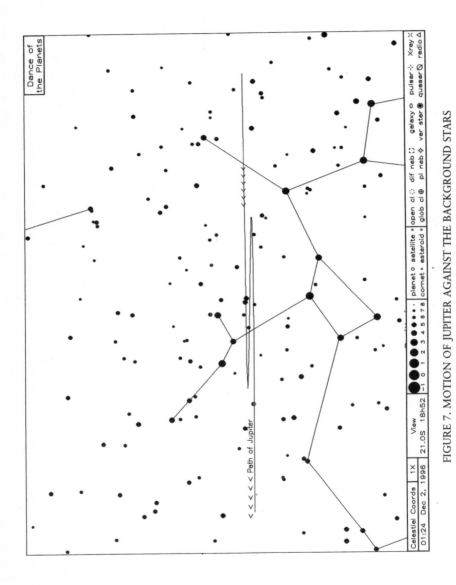

FIGURE 7. MOTION OF JUPITER AGAINST THE BACKGROUND STARS

above, are the most important changes which could be and were observed by sky watchers from the time of the earliest major ancient civilisations. Indeed, they would certainly have been known to the Magi. However, it is also important to realise that the sky looks different from different places on the earth's surface. Figures 8a, b, c and d show some examples of this: the sky as seen from the North Pole, with Polaris almost directly above our heads; the sky from latitude 45 degrees north; at latitude 45 degrees south; and the sky from the South Pole. Figure 8e shows the Southern Cross and the two pointers to the Cross. The ancient mariners used their knowledge of the movements of the patterns in the night sky to navigate on the great voyages of discovery.

The seasons, equinoxes and solstices

The night sky also changes as we pass through spring, summer, autumn and winter. This can be explained by looking at the movements of the earth on its axis and its movements around the sun as seen from outer space (figure 9). The northern end of the earth's axis points towards Polaris. As seen from outer space this axis will point to this star as earth orbits the sun. During the northern winter, the North Pole is angled *away* from the sun, whereas in the northern summer it is angled *towards* the sun. In spring and autumn the two Poles will be *equidistant* from the sun.

Figures 10a, b, c and d show the sky, again at the latitude of Greenwich, UK, at 2200 hours on 21 March, 21 June, 23 September and 21 December 1999.

1. 21 March is the *spring equinox*. On this day the sun rises exactly in the east and sets exactly in the west, creating equal hours of daylight all over the world.
2. 21 June is the *summer solstice*. This refers to summer in the northern hemisphere. On this day the sun will rise somewhere between the east and the north, depending on our distance from the equator, and we will have the longest day and the shortest night of the year. In northern Scandinavia, the sun does not set below the horizon, but merely makes a dip in the sky, so it does not get dark at all.
3. 23 September is the *autumn equinox*. Once again the sun rises exactly in the east and sets in the west, meaning equal hours of daylight and night.

23

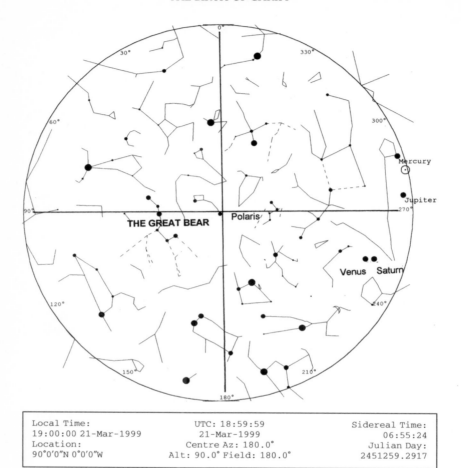

Local Time:	UTC: 18:59:59	Sidereal Time:
19:00:00 21-Mar-1999	21-Mar-1999	06:55:24
Location:	Centre Az: 180.0°	Julian Day:
90°0'0"N 0°0'0"W	Alt: 90.0° Field: 180.0°	2451259.2917

FIGURE 8A. LOCATION DIFFERENCES: THE NORTH POLE

4. 21 December is the *winter solstice*. This refers to the
   northern winter. On this day the sun rises towards the
   south-west. We therefore experience the shortest day and
   the longest night of the year. Above the Arctic Circle there
   is no daylight at all for a period.

The map for Greenwich on 21 March (figure 10a) shows the
constellations of Virgo in the E-SE sector, Leo in the S-SE sector,
Cancer in the S-SW sector, and Gemini in the W-SW sector. The
constellation of Orion is just about to set in the W-SW
sector and Sirius is in the south-west. Ursa Major is very close to
the zenith. By June 21 – the summer solstice – things have

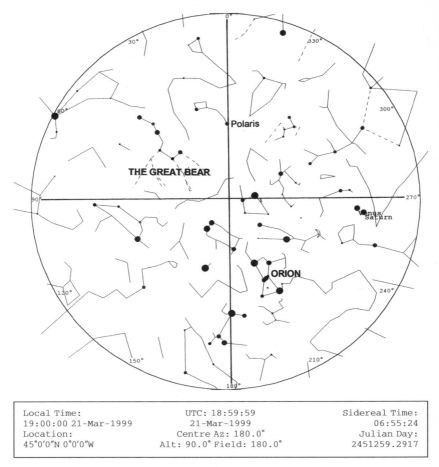

Local Time:	UTC: 18:59:59	Sidereal Time:
19:00:00 21-Mar-1999	21-Mar-1999	06:55:24
Location:	Centre Az: 180.0°	Julian Day:
45°0'0"N 0°0'0"W	Alt: 90.0° Field: 180.0°	2451259.2917

FIGURE 8B. LOCATION DIFFERENCES: LATITUDE 45 NORTH

changed (figure 10b). Leo is now in the west and Virgo is in the south-west. Scorpio and Libra are now to be seen in the south, and Sagittarius is very low in the south-east. Ursa Major straddles two sectors between the north and west, but is still fairly high up in the sky. With the coming of the autumnal equinox (figure 10c), the September sky shows Ursa Major in the N-NW sector. Taurus has appeared in the N-NE sector and Pisces is now to be seen mainly in the E-SE sector, with Aquarius in the S-SE and Capricornus in the S-SW sector. As Christmas arrives, at the time of the winter solstice (figure 10d), Orion is once again halfway up in the S-SE sector. Sirius is almost due south, Leo is just about to rise in the E-NE sector, Gemini is in the E-SE, and Ursa Major is in the N-NE sector.

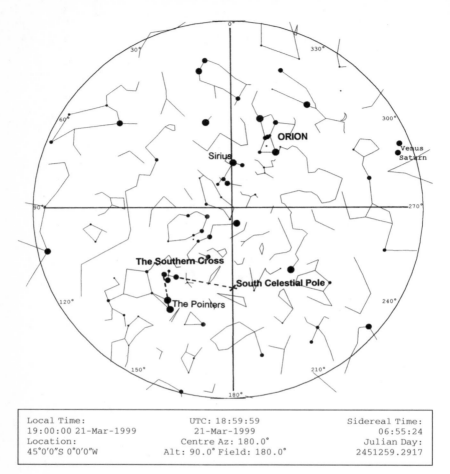

Local Time:	UTC: 18:59:59	Sidereal Time:
19:00:00 21-Mar-1999	21-Mar-1999	06:55:24
Location:	Centre Az: 180.0°	Julian Day:
45°0′0″S 0°0′0″W	Alt: 90.0° Field: 180.0°	2451259.2917

FIGURE 8C. LOCATION DIFFERENCES: LATITUDE 45 SOUTH

These star maps show the sky visible in the northern hemisphere of earth. The pattern of constellations in the southern hemisphere is different: the familiar constellations of the zodiac may be seen, but at different seasons of the year; there are other important constellations, such as the Southern Cross; and there is no equivalent to Polaris above the South Pole. The arts of navigation began in the so-called 'cradle of civilisation' around the Mediterranean Sea, which is in the northern hemisphere. For that reason, as well as the fact that Polaris so conveniently indicates north, the development of navigation and the system of latitude and longitude developed around the north point.

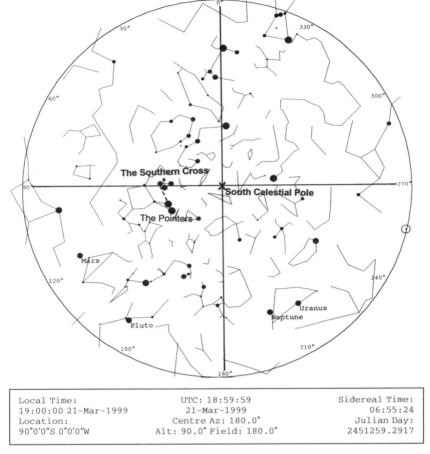

Local Time:	UTC: 18:59:59	Sidereal Time:
19:00:00 21-Mar-1999	21-Mar-1999	06:55:24
Location:	Centre Az: 180.0°	Julian Day:
90°0'0"S 0°0'0"W	Alt: 90.0° Field: 180.0°	2451259.2917

FIGURE 8D. LOCATION DIFFERENCES: THE SOUTH POLE

Therefore, at 2200 hours on any night, those constellations which are visible at any point on earth will change throughout the year. Some groups of constellations will dominate the night sky during one season whilst others will become visible during a different season. These seasonal differences will repeat themselves year in, year out, over generations and very little change will take place – at least at a rate that can be noted with the naked eye, even over a human lifespan.

The Magi would, as a matter of course, have observed all of these changes. Even a shepherd or a fisherman in Judea 2000 years ago would not have needed an extensive education to be able to tell the time, the date and the season by looking at the sky

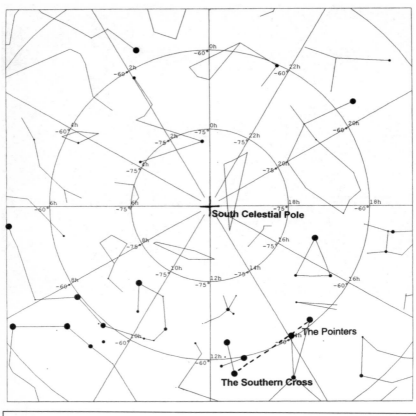

Local Time:	UTC: 17:06:27	Sidereal Time:
17:06:27 11-Apr-1998	11-Apr-1998	06:15:13
Location:	RA: 0h00m00s	Julian Day:
53°27'0"N 2°31'0"W	Dec: −90°00' Field: 75.0°	2450915.2128

FIGURE 8E. THE 'SOUTHERN CROSS' CONSELLATION

clock above his head. For most of human history the sky has provided a permanent and regular indicator by which life and work could be structured.

Despite this wonderful regularity, however, some very slow, but constant, changes are taking place over extremely long periods of hundreds and thousands of years. The most important of these changes is called 'the precession of the equinoxes'.

Precessional motion of the sky

To understand the concept of precessional motion, a brief definition of certain astronomical terms is necessary. It is also

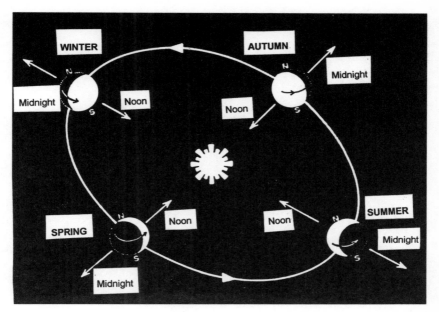

FIGURE 9. THE POSITION OF THE EARTH AROUND THE SUN AT THE FOUR
SEASONS

important to be aware of the observations which would have
made the ancient sky watchers aware of the changes associated
with precession.

The north celestial pole of the sky is the point around which
the whole sky seems to move in the northern hemisphere, while
the celestial equator is the projection on to the sky of the equator
on earth. The pathway made as the sun crosses the sky against the
background stars is known as 'the ecliptic'. In the same way that
distance is measured in degrees from the equator on earth, so the
distance from the celestial equator (known as 'declination') is also
measured in degrees. The ecliptic crosses the celestial equator at
two points, one of which is the point of the vernal equinox. This
point is very important in astronomy as it denotes the position of
the sun against the background stars at the start of spring in the
northern hemisphere. This is highly relevant to the Magi's
understanding about the Star.

Figure 11 shows the positions of Polaris over the last 6000
years with respect to the actual pole of the sky. As this figure
shows, although the north point of the sky and Polaris are very
close to each other at the moment, since 4000 BC Polaris has

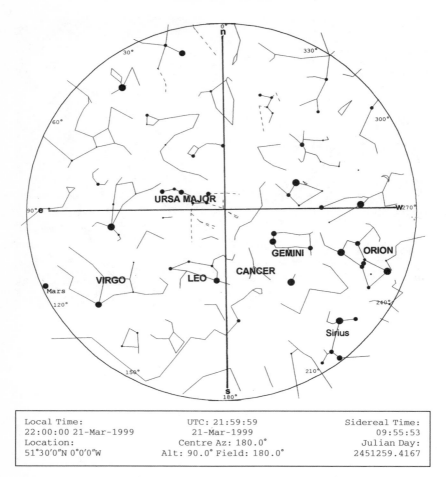

Local Time:	UTC: 21:59:59	Sidereal Time:
22:00:00 21-Mar-1999	21-Mar-1999	09:55:53
Location:	Centre Az: 180.0°	Julian Day:
51°30'0"N 0°0'0"W	Alt: 90.0° Field: 180.0°	2451259.4167

FIGURE 10A. SEASONAL CHANGES: THE SPRING EQUINOX

moved through a large angle. This is one of the effects of precessional motion.

The sun makes its annual path across the sky through a set of constellations known as 'the zodiac'. Each of these constellations is estimated to measure 30 degrees, a somewhat arbitrary figure, but very convenient. These constellations are very well known: Aries, Taurus, Gemini, Cancer, Leo, Virgo, Libra, Scorpio, Sagittarius, Capricornus, Aquarius and Pisces. The sun progresses through the zodiac in this order, but in the phenomenon of precession, its position at the vernal equinox is actually moving backward through each constellation. Figure 12 shows how the position of the vernal equinox has changed over the last 4000 years.

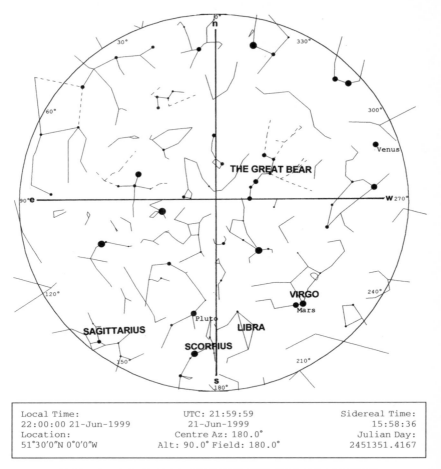

Local Time:	UTC: 21:59:59	Sidereal Time:
22:00:00 21-Jun-1999	21-Jun-1999	15:58:36
Location:	Centre Az: 180.0°	Julian Day:
51°30′0″N 0°0′0″W	Alt: 90.0° Field: 180.0°	2451351.4167

FIGURE 10B. SEASONAL CHANGES: THE SUMMER SOLSTICE

It used to be accepted that precession could not have been known about before Hipparchus discovered it 'scientifically' at his observatory on the island of Rhodes sometime between 190 BC and 120 BC. However, modern scholarship has demonstrated convincingly that ancient civilisations did indeed observe the precession of the equinoxes, and, more than that, it formed part of the mythology of cultures right down to the time of the Magi.

Eclipses of the moon

Lunar eclipses need to be considered here very briefly, mainly because it is a way of putting limits on the date of Christ's birth

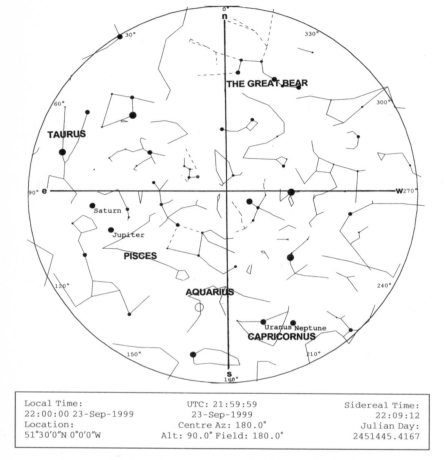

Local Time:	UTC: 21:59:59	Sidereal Time:
22:00:00 23-Sep-1999	23-Sep-1999	22:09:12
Location:	Centre Az: 180.0°	Julian Day:
51°30'0"N 0°0'0"W	Alt: 90.0° Field: 180.0°	2451445.4167

FIGURE 10C. SEASONAL CHANGES: THE AUTUMN EQUINOX

and will support my argument about the Star of Bethlehem. St Matthew's gospel mentions an eclipse of the moon at the time of Herod's death. If the possibilities for this particular eclipse can be narrowed down, it is possible to work towards a year for Christ's birth.

An eclipse of the moon occurs when the earth comes between sun and moon and blots out the sunlight which would otherwise be lighting it up. However, because of the earth's atmosphere, a certain element of red light is bent, or refracted, around the earth, which gives the moon a dark, reddish appearance during a total eclipse. This is shown in figures 13a and b.

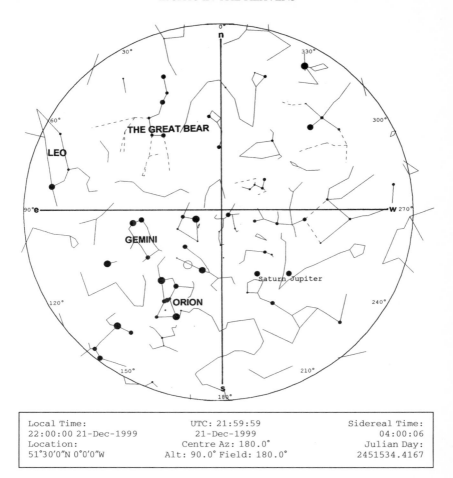

Local Time:	UTC: 21:59:59	Sidereal Time:
22:00:00 21-Dec-1999	21-Dec-1999	04:00:06
Location:	Centre Az: 180.0°	Julian Day:
51°30'0"N 0°0'0"W	Alt: 90.0° Field: 180.0°	2451534.4167

FIGURE 10D. SEASONAL CHANGES: THE WINTER SOLSTICE

Egyptian star clocks and Babylonian calendars

We inherited our 24-hour day/night period from the Egyptians, although it has undergone modification since then. The Egyptians knew how to tell time by the sun, and invented a shadow clock with a system of twelve daylight hours (figure 14). But for the hours of night they needed something else. They therefore used a sequence of 36 stars, more or less evenly spread across the middle part of the sky – the part that is known as 'the celestial equator'. On a particular night the first star rising after dusk would mark the first hour of the night; the second star in the sequence would mark the second hour, and so on. However, as shown earlier, this apparently unchanging belt of fixed stars rises above the eastern

33

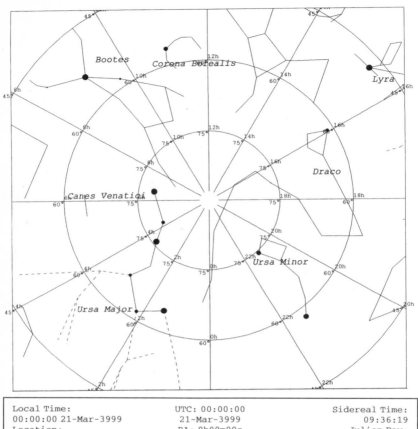

Local Time:	UTC: 00:00:00	Sidereal Time:
00:00:00 21-Mar-3999	21-Mar-3999	09:36:19
Location:	RA: 0h00m00s	Julian Day:
53°27′0″N 2°31′0″W	Dec: +90°00′ Field: 80.0°	260502.5000

FIGURE 11A. PRECESSIONAL CHANGES IN THE POSITION OF POLARIS OVER 6000 YEARS.
21 MARCH 4000 BC

horizon slightly earlier each night. Although the ancient Egyptians recognised this occurrence, they were not aware that this was due to earth's progress around the sun.

The Egyptians did not have scientific understanding as we know it today, but, as expert watchers of the stars, they knew that after about ten days the first of the 36 stars would *not* rise at dusk, but the second star would. This second star would therefore become the marker for the first hour of the night. After another ten days or so the third star of the 36 would become the marker for the first hour, and this pattern would then continue throughout the year.

They also observed that days and nights were of equal lengths

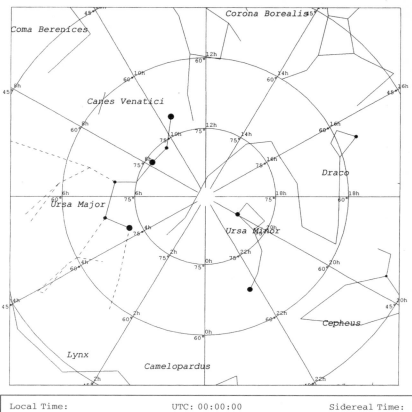

Local Time:	UTC: 00:00:00	Sidereal Time:
00:00:00 21-Mar-1999	21-Mar-1999	10:34:46
Location:	RA: 0h00m00s	Julian Day:
53°27'0"N 2°31'0"W	Dec: +90°00' Field: 80.0°	991002.5000

FIGURE 11B. PRECESSIONAL CHANGES IN THE POSITION OF POLARIS OVER
6000 YEARS.
21 MARCH 2000 BC

during the spring and autumn equinoxes, but that during the summer the nights were shorter. Therefore, eighteen of these sequential stars would rise above the eastern horizon at the equinoxes during the course of the night, but only twelve would rise above the eastern horizon during the shorter summer night. Consequently, the Egyptians settled for a clock system of 12 hours of night and 12 hours of day for the whole year, the origin of our own 24-hour day and night.

There is, however, an important variation between the ancient Egyptian system and our own: the lengths of the 'hours' varied from one season to the next. The daylight period consisted of four

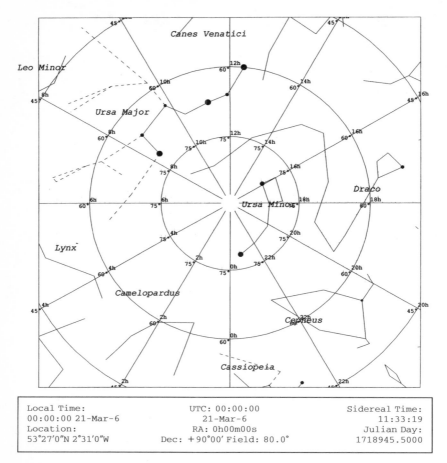

Local Time:	UTC: 00:00:00	Sidereal Time:
00:00:00 21-Mar-6	21-Mar-6	11:33:19
Location:	RA: 0h00m00s	Julian Day:
53°27'0"N 2°31'0"W	Dec: +90°00' Field: 80.0°	1718945.5000

FIGURE 11C. PRECESSIONAL CHANGES IN THE POSITION OF POLARIS OVER
6000 YEARS.
21 MARCH 7 BC

periods: two hours for dawn; four hours for morning; four hours
for afternoon; and two hours for dusk. The night period consisted
of twelve hours as marked by the stars rising above the eastern
horizon.

It may seem incomprehensible that an 'hour' could be a
variable amount of time, but this was not uncommon in many
timekeeping systems before the development of mechanical
timekeeping systems. The ancient Egyptians had several different
clock- and calendar systems, each of which was used for different
practical purposes. This 24-hour system seems to have been
reserved for ritual and religious use only. Our lives today are

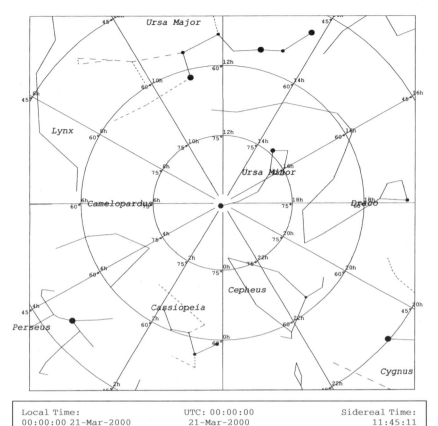

Local Time:	UTC: 00:00:00	Sidereal Time:
00:00:00 21-Mar-2000	21-Mar-2000	11:45:11
Location:	RA: 0h00m00s	Julian Day:
53°27'0"N 2°31'0"W	Dec: +90°00' Field: 80.0°	2451624.5000

FIGURE 11D. PRECESSIONAL CHANGES IN THE POSITION OF POLARIS OVER
6000 YEARS.
21 MARCH AD 2000

fundamentally dependent on advanced technology where measurement of everything, including time, is exact and needs no direct reference to natural standards. It is therefore difficult to understand different concepts of timekeeping or calendar-making, yet it is important to be able to do this to see the sky and understand it as the ancients saw and understood it.

The Babylonians invented a form of astronomy that was based on arithmetic. This system was very sophisticated when compared to other approaches to the subject around at that time. Current knowledge of Babylonian astronomy is based largely on various clay tablets covered with a cuneiform script. These were in use in

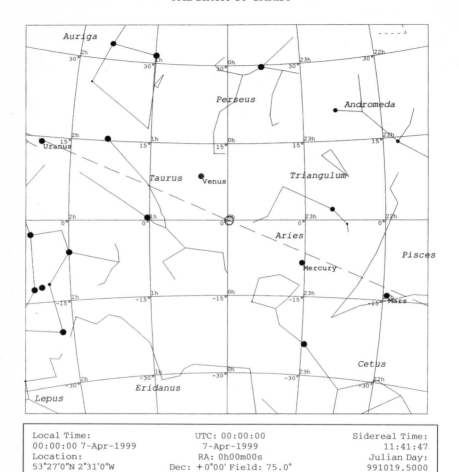

Local Time:	UTC: 00:00:00	Sidereal Time:
00:00:00 7-Apr-1999	7-Apr-1999	11:41:47
Location:	RA: 0h00m00s	Julian Day:
53°27'0"N 2°31'0"W	Dec: +0°00' Field: 75.0°	991019.5000

FIGURE 12A. PRECESSIONAL CHANGES IN THE POSITION OF THE SUN AT THE VERNAL EQUINOX OVER 4000 YEARS.
[(A) 7 APRIL 2000 BC]

ancient Mesopotamia for around 3000 years, until the first century of our own era.

At this stage, the Babylonians did not try to make a geometrical model of how the sun and moon were arranged in space. Instead they saw the zodiac as a road which they divided up into sectors, and each part of the road was given its own numbered 'address'. The positions of the sun, moon and planets were then given in terms of these addresses, and their motions in terms of changes in the addresses. Patterns in these changes were mimicked using mathematical sequences of numbers. The Babylonians were

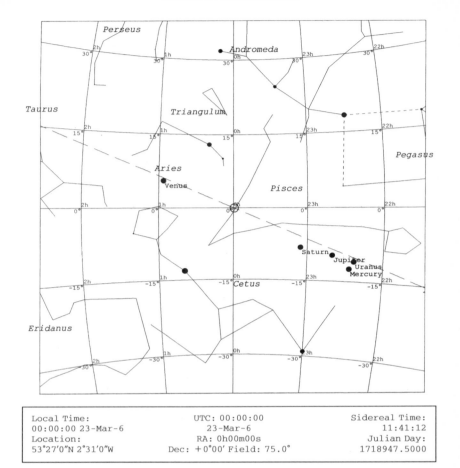

Local Time:	UTC: 00:00:00	Sidereal Time:
00:00:00 23-Mar-6	23-Mar-6	11:41:12
Location:	RA: 0h00m00s	Julian Day:
53°27'0"N 2°31'0"W	Dec: +0°00' Field: 75.0°	1718947.5000

FIGURE 12B. PRECESSIONAL CHANGES IN THE POSITION OF THE SUN AT THE VERNAL EQUINOX OVER 4000 YEARS.
[(B) 23 MARCH 7 BC]

therefore able to work out lunar calendars for everyday use, and solar and planetary almanacs, which they used for astrological predictions. Their approach was a considerable advance over those from earlier periods and the methods used by their neighbouring countries.

Calendars before Christ's birth

The triple conjunction of Jupiter and Saturn in Pisces, which occurred around the time of Jesus' birth, is a matter of record. It can be accurately dated in an astronomical sense, and with a planetarium we can take ourselves back in time to look at the very

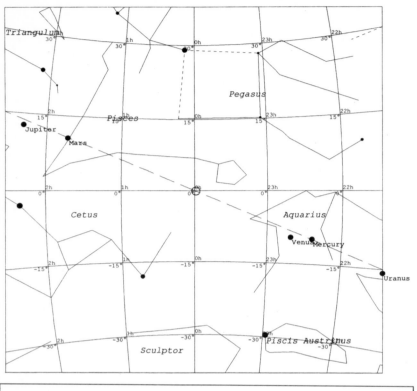

Local Time:	UTC: 00:00:00	Sidereal Time:
00:00:00 20-Mar-2000	20-Mar-2000	11:41:15
Location:	RA: 0h00m00s	Julian Day:
53°27'0"N 2°31'0"W ·	Dec: +0°00' Field: 75.0°	2451623.5000

FIGURE 12C. PRECESSIONAL CHANGES IN THE POSITION OF THE SUN AT THE
VERNAL EQUINOX OVER 4000 YEARS.
[(C) 20 MARCH AD 2000]

same sky patterns which shone over Bethlehem on the evening
when Jupiter and Saturn, conjunct for the third time, rose above
the horizon in the east just as the sun in Virgo was setting in the
west.

Using our modern-day calendar system, it is possible to
pinpoint this night as being 15 September 7 BC. There have,
however, been many different calendar systems since Christ's
birth, and calendar dating is by no means as simple as it may
seem. In order to know what is meant when it is said that Christ
was born on 15 September 7 BC, it is necessary to know something
about calendars in the ancient world and how they developed.

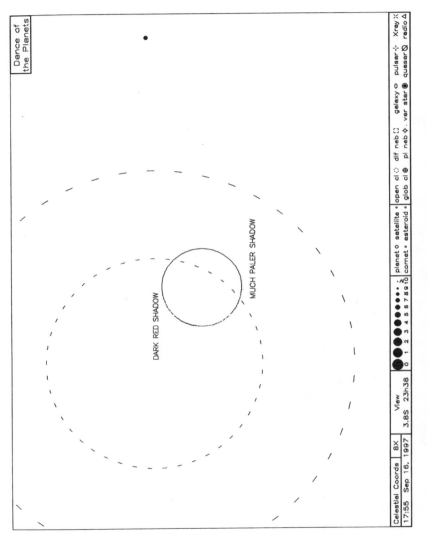

FIGURE 13A. AN ECLIPSE OF THE MOON AS SEEN FROM EARTH

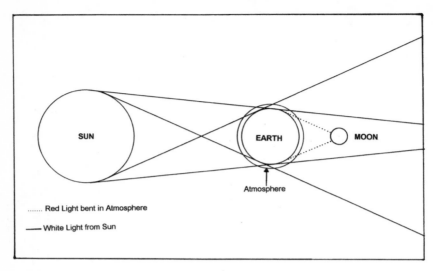

FIGURE 13B. AN ECLIPSE OF THE MOON AS SEEN FROM SPACE

As was seen earlier, seasonal changes in daylight hours and climate arise because the earth tilts on its axis. As a result of this tilt, each hemisphere is sometimes nearer and sometimes farther from the sun. In early times people depended on hunting or gathering their food from the trees and plants around them. They would have realised quite quickly that particular animals or species of plants were not constantly available, but perhaps disappeared in colder weather, only to return again when the longer days and warmer weather returned. Days lengthened and shortened, then lengthened again; the sun-god made cyclical progress which was constant and predictable; available food sources clearly tied in with this cycle, and so did the patterns in the night sky.

As civilisations began to develop, people began to use the sky as a calendar. The myths and legends of early cultures describe divisions of time and seasonal changes in terms of celestial deities, above all, the sun-god, without whom life could not exist.

Subsequent development of agricultural civilisations all over the world made greater demands on the calendar-makers. The whole problem required a series of astronomical observations which spanned a long period of time. All the great agricultural communities had one feature in common: they started along the plains of great rivers. In Egypt it was the Nile, in Mesopotamia

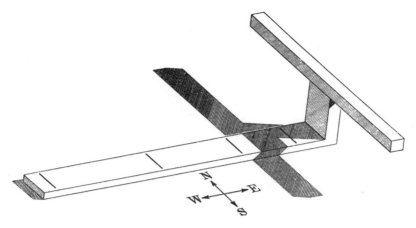

FIGURE 14. AN EGYPTIAN SHADOW CLOCK

the Euphrates, and in China the Hwang that provided the water for these great civilisations.

The amount of water available in these rivers had a seasonal flow, so more accurate calendars were needed to predict when the rivers were likely to flood. Why was such precision necessary? Because in all ancient cultures and civilisations agricultural activities were accompanied by religious rites, ceremonies and festivals. The gods in whom people believed represented the dominant natural forces, which imposed regularity on the social structures of the day. Observance of rituals had to be precise, and the calendar was essential to their chronological ordering.

The two most obvious objects on which to base a calendar are the sun and the moon, and both solar and lunar calendars existed from early times. Star clocks were also very important. As the great civilisations developed, so did the complexity of their calendars, and this led to problems.

The difficulty arose because the cycles involved are not simple fractions of each other. For example, the average time for the moon to go from one new moon to the next is 29.53 days. On the other hand the solar year, crucial to calendar-making, is 365.2422 days. This is not even a whole number of days, let alone a convenient multiple of the moon cycle. Twelve lunar months amount to 354.367 days, which is eleven days short of one solar year, and so after three years a calendar based on the moon becomes thirty-three days short of three seasonal cycles. To bring such a lunar calendar back in step with the seasons, it was necessary to include an extra month of thirty-three days every three years. Different cultures found different working solutions to the difficulties of making a useful calendar.

All early communities for which we have evidence used the moon for making their calendars. Unlike some of their neighbours, the Egyptians did not begin their lunar month with the first appearance of the new crescent in the west at sunset. Instead, they began it with the morning when the old crescent of the waning moon could no longer be seen in the eastern sky just before sunrise. They divided their lunar year into three seasons, each consisting of four lunar months: four months of the inundation, during which the Nile overflowed and covered the Valley; four months of planting and growing; and four months of harvest and low water. In order to keep this lunar year in step with the seasons, a thirteenth intercalary month was introduced every three years. Later on the Egyptians used the bright star Sirius to regulate the inclusion of this extra month.

Early Egyptian astronomers – usually known as 'hour-watchers' – noticed that about the time that the Nile water levels began to rise, Sirius could be seen in the east, just before the sun appeared above the horizon. Although the glow from the sun was already becoming visible, Sirius was still bright enough to be seen at this time. Such a rising is called 'a heliacal rising', and it follows a period of invisibility, when Sirius was virtually rising and setting with the sun and could not be seen. To the Egyptians, Sirius was the goddess Sopdet or Sothis, the appearance of whom heralded the inundation.

This calendar was used for centuries in the early period of Egyptian civilisation. Early in the third millennium BC, a new calendar was introduced, most probably for administrative purposes. This calendar consisted of three seasons of four 30-day months each, with five additional 'epagomenal days' or 'days upon the year', which were considered to be festival days, giving 365 days in all. The Egyptians were also aware, soon after the introduction of this calendar, that the real solar year was longer than their civil year by about a quarter of a day, but they chose not to do anything about it. Presumably they would have introduced an extra intercalary day when it became absolutely necessary to do so. However, they had determined the length of the natural year and had invented one of the most sensible and practical calendars of the ancient world.

The Babylonians' arithmetical astronomy enabled them to predict the motions of sun, moon and planets with some precision. It also enabled them to work out the likelihood of eclipses of the sun and moon. Their approach to theoretical astronomy was very important in the subsequent developments of mathematical astronomy in many parts of the Western world. Initially, this form of Babylonian astronomy was invented to cope with the fact they they had a strict adherence to a lunar calendar. The calculation problems raised by this commitment demanded the development of powerful numerical techniques, which would later be applied to the movement of other celestial bodies.

In Babylon the month began on the first day the thin crescent of the moon appeared in the west just after sunset. Consequently, the Babylonian calendar, at least in this respect, was more in keeping with those of neighbouring cultures than it was with that of the Egyptians. The inconvenience of starting the month with the actual sighting of the thin crescent is obvious, because it is so dependent on conditions in the atmosphere. For this reason, the Babylonians needed to develop a theoretical astronomy to predict when, in principle, they should be able to see the crescent moon. They would then be able to start their month without having to wait for an actual sighting. Unfortunately, the problems associated with this aim were considerable.

As earth orbits the sun, so the sun will seem to change its position against the background stars (assuming, of course, that the sun and stars could be seen at the same time). The moon is circling earth, so it, too, has a pathway against the background stars, which is different from that of the sun. The apparent speeds with which the sun and moon move are different: the average apparent speed of the sun against the background stars is about one degree per day, while the moon moves through about thirteen degrees per day. These are, however, average speeds and there are some deviations from them. The speeds at which the sun and moon move against these stars are important in calculating the appearance of the crescent moon.

Firstly, for the crescent to be seen in the sunset glow, the moon must be a certain distance from the sun. Also important is the angle made where the line joining the sun and moon meets with the horizon. If this angle is too small, the moon will be too close to the horizon to be seen in the sunset glow. The Babylonian astronomers therefore had to make a careful study of the movements of both the sun and moon. In order to do this they had to invent a method of describing the positions of both bodies against the stars, which would form a natural map against which the sun, moon and planets moved. Just as the postman needs an address before they can deliver a letter to a given house, so astronomers had to define addresses for the sun and moon in the sky. This was normally done by giving the number of degrees each body had moved into a certain constellation of the zodiac.

To describe the motion of, for example, the moon, it was necessary to give a list of the number of degrees by which it had moved into a given constellation on a number of different dates. In order to predict where the moon would be at a particular point in the future, it was necessary to be able to predict these numbers. The Babylonians did this by observing the patterns in these sets of numbers, and then trying to reproduce these patterns using numerical sequences. Once a successful sequence had been obtained it was possible to project these forward into the future. The Babylonians' theoretical astronomy was based purely on arithmetic, and at no time did they seek to picture how the celestial objects were arranged in space. However, their approach did allow them to work out a predictable lunar calendar, and it also helped them to predict some of the eclipses that were eventually observed.

At the time of the Magi of our story, Jerusalem was under the domination of Rome. In his campaigns to Egypt, Julius Caesar had become familiar with the civil and administrative advantages of the Egyptian calendar. In 46 BC, knowing of the need to add a quarter day to the 365-day year, he enlisted the help of Sosigenes of Alexandria to incorporate this extra quarter day into the calendar in a systematic way. He introduced this new calendar to the Roman world, decreeing that the Julian calendar should consist of three common years of 365 days each, and a fourth year of 366 days.

Unfortunately, Caesar's decree was misinterpreted, and for many years every *third* year was made a leap year. It was therefore left to Augustus Caesar to realise that an error had been made, and he took the necessary steps to correct this mistake, although leap years were not correctly inserted into the calendar until AD 8. The Jewish people of Christ's time were therefore operating under the uncorrected Julian calendar, while the Magi would have been following the Babylonian lunar calendar.

The seven-day week

The cycles of night and day, the lunar month and the seasons are all natural in that they are determined by repeatable astronomical events. The seven days of our week are not a natural cycle, but something introduced into the calendar by people. Although it is not entirely clear how this particular division of the calendar started, some suggestions have been made with regard to its origin.

According to A. A. Dickson in an article on *The History of the Calendar*, the Babylonians are thought to have divided their lunar month into seven-day periods. The time between any two consecutive phases of the moon, for example between first quarter and full moon, is seven days, nine hours and eleven minutes. Seven days is therefore the nearest whole number. This is why the Babylonians introduced the seven-day week into their calendar, which was always strictly a lunar one. Dickson does, however, suggest another possibility:

> A possible alternative explanation may lie in the number seven itself and in the special sanctity that has adhered to this particular number from earliest times, when primitive man first discovered that the Sun and Moon were not the only visible heavenly bodies that 'wandered' around the heavens but that there were five others (which we now call Mercury, Venus, Mars, Jupiter and Saturn), making seven in all and coinciding with the number of visible stars in the Pleiades, the Great and Little Bears, and other familiar constellations.

Ideas about the sanctity of certain numbers will be returned to later on.

The most likely source of the week, as regards its adoption by Judaism and Christianity, is the biblical story of Creation told in the Book of Genesis:

> On the sixth day God completed all the work he had been doing, and on the seventh day he ceased from all his work. God blessed the seventh day and made it holy, because on that day he ceased from all the work he had set himself to do.
>
> (Genesis 2:1–2, New English Bible)

Christian calendars

Over the centuries, astronomers have measured the length of the year with ever-increasing accuracy. It is now known that the natural year is 365.2422 days long. Consequently, this meant that even the corrected Julian calendar was slightly inaccurate, and by the year 1582 an error of ten days had accumulated. A decree was issued by Pope Gregory XIII in that year which introduced a new calendar and rectified the mistake. This document stated that the day following 4 October would be called 15 October. It was also decreed that leap years falling at the end of a century would not be counted as a leap, unless the first two figures were divisible by four. This was how the Julian calendar, itself of Egyptian origin, gave rise to the Gregorian calendar.

Differences between Protestants and Catholics, and divisions of the Eastern and Western Christian churches, meant that, in many countries, the advantages of the Gregorian calendar were not accepted straightaway: France, Italy, Luxembourg, Spain and Portugal adopted the new calendar in 1682; the Catholic states of Germany, the Netherlands and Belgium followed in 1684. Although in Switzerland the changeover began in 1583, it was not completed until 1812, while in the United Kingdom and its colonies the change was made in 1752, 170 years after the papal decree.

The calendar used by most Christian churches today, at least in the Western world, is a mixture of the Hebrew lunar calendar and the Gregorian solar calendar. Easter Day is a movable feast, and all the other movable feasts, for example Rogation and Ascension, follow in a fixed sequence from that. The rules to be used for the calculation of Easter Day are found in the Book of Common Prayer. Here we find that Easter Day: 'Is always the first Sunday after the full Moon which happened upon or is next after the twenty-first of March; and if the full Moon happens upon a Sunday, Easter Day is the Sunday after.'

Christmas Day is a fixed feast, determined solely by reference to the Gregorian calendar. The use of 25 December was really based on a pagan festival that had its roots in an astronomical phenomenon. As we move from the northern summer towards winter, the sun gets closer to the south-western part of the horizon, and the days get shorter. On 21 December, the sun sets farther to the south-west than on any other day of the year, resulting in the shortest day in the northern hemisphere, which is known as the winter solstice. On 25 December there is a noticeable lengthening of the day, and the point on the horizon at which the sun sets seems to be moving back from its most south-westerly position. Many people who worshipped the sun as a god saw this day as the one on which the sun-god returned from the south. Therefore, 25 December became a festival day. Although spring and the warmer weather were still a few months away, the days were beginning to increase in length, heralding the rebirth that would occur near the vernal equinox.

In the second century AD, the Christian Church made a decision to adopt this date as the day on which Christ was born. Thus there is no historical reason to believe that Jesus was actually born on 25 December.

When the Gregorian calendar was introduced, there was a lot of debate over the date of Easter. It was therefore decided to set the rules from which it would be possible to calculate the date of Easter for years to come. The approach that was chosen completely dispensed with the need to undertake any complicated astronomical observations. However, from the point of view of the astronomer, these rules are not as simple as they initially seem. The moon used to fix the date of Easter is known as an idealised 'ecclesiastical moon'. It is defined by sets of tables and does not correspond precisely to the position of the 'real moon' in the sky. The vernal equinox does not always fall exactly on 21 March – it can vary by a day on either side – so once again it is an idealised equinox that is used in the calculation. In 1923 the Congress of the Eastern Orthodox Churches decided not to follow these rules, but chose to determine the date of Easter by the real moon at the meridian of Jerusalem.

Many different calendars existed in the ancient world, and when trying to connect the chronologies associated with these ways of marking the passage of time, considerable difficulties arise. This is not only because some calendars were based on the moon, the stars, the sun, or on a complex combination of these objects, but also because of the differentiation in the dates from which these calendars all begin. Sometimes a correlation may be made using events which occurred in more than one calendar. Another, very natural, way, since all calendars are based on celestial phenomena, is to use astronomical records of solar and lunar eclipses and listings of planetary positions. This method has proved very fruitful and has shed light on the timing of events for which no specific dates have been given.

This approach is essential to developing many of the ideas in this book. Although the reasons for choosing the date of 25 December for Christmas Day have been looked at, it is important to consider briefly the concept of AD and BC to support the real date for the birth of Christ. The calendar in use today is commonly assumed to begin from that very day, but the reality is not that simple. However, any calendar system has to have a starting point, so how was the start of the calendar we use today – the Christian calendar – decided upon?

The Jewish calendar used a system based on the Era of Creation. Using the Book of Genesis and today's dating mechanism, Jewish scholars have calculated the day of the Creation of the world as being 21 September. In our present reckoning, this would have occurred 3761 years before the start of the Christian era. They subsequently counted the passage of time from this date.

Events in Greek history were dated using the Era of the Olympiads, which using our present dating system, began on 17 July in the year that we would now call 776 BC, the date on which Coraebus won the foot race at the first Olympic Games.

The Roman calendar began with the foundation of Rome. This was calculated by M. Terentius Varro, a Roman author who lived in the first century before Christ was born. The first year of the Roman calendar was called *ab urbe condita* 1, or AUC 1, and this system was used for several centuries, even after the introduction of the Julian calendar during the early years of the Christian Church. This system was eventually superseded by one which was supposed to reflect the Christian Era or the Era of the Incarnation of the Word.

The starting point of this calendar was decided upon by a Christian monk, Dionysius Exiguus, who lived about 500 years after the birth of Christ. Accepting the orthodox doctrine that 25 December was Christ's birthday, he calculated that Christ was born on 25 December 753 AUC and therefore that the Christian era should begin on 1 January 754 AUC, and that this should be called 1 *anno Domini* (AD). In his calculations he neglected to include the four years when Augustus Caesar ruled under the name of Octavius. It was therefore decided later on that Christ was probably born in 750 AUC, although no adjustment was made for the discovery of this error.

The years before the birth of Christ were subsequently labelled before Christ (BC) and the years after this event are called AD. However, this method of calculation has no zero: it goes from 1 BC to AD 1. This has led to all sorts of difficulties, which are demonstrated by the following example: along a coast the heights

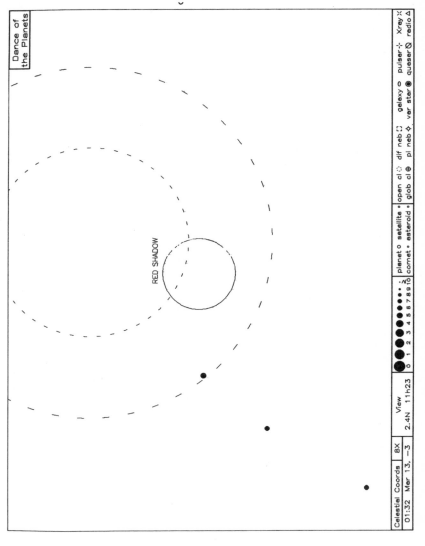

FIGURE 15A. ECLIPSE OF THE MOON, 13 MARCH 4 BC

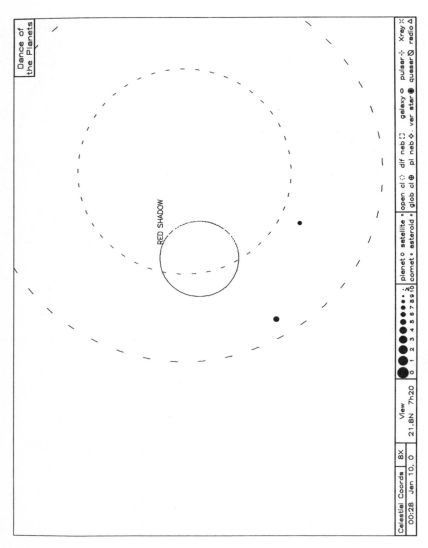

FIGURE 15B. ECLIPSE OF THE MOON, 10 JANUARY 1 BC

of cliffs and hills are given with respect to the average sea level, which is taken as zero. The depths of different parts of the ocean floor are also given with respect to sea level, but whereas the hills are taken to be so many positive metres above this level, the valleys in the ocean floor are counted as negative, i.e. so many negative metres below sea level.

It is impossible to make historical and astronomical calculations without having a datum line, i.e. a zero point. For this reason, astronomers have decided to call 1 BC the year zero. This means that for the purposes of calculations, 2 BC should be called −1, and AD 1, 2, 3 and so on should be labelled +1, +2, +3 respectively. Using such a system would make it possible to calculate when events occurred. It is unfortunate that no uniform dating system exists, because the dates historically used by scholars within different disciplines, different cultures, and even different periods of Christian history have led to a great deal of muddle and confusion.

However, since the beginnings of Christianity, scholars have tried to fix the year of Christ's birth. David Hughes gives an interesting graph of authors who have provided a range of dates which vary from 12 BC to AD 1. Ancient scholars mostly centre around 3 BC, while modern scholars tend to prefer a date around 6 BC. Whatever the method of calculation, in most cases the death of Herod the Great, who reigned when Christ was born, is taken as an important clue.

According to Flavius Josephus, the Jewish historian, Herod died within a few days of an eclipse of the moon, which was visible from Jericho. Most authors believe that the most likely explanation for this astronomical event is that it was the partial eclipse which took place on 13 March 4 BC between 1 a.m. and 3 a.m. However, other authors believe that the total eclipse of 10 January 1 BC is more likely. Both eclipses would put the birth of Christ before the normally accepted date of AD 1 and are shown in the computer-generated diagrams of figures 15a and b.

Astronomy and calendar-making gave a framework to people's lives but behind that numerical structure lay the world-view, or cosmology, of a people's culture. But what was the world-view in which the Magi lived and worked, the one that led them to the birthplace of Christ?

TWO

THE ABODE OF THE GODS

The question of all questions for humanity, the problem
which lies behind all others and is more interesting than
any of them is that of the determination of man's place
in Nature and his relation to the Cosmos.
(Thomas Huxley)

Religious belief systems, philosophical frameworks, political ideologies, mathematical structures and scientific theories all have something in common: they are creations of the human intellect. Scientific theories and religions, in particular, have two overriding similarities. Firstly, they both attempt to answer what Thomas Huxley called the 'question of all questions', as in the quotation above. Secondly, they are both products of human minds and so are dependent on our mental capabilities and the societies in which we live.

The word 'cosmology' can be defined as a set of beliefs about the universe: the sun, moon, planets and stars, and their motions in the sky. All the major civilisations, possibly almost all cultures, who seek answers to Huxley's question of questions, do this in terms of their cosmologies. And their ways of understanding and explaining events in the sky always invoke the gods and the heavens. For example, the Milky Way may be a river or a celestial field of wheat; the moon may be a goddess ruling childbirth; above all the sun is the sun-god, the giver of life. It has always been known that civilisations, both old and modern, have their gods. But it is very interesting to see what the new generation of archaeologists and historians of science are discovering about ancient ideas.

Like thinkers of any time, the Magi were on a quest, and they were the broadcasters of the cosmology of their world. The Magi were learned men from Babylon, and believed in the Zoroastrian faith. This religion was pre-Islamic and was founded by Zoroaster, a prophet who lived from 628–551 BC. Zoroaster was probably born in Tehran, and it is often claimed that he was a priest in the existing ancient polytheistic religion who received a vision instructing him to preach a new faith. This religion, named Zoroastrianism after him, recognised the two fundamental principles of Good (personified by Ahura Mazda) and Evil (personified by Ahriman). According to Zoroastrianism, Ahura Mazda would eventually triumph, resurrecting the dead and creating paradise on earth, an event presaged by the return of Zoroaster the Messiah. A lunar calendar and a belief in astrological influences was a central part of this faith. At the time of the birth of Christ, however, Babylon was very much under the influence of Hellenistic Greece. The Empire established by Alexander the Great in the fourth century BC had spread the cosmological, philosophical and scientific learning of Greece far and wide. Plato, Pythagoras and Aristotle were acknowledged as among the great teachers, and the Magi were steeped in the cultural ideas of the age as well as their own particular Zoroastrian discipline.

The Greeks offered a completely new way of thought. The excellence of the individual was glorified, and it was considered that man (by which was meant free men, not women and not, usually, slaves) was a rational, social and political being, capable of using his own reasoning powers to understand and to make judgments, regardless of his status. With the limits described above, men were equal and this extended to humanistic tolerance of other religions and other mythologies.

This emphasis on individual and personal significance was new. The Greeks felt free to ask questions and even challenge their gods in trying to make sense of the world around them. Until this time, the development and expansion of human critical thinking, philosophy, geometry and science as we know them had not existed. However, new research is proving that although this alternative way of thinking was quite radical, the foundations of Greek religious and mythological ideas – from which their philosophical and scientific concepts sprang – were based upon other, older religious and mythic themes.

It is important to understand the cosmology and myths from the Magi's Hellenistic world. But to really comprehend the astrology and astronomy which shaped the world-view of the Magi, it is necessary to travel back in time to the ancient mythologies which lay behind both the world-view of the Babylonians and the cosmologies of the Greeks at the time of Christ's birth.

The abode of the gods

A new and flourishing approach to the study of religious and mythical ideas of ancient civilisations has recently developed. Modern scholarship, making use of modern ways of thinking and using modern scientific tools, is offering exciting and vivid new insights into the ancient world and is showing the limitations of earlier historical approaches.

Hamlet's Mill, by Giorgio de Santillana and Hertha von Dechend, is a fascinating book which re-examines myth and legend from all over the world. In the preface, de Santillana says, 'Over many years I have searched for the point where myth and science join. It was clear to me for a long time that the origins of science had their deep roots in a particular myth, that of *invariance*.'

The cycle of day and night, the seasonal cycle, the lunar cycle and even the complex cycles of the planets all repeat themselves over time spans of varying length. Giorgio de Santillana and Hertha von Dechend claim that the observers of the ancient skies had discovered that certain changes that took place did not repeat even over what appeared to them to be very long periods of time. They collected evidence from ancient cultures all over the world to prove that these people were adept in astronomical observation, and that their religions and mythologies were their ways of expressing what they saw above them.

It is widely assumed by historians of science that knowledge of precession could not have existed before its discovery by Hipparchus in Greece in the second century BC. Otto Neugebauer was an erudite scholar who rejected any claim that the Babylonians had made this discovery. He did this on several grounds, including an argument about the lack of any contemporary textual evidence. Another scholar, A. Pannekoek, agreed. As he said in *A History of Astronomy*:

> It [precession] appears in the tables of the Chaldeans [the astrologer-astronomers of Babylon] in such a way that at different times different longitudes have been adopted as zero points; hence the Chaldeans are sometimes claimed to be the true discoverers, from whom Hipparchus borrowed the knowledge. There can be no doubt, however, that it was Hipparchus who recognised it as a continuous regular progress; he derived its amount from a comparison of earlier Alexandrian observations with his own.

No doubt these scholars are correct in bestowing a scientific understanding of precession on Hipparchus and the Greeks. But today we are having to reconsider the assumption that the phenomenon of precession was unknown to older civilisations. Even more than that, it would appear that the very ancient civilisations, which existed long before Hellenistic Greece, used observations of precessional effects in their own cosmologies and myths.

Looking at recent discoveries, which concern a knowledge of the effects of precession amongst ancient peoples, including the Egyptians, it appears that the slow movement of precession did manifest itself to the ancient watchers of the sky. Consequently, it became enshrined in their monuments, mythology and cosmology.

Some scientific historians – notably Professor Otto Neugebauer – claim that this knowledge does not appear in the mathematical astronomy of the time. However, this is not necessarily surprising: people may have had a mythologising approach to celestial events without possessing scientific or mathematical information. Its inclusion in their mathematical calculations might be a much slower and, in a technical sense, more difficult task. This is very much in keeping with what is known about scientific progress.

At certain stages in the history of science, observational and experimental measurements can outstrip contemporary theories and are only gradually and painstakingly incorporated into the theoretical frameworks used in mathematical calculations. In day-to-day calculations for a lunar calendar, or for astrological work on the relative positions of the sun, moon and planets, there is no great need to take the slow effect of the precession of the equinoxes into account. A similar situation now exists in geophysics, where it is known that the continents are slowly moving with respect to each other, but the shift is extremely slow. As a result, it is not necessary to take it into account when drawing up maps and charts for pilots and navigators.

The authors of *Hamlet's Mill* claim that all cultures for whom records exist have been interested in astronomy and have explained events in the sky in terms of gods and the heavenly land they inhabit. They also claim that ancient civilisations knew about precession, a fact which may be deduced from a study of the religious and mythological stories of cultures far older than Greek civilisation. Moreover, the authors demonstrate that myths and legends from diverse parts of the globe contain similarities and parallels, however widely the cultures may differ, and however separate the different cultures may seem to be from each other.

The argument is that the ancients made skilled and accurate astronomical observations, and correlated celestial objects (such as the sun, moon, planets and stars) and the motions of these objects with their deities. The discovery of the effects caused by precession damaged belief in the 'principle of invariance'. This principle was at the basis of all ancient science and can be found in a modified form today. It revolves around the deep conviction that while changes may be found to occur in the real world, they can only be short term, and of a cyclical nature. It is believed that the universe cannot be subject to long-term progressive change and is stable and changeless over long periods of time. This principle is closely tied in with the Aristotelian cosmological view (explained later in this chapter) that the cosmos is perfect and harmonious, unchanging and unending. This belief was held by many ancient societies, not only those influenced by Greece, and is a very human and philosophical belief about God and His universe. However, the development of astronomical knowledge led to a great cultural shock for the early pre-scientific communities. Something had happened in the celestial heavens, which had previously seemed so eternally stable and unchanging, and had travelled down through all the generations of the tribe or society. Security in the reigning order of gods had been severely shaken. Giorgio de Santillana and Hertha von Dechend therefore believe that legends and religious stories were developed to deal with this shocking fact.

They consider the greatest gap between archaic thinking and modern thinking to be found in the use of astrology, and they are at pains to define their terms:

> By this is not meant the common or judicial astrology which has become once again a fad and a fashion among the ignorant public, an escape from official science, and for the vulgar another kind of black art of vast prestige but with principles equally uncomprehended.

They are talking about astrology as it was understood in the ancient world:

It is necessary to go back to archaic times, to a universe totally unsuspecting of our science and the experimental method on which it is founded, unaware of the awful art of separation which distinguishes the verifiable from the unverifiable. This was a time, rich in another knowledge which was later lost, that search for other principles. It gave the *lingua franca* of the past. Its knowledge was of cosmic correspondence, which found their proof and seal of truth in a specific determinism, nay overdeterminism, subject to forces without locality.

It is very important to bear these points in mind. The astrology of the ancients gave the world a rich set of signs and symbols. It also provided a language that often cut right across geographical boundaries and cultural divisions. It is in this respect that astrology has affected our art, literature, religious beliefs and philosophies. This aspect of the astrological *lingua franca* has been more enduring than belief in astrology as a possible means of understanding correspondence between terrestrial events and certain cosmic cycles.

Astrology needs to be looked at without prejudice; it needs to be understood as a genuine attempt to make sense of 'man's place in nature and his relation to the cosmos' (Thomas Huxley). If this can be done, a richer picture will be painted of the religious and mythological world into which Jesus was born, and the kind of knowledge the Magi would have had and used in predicting the coming of the Messiah for the new age. It also will have a bearing on the claim that the Magi knew about the phenomenon of precession and would have incorporated this phenomenon into their predictions about the future.

Mythic time
Joseph Campbell has a section entitled 'Mythic Time' in his four-volume work, *The Masks of God*. It is here that he draws out a most interesting fact about peoples of the world 3000 years ago. In this period, the Sumerian and Egyptian cultures were thriving, Pythagorean and Greek ideas had not been heard of, and the Jews as a race did not exist. The journey of the Magi and the birth of Christ were events which were a long way in the future.

Campbell describes various cultural concepts of the progression of time which have a fundamental bearing on how we understand humanity's place in the cosmos. Firstly, he points out that two numbering systems existed in ancient Mesopotamia: the decimal system, based on 10, and the sexigesimal system, which is based on 60. The sexigesimal system is still used in calculating time: 60 seconds to the minute, 60 minutes to the hour. It is also used in measuring: 60 seconds make a minute of arc, 60 minutes make a degree, 360 (6 × 60) degrees make a circle. But the Mesopotamians took this further: space was a circle, and in the centre of the circle were the five points of their sacred ziggurat, i.e. four corners angled to north, south, east and west, and the fifth directed to the sky, by which divinity was brought into the world. They believed that the year consisted of 360 days (6 × 60), plus five festival days, and that when the old year died, the new year was born, and divinity was restored to the world. Furthermore, claims Campbell, there was the concept of a Great Year – a year of years: 'As the day was in proportion to the year, so was the year in proportion to the great year; and at the close of each such eon or great year there was a deluge, a cosmic dissolution and return.'

Campbell here refers to the Mesopotamian year of 360 days, and therefore to a Great Year of $360 \times 360 = 129,600$ years. Scholars have verified beyond reasonable doubt that Sumerian multiplication and division tables were based upon 12,960,000.

According to Campbell, Mesopotamian legend told of ten mythological kings who had each ruled for long periods of time between the 'first descent of kingship from the courts of heaven upon the cities of men and the coming of the Flood'. Various lengths of time were mentioned, but much later, in the third century BC, a Babylonian priest by the name of Berossos wrote that the legendary kings had ruled for a total period of 432,000 years.

Campbell revives a controversial idea, put forward before World War I, that there is a relationship between the Mesopotamian number system and the precession of the equinoxes:

> In one year . . . the precessional lag is 50 seconds, in 72 years it is 1 degree, and in 2160 years, 30 degrees; hence, in 25,920 years it would be 360 degrees, one complete cycle of the zodiac, . . . one 'Great' or 'Platonic Year'. But 25,920 divided by 60 (one soss) yields the figure 432.

It therefore appears that there is a profound relationship between the number of years assigned by Berossos to the cycle of his ten ancient kings of Mesopotamia and the length of time it takes for the sun to move once through the zodiac at the vernal equinox.

As Campbell points out, these mathematical figures of legend are not to be read as accurate references to historical events. They are mythological, but, he suggests, they should be regarded as more than simple expressions of mythological themes. They indicate a carefully worked out and seriously regarded mathematical order. In Campbell's belief, the highest concern of the Mesopotamian mythology must have been 'some sort of mathematically ordered, astronomically referred notion about the relationship of man and the rhythms of his life on earth, not simply to the seasons, the annual mysteries of birth, death and regeneration, but beyond those to even greater, very much larger cycles: the great years.'

He then goes on to say that the cosmic order is known deeply and essentially through number:

> . . . which becomes audible – as Pythagoras held and the harps of
> Ur suggest – in the harmonies and rhythms of music; specifically,
> the number system of:
> 60 – the soss
> 600 – the ner
> 3600 – the sar
> 216,000 – the great sar ($= 60 \times 3600$)
> two great sars yielding that interesting 432,000 of Berossos' eon.

Joseph Campbell has therefore provided a guide from the number systems and mythological schemes of early Sumerian culture, through the late Babylonian period of Pythagoras and then Berossos, down to the Hellenistic world of the Magi and the Greek scheme of the Platonic Great Year. He has shown that there is a relationship between the number system used in early Sumerian mythology, in Pythagorean harmonies, and in the Platonic scheme which formalised the Greek scientific description of precession of the equinoxes.

As Campbell has pointed out, the Babylonian festival year was calculated mathematically, and the Great Year has been found in the same way. This happens to coincide with the *observable* astronomically-calculated Platonic Great Year which, according to Campbell, 'might indeed have been the result only of a sheer (but then how really wonderful!) accident'. Approximately 3000 years separate the early Sumerians from Pythagoras and after him,

Hipparchus and the Greeks who 'discovered' precession and formulated the Platonic Great Year.

It has been argued that these numbers are merely a consequence of using a sexigesimal system. They claim that any similarities with the figures, which arise from the effects of precession, can only be a coincidence. But could 'coincidence' really be the only explanation? The Mesopotamian scheme also uses numbers which bear a profound relationship to numbers associated with precession of the equinoxes.

The fact is that this figure occurs time and again in other ancient mythologies. In the Icelandic sagas, the cosmic battles between good and evil gods follow a cyclical round which is called the 'war with the Wolf':

> 'Five hundred doors and forty there are,
> I ween, in Valhall's walls;
> Eight hundred fighters through each door fare
> When to war with the Wolf they go.'
> (Taken from The *Masks of God* by Joseph Campbell)

Therefore, $540 \times 800 = 432,000$, the number of years in one cosmic cycle of time. The Indian cycle of four world ages is 12,000 'divine years' of 360 'human years', i.e. 4,320,000 human years: we inhabit the last tenth of that period, i.e. 432,000 years. As we see, these numbers correspond with the Mesopotamian numbers for the mythological kings.

We therefore have evidence from three, quite separate, cultures of the use of the same particular numbers, and multiples of numbers, and these numbers bear an obvious relationship to precession of the equinoxes. What does this mean? Why should three completely different kinds of society choose exactly the same figure as part of the framework of their mythology?

Is it beyond belief that the precessional movement of the sun was known about long before Hipparchus discovered it? The Babylonians, or indeed any early civilisation, may not have understood precession in the scientific sense in which the Greeks understood it, or in which we understand it today, but since many early calendars made use of observations on the sun and stars, it seems likely that they would have noticed long-period shifts in the stars that arose just before the vernal equinox. This would have meant they were aware of the observational changes now attributed to the precession of the earth's axis.

Egypt

Contrary to the orthodox views of many historians, it is becoming increasingly clear that the civilisation which built the pyramids *had* discovered precession of the equinoxes. Many Egyptologists have, until recently, been dismissive of claims about the possible astronomical significance of the pyramids. There is, however, plenty of evidence that their positions and construction are both closely influenced by, and linked to, astronomical knowledge.

In 1938 an eminent scientist, Lancelot Hogben, wrote:

> The Pyramid of Cheops and that of Sneferu are constructed on a common geometrical plane . . . the rays of Sirius the Dog star, whose heliacal rising announced the Egyptian New Year and the flooding of the sacred river which brought prosperity to the cultivators, were perpendicular to the south face at transit, and shone down the ventilating shaft into the royal chamber while building was in progress. The main opening, and a second shaft leading to the lower chamber, conveyed the light of the Pole Star, which was then the star Thuban in the constellation of Draco, at its lower transit, three degrees below the true celestial pole.

This was controversial stuff in those days. The so-called 'ventilation shafts' were considered to be just that, despite the obvious care and extreme attention to detail that had been used in their placement and construction. To suggest that they might be significant in some way went against the orthodox view. Other academic Egyptologists were consequently dismissive of these and other assertions that the pyramids were built with astronomical knowledge in mind.

It was already known that the majority of the pyramids faced the four cardinal points of north, south, east, west with a very high level of accuracy of less than 0.10 degrees. Interestingly, the Sumerian ziggurat was also aligned to the cardinal points. It was widely accepted that the Egyptians were fascinated by the stars. The Egyptian name for the stars around the pole of the sky was 'the stars which know no death'. These stars, as seen earlier, do not appear to rise in the east, move across the sky and set in the west, as the other constellations do; instead they seem to circle around the north pole of the sky and are therefore never out of view below the horizon.

The Egyptians believed that their Pharaoh was divine, the god

Osiris incarnate on earth, and that the sky was heaven, the abode of the gods. Orion was a very important constellation for the ancient Egyptians, as was Sirius. Orion's importance came from the fact that this constellation rose in the east at the vernal equinox c. 4500 BC. By 1000 BC, Sirius was rising in the east just days before the start of the floods of the Nile. When the Pharaohs came to the end of their allotted time on earth, their earthly bodies were preserved with great care and ritual so they could abide for eternity within the pyramids, and their heavenly presence could be viewed in the sky above. It was an important part of Egyptian religion that each Pharaoh in turn was the god incarnate; he had to re-live, and re-die, as the story of Osiris told.

None of this is new or controversial knowledge, but it does seem strange that Egyptologists have traditionally refused to consider the implications of astronomical discoveries. The pyramids were built 4000 to 5000 years ago by a society that we would call technologically unsophisticated. However, the scale of building, the precision of the positions of interior chambers, and the accuracy of the angles of the shafts to star positions, all combine to raise many questions. Established academic Egyptologists find it surprising that people should be so fascinated, even overwhelmed, by the pyramids. They acknowledge that astronomy must have been important, but seem surprisingly uninterested in the implications of the discoveries. However, a recent upsurge of interest in ancient Egyptian astronomy and mythology has led to some fascinating developments in this field. In order to appreciate fully the advances which are being made, it is important to know the story of the supreme Egyptian god, Osiris.

The story of Osiris

There were two brothers, sons of the Earth-god and the Sky-god. One brother, Osiris, was good. He travelled abroad, civilising the whole world. The other brother, Seth, was evil, and in his jealousy he killed Osiris. Isis was sister and wife of Osiris, and she represented motherhood and healing. She magically restored the dismembered body of Osiris to life and conceived Horus, son of Isis. Horus avenged his father's death in an 80-year battle with Seth. The Pharaohs were considered to be the earthly incarnation of Horus during their lives on Earth, and they became rejoined to Osiris upon departing from their earthly lives. The constellation Orion is Osiris seen in the land of the gods.

In 1994 a BBC television programme was made about the pyramids, based on the book, *The Orion Mystery*, by Robert Bauval and Adrian Gilbert. Robert Bauval, a construction engineer who lived in Egypt, became interested in the questions raised by the pyramids, but his explorations were dismissed by orthodox Egyptologists. He then met Adrian Gilbert, an author interested in the astronomical and astrological tradition of Egypt, and together they threw light on the fascinating discoveries that were being made.

In *The Orion Mystery*, Bauval and Gilbert raised the important contribution made by Virginia Trimble, an American astronomer. In 1964 she confirmed the significance of the northern passage of the pyramid of Cheops. This passage pointed directly to the north celestial pole, the area of the circumpolar stars, the stars which knew no death. Why should this passage point so accurately to that part of the sky? This was a vital question, ignored by Egyptologists.

Trimble had discovered a fascinating relationship between the southern shaft and the three stars of the belt of Orion, a constellation which has many associations with ancient Egypt. According to Bauval and Gilbert, and also Jane Sellars, the sky image of Orion (or Sahu) is depicted as a human figure in many places, including the ceiling in the Tomb of Senmut. In some representations Orion is shown with three large stars just above his head, stars which have been identified with the three stars of Orion's belt. Using the phenomenon of precession, Trimble calculated the positions of the three stars as they would have appeared in the sky at the time of the building of the Great Pyramid (*c.* 2600 BC). An astonishing fact emerged:

> These three stars . . . passed once each day, at culmination directly over the southern shaft of the Great Pyramid at the time it was built. Thus considerations of Egyptian religion and modern astronomy combine to indicate that the 'air shafts' of Cheops's Pyramid were actually intended as ways by which the soul of the deceased king might ascend to join the circumpolar stars and the god constellation Sah.

This is a significant discovery for two reasons. Firstly, it indicates that the Egyptians believed that precise alignment of the pyramids with certain stars was of great importance. But why did the Egyptians use such immense human resources and astronomical knowledge to construct the pyramids? And why did they take such care in the alignment of the pyramids? These questions are of paramount importance, especially for Egyptologists.

The second reason why Trimble's discovery is so important is the implication of the statement. The pyramids were built to house the earthly body of the pharaoh, and scholars have tended to state that they were merely a part of the complex funerary rites associated with the Pharaoh's death. However, they clearly give us more information than this: they point to the part of the sky that was important – they seem to point to Orion. Why?

Bauval received very little help from the experts, but discovered something else. It occurred to him that the three pyramids at Giza might have been built to represent the three stars of Orion's belt, as these three stars were in exactly the same line with respect to each other as the pyramids. Also, the third star, which is fainter than the other two, corresponds to the third, smaller pyramid, and what is more, the orientation of the pyramids with the east-west line was equal to that of the three stars of Orion's belt with the eastern horizon in 2450 BC.

Further investigations showed that two other pyramids, one at Zawyat Al Aryan and another at Abu Ruwash, might also be seen as two further stars of Orion (Bellatrix and Saiph respectively) on the same scale as the other three pyramids. Also on the same scale, two pyramids at Dashour might be seen as the eyes of Taurus, the Bull.

There are, however, some prominent stars which are not represented by pyramids. This raised the question that if the pyramids do represent stars, why should some stars be represented and not others? Scholars have criticised the findings of Bauval and Gilbert, claiming that the absence of pyramids corresponding to important stars detracts from their claim that the Egyptians were attempting to represent the constellations of Orion (which they called Osiris) and Taurus (which they called Seth) on earth. However, when one looks at the relationship between the pyramids in relation to the course of the Nile, another interesting fact emerges. The pyramids' position correlates closely to positions of the relevant stars in relationship to the path of the Milky Way across the sky. So what were the Egyptians aiming to achieve?

The work of Bauval and Gilbert on the pyramids and the Orion constellation has been dismissed as a pyramid marketing ploy by

Krupp, an astronomer at the Griffith Observatory in America. He claims that this representation of Orion by five pyramids is upside down in relation to the real constellation: in the sky, the head of Orion is in the north and his feet in the south, whereas in the supposed representation the head of Orion would be towards the south and the feet in the north.

Krupp's comments show the difficulties that arise when modern knowledge is used to criticise a suggestion concerning the way in which the ancients might have seen themselves in relation to the universe. However, Krupp makes the mistake of assuming that the Egyptians thought in terms of latitude and longitude, north and south. The overwhelming evidence is that latitude and longitude came much later in the history of geography. His objection is weakened by the fact that there is no evidence that the Egyptians saw the earth and sky as spheres. To them, the constellations around the north pole were the stars that knew no death, but this did not have to be (and apparently was not) understood in modern terms. It is possible that they were simply representing the position of Orion with respect to the Milky Way on the banks of the Nile, as they saw these features rising in the east.

Other scholars continue to be sceptical of these findings. One of their main arguments is that there are hundreds of pyramids all over Egypt. However, it is worth staying with the mystery of Orion and the pyramids a little longer.

Jane Sellars is a modern scholar who questions established notions about mythology in the ancient world. In her book, *The Death of Gods in Ancient Egypt*, she acknowledges her debt to *Hamlet's Mill*. On the subject of Orion–Osiris mythology, she suggests that 'Orion's precessionally caused failure to appear in "his place" at "his proper time" gave rise to long centuries of an oral tradition of Osiris's death.' In other words, the Egyptian sky watchers did know of precession. They observed, over centuries, that the motion of the stars, which had seemed so constant, was changing very slowly, and therefore the constellation of Orion did not continue to rise at the expected time.

The myths of a culture reflect the deepest questions which can be posed about nature and the place of human beings in it. Like the authors of *Hamlet's Mill*, Sellars believes that astronomical observations not only gave ancient people a 'sky picture' of their mythology, but at times necessitated revision of this mythology when the sky picture provided new and disturbing information.

According to Sellars, Orion–Osiris had been 'alive' during the long period when the constellation of Orion was visible in the east at sunrise at the vernal equinox. However, as a result of precession, a time came when Orion was not completely visible, and eventually none of the stars of Orion could be seen at the crucial moment of dawn at the vernal equinox. The argument is therefore being made that the mythology of Osiris was a method of rationalising, or explaining, certain astronomical events. The ancients' reliance on what they saw as the eternal and immutable order of the night sky had suffered a huge shock with the discovery that the Orion constellation had ceased to rise in accordance with this unchanging order. Astronomically, they had observered precession. They had to explain it, and as Sellars and others such as de Santillana, von Dechend and Joseph Campbell show, they used their myths to give meaning to the acts of the gods which they could see in the sky above their heads. Therefore, if Orion was no longer constant, it was because evil, in the form of his brother Seth, was killing him. But evil was not stronger than good. Isis was goddess of healing and motherhood, the original and ever-living mother of all things, and she restored the god to life. Astronomically, this was demonstrated by the eventual reappearance of the constellation Osiris on the eastern horizon at dawn, but no longer at the time of the equinox. As Sellars explains:

> The confusion, the grief and the fear, when this lag [the precessional lag] at last claimed all of the stars of Orion, were great . . . Myths from divergent cultures all point to the intense loss, but in these myths, it is a loss that is always followed by great relief and great joy. Stars rise four minutes earlier each night and in a short time the stars of Orion once again appeared before dawn, but on a later date . . . Osiris was given the Netherworld as his new 'office' . . .

Clearly, the Egyptians had a sophisticated knowledge of astronomy, and there is evidence that they observed precession of the equinoxes. It is also evident that, contrary to orthodox scholarship, they understood the effects of precession, even if they did not have the scientific explanation of it which we call understanding today, the discovery of which is usually ascribed to Hipparchus.

Pythagoras

From around 600 BC, the Mediterranean and Middle Eastern world saw a change taking place in the way people understood the cosmos. Egyptian civilisation was ancient and rich, but the development of a very different way of thinking was beginning to spread throughout the area. The rise of Greek civilisation and the Greeks' flair for a special kind of 'rational' thinking was to profoundly affect all aspects of culture, including religious ideas.

Pythagoras is a mysterious figure about whom little is known for certain, although much is attributed to his teaching. He was the master of a mystery cult in the sixth century BC whose teachings were secret, and perhaps because of this it is difficult to say exactly what the teachings of Pythagoras were. However, the ideas generally ascribed to Pythagoras and his followers had a profound impact on both the scientific developments of the Greeks who came after him, and on the history of scientific thought. Jacob Bronowski, author of *The Ascent of Man* said: 'I find both a pleasure and constraint in describing the progress of mathematics, because it has been part of so much human speculation: a ladder for mystical as well as rational thought.'

Human fascination with numbers and their possible magical properties goes back to very ancient times, long before the more formal approach associated with Euclid and the Greeks. Euclid was a third century BC mathematician from Alexandria in Egypt. He was the author of *Elements*, which set out the principles of geometry, and remained an important text until at least the nineteenth century. The ancient, pre-Euclid concern with 'arithmetical magic' is more properly the realm of what could now be called numerology, rather than systematic mathematics.

Pythagoras was a man who stood with one foot in the ancient world of numerology and one foot in the modern world of pure mathematics and the application of mathematics to the physical world. He was a mathematician, scientist and philosopher. He is important to this story because he made new and important contributions to astronomy, cosmology, mathematics and the physics of music, learning which would have been part of the intellectual inheritance of the Magi. Pythagoras founded a religious brotherhood that included mysticism and rational science, and the Magi would have accepted both these approaches to truth in a way most people find impossible today.

Pythagoras developed theories about number and geometry in a different way from preceding methods. He inherited much of his thinking about numbers from the Babylonian culture, and he and his followers made a substantial contribution to the development of astrology as it was known at the time of Christ's birth. The Pythagoreans are best known for developing important concepts about music, geometry, and the inherent harmony of numbers. Firstly, they realised that basic frequencies produced by musical instruments were related by simple mathematical ratios. For example, if a string, fixed at each end, is plucked in the middle, the string gives off a note at a certain vibration – its fundamental or ground note. The ends of the string do not move, and such points are called the nodes. If the string is plucked a quarter of a length from the end, it will not vibrate in the middle, and this gives the octave above the ground note. Pythagoras showed that all notes which were in harmony with a fundamental note, divided the string in a whole number of equal parts of two, three, four and five, while notes which occurred when the string was divided up in other ways were out of harmony with the fundamental note. Pythagoras and his school developed this work on music, and extended their discoveries about ratios to geometry, movements of the planets, and the application of arithmetic and logic to geometry.

A very important contribution attributed to the Pythagoreans was that they knew how to construct the first three of the five regular solids: the tetrahedron, cube and octahedron (the other two being the dodecahedron and the icosahedron). They tried to combine these concepts into a unified model of the solar system, and believed that they should be able to calculate the orbits of the sun, moon and planets by relating them to musical intervals. These movements of the heavenly bodies were later to be described as 'the music of the spheres'.

People asked why this 'music' which Pythagoras claimed to exist throughout the cosmos could not be heard. The answer was that humans, belonging to the imperfect and sublunar area upon earth, are unable to appreciate the perpetual sound because their souls are not in complete harmony with the music of the perfect, superlunar regions of the universe. The next section will explain this profoundly Greek development of belief in perfect and rational natural order.

This Greek belief in the value and power of rational thought changed human understanding once and for all. The gods might be capricious and wayward, yet humans could, by using their ability to think rationally, discover and understand the fundamental order of the universe and everything in it. In this, the Greeks differed from their neighbours because they were developing the notion that humans could equal (and even exceed) the gods in understanding. We might be subject to the influence of fate upon our destinies, yet if we chose we could develop a powerful understanding which would show us how the universe worked. This philosophical idea was not quite the same as other religions where a human might achieve perfect bliss or immortality by virtue of faith in his gods and/or appropriate behaviour throughout his life. The Greeks were to foster the notion that man could achieve wisdom and happiness by virtue of his ability to think philosophically, make discoveries, and formulate a rational view of the world. This was the start of scientific thought as the phrase is understood today.

The Pythagoreans also adopted another concept from the Babylonians: the Great Year. This is not the same idea of a Great Year as that of the later Greeks, based upon the gradual movement of the sun at the vernal equinox and relevant to the astrology of the Magi. The Pythagoreans argued that because the periodic motion of the planets (with respect to the background stars) was related by simple proportions, special alignments of the planets would repeat after a certain length of time. They believed that all the heavenly bodies would eventually complete a round of all their differing and interacting movements, returning to an original point. And since all earthly events were largely under the control of planetary motion, it followed that history would also eventually repeat itself. This period of time was called a Great Year, and many ancient cultures and their own version of this concept.

In his book *The Great Year*, Nicholas Campion says:

> The Pythagoreans maintained that the same process of creation, indeed all existence, could be explained by the successive subdivision of the monad, the one. The single original point split into the two. These two points then interacted to produce a third, and the three then combined to produce the four. The figure thus obtained, the tetratys, is the model of creation in Pythagorean philosophy.

The tetratys is also the sum of $1+2+3+4$ which equals 10. The number 10 was considered to be a perfect and a sacred number in its own right.

These ideas were then taken up by Greek scholars such as the astronomer and mathematician Eudoxus (c. 406–355 BC) and Plato. From Pythagoras' teachings the Greeks developed the concept of the Platonic Great Year. For the first time they also formally expressed ideas about precession of the equinoxes – the sun's gradual movement on the first day of spring from one zodiac constellation to another.

It is, however, important not to forget the mystical aspect of Pythagorean concepts – ideas embodied the old learnings as well as the new. All this knowledge formed an important part of the Magi's thinking. A deeper understanding of the Pythagorean/ Platonic concept of the Great Year included the belief that mankind was not only at the end of one age, but was at the beginning of another. But far more than that, for educated people living at the time of the Magi there was the realisation that one whole Great Year, which was made up of the twelve ages of the sun's progress through the zodiac, was coming to an end.

Apocalyptic times were therefore expected, and everyone, including the Magi, anticipated hugely significant events. These included the birth of a great leader, the Messiah, which would take place as the vernal equinox moved from the age of Aries into the new age of Pisces. The path of the sun moves backwards through the zodiac, and Pisces was the first sign of the zodiac – the new 'Great Month' of a new Great Year.

The links between ancient cosmology, numerology and the work of the Pythagorean school are discussed at length by Gordon Strachan in his book *Christ and the Cosmos*. Here he quotes from *Towards Aquarius (A History of the Zodiacal Ages)* by Vera Reid:

> The transition between the ages of Aries and Pisces marked a turning point both in human evolution and in world history for it coincided with the close of one Great Year and the opening of another.

Strachan adds:

> Thus it would appear from these authorities that we have established a strong case for maintaining that the star of Bethlehem

marked not only the end of the age of Aries but also of a complete Great Year, and that it therefore also marked not only the beginning of the age of Pisces, but also of a whole new Great Year.

So for many, the coming of Jesus the Messiah was the coming of a saviour who would rescue the people from their persecutors (specifically the Romans). For some, the new figure was a representative of a completely new order: the Fisherman, the representative of the Piscean age. He could also be said to be a new kind of man for a new cosmic beginning. The link between this religious belief in a messiah and the contemporary Greek-inspired belief in rational man, is that both ideas occur at a historically unique moment in the history of mankind. Modernity had begun with the dawning of the new Great Year, a beginning shared by both Christianity and scientific thought.

The Greek cosmos

The Aristotelian description of the universe was a profoundly convincing cosmology which gave a framework both to the ideas of Western civilisation and Christian theology, right up to the time of Copernicus in the sixteenth century. Plate 3 shows this plan.

According to Aristotle's cosmology, the universe consisted of a series of spheres, one inside the other. The outer sphere, called the 'celestial sphere', contained all the 'fixed' stars, i.e. those that do not appear to move relative to each other. Earth was a sphere fixed at the centre of this universe. Between earth and the celestial sphere were seven other crystalline spheres of the planets. To the sphere below the fixed stars was attached the planet Saturn, Jupiter's sphere came next, then the spheres of Mars, the sun (the Greeks considered the sun and moon to be planets too), Venus, Mercury, and finally, in contact with earth, was the sphere of the moon.

The spheres nestled within each other, rather like Russian dolls, and each moved as a result of friction with the sphere above. All the spheres ultimately received their movement from the celestial sphere which, in turn, was moved by the 'prime mover'. The 'prime mover' was the unseen, unquantifiable force which existed outside and beyond the universe. However, it was also the ultimate cause of all motion and existence within the universe. The prime mover could not be known or recognised by mortals, except as the *a priori* notion from which all else followed that could be experienced or discovered. As a result of this cosmology, the movement of the stars and planets could be understood by an observer on earth who could gaze up through these crystalline spheres and observe the workings of God.

In mechanical terms, the celestial sphere transmitted its motion to Saturn by friction. However, Saturn would not move as fast as the celestial sphere, because the friction drive was not totally efficient. The motion of Saturn's sphere was transmitted to that of Jupiter by the same mechanism. Consequently, Jupiter was moving even more slowly than Saturn, or, in other words, it was slipping more with respect to the sphere of the stars. Whereas the sphere of the stars moved around the earth once in 23 hours 56 minutes, the moon moved around in almost 25 hours. This was due to the way in which the sphere of the moon was in contact with the earth, and the friction drive, transmitted between neighbouring crystalline spheres, was becoming less effective by the time it got down to the moon.

From a present-day, astronomical point of view, this may seem odd and contrived, but it was a serious attempt to reconcile astronomical observations with philosophical and religious beliefs. The universe was in two parts, and different physical 'laws' applied in each division. The area above the moon, containing the stars and the other planets including the sun, was the superlunar region, and here all was perfect. Motion therefore had to be circular, with no permanent change, only cyclical change repeating itself. Neither could there be any corruption, decay or alteration.

This perfect region consisted of only one element: aether. The other division of the universe was the sublunar region, that of the moon and earth. In contrast to the superlunar region, in the sublunar region, imperfection did exist. Consequently, change, corruption and motion in a straight line took place. All the material objects in this region were composed of four elements: earth, water, air and fire.

There were difficulties with this simple and aesthetically very pleasing scheme, and as a result, important refinements were made to it by the astronomers and mathematicians Eudoxus (in the fourth century BC) and Ptolemy (in the second century BC). At this stage in the history of ideas, a clear distinction was accepted between physical reality and the mathematical models used to calculate planetary positions. Aristotle's cosmology was designed to represent the ways in which celestial objects were actually ranged in space, while the refinements of Ptolemy were considered to be merely mathematical devices useful for calculations, but not part of the pure and harmonious order represented by Aristotle's scheme.

Aristotle's vision harmonised the extraordinary astronomical, geometric and philosophical developments of the Greeks. All parts of the world which subsequently came under the influence of the Greeks were inspired by this Aristotelian expression of cosmology. The Greek view of the order of things held sway throughout the Alexandrian Empire, and in Europe for many centuries after that, until the Copernican Revolution in the seventeenth century AD.

The Platonic Great Year

The concept of the Platonic Great Year arose from knowledge of precession of the equinoxes, a concept which would certainly have been a part of the Magi's learning. The Platonic Great Year was a measure of the length of time it took the sun's position on the first day of spring to progress through the zodiac constellations. In this ideal scheme, the twelve constellations form a 360-degree circle, and each constellation covers 30 degrees of arc. The vernal equinox moves through 1 degree of a constellation in 72 years; it therefore moves through a whole constellation (30 degrees) in 2160 years (i.e. 30 × 72); it moves through all twelve constellations in 25,920 years (i.e. 360 × 72). It is, however, important to remember that this scheme depends upon 30 degrees of arc being assigned to each constellation. This was therefore a late development in use of constellations, which previously could vary considerably in size. Modern astronomical calculations, using highly sophisticated technology, give a value for this equinoctial period of 25,800 years. The Greek system was out by only one per cent, a tribute to their geometrical skills and observation. However, the Greek figure of 25,920 turns out to be a fascinating figure when compared to other significant figures in ancient numerology.

In the Platonic Great Year, one Great Day is 72 years, one Great Month is 2160 years, and the Great Year is 25,920 years, consisting of the twelve Great Months. This Platonic system underlies the astrological zodiac as it is known today. When, for example, the Age of Pisces or the Age of Aquarius is discussed, we are referring to one Great Month of the Platonic scheme, the length of time that the sun at the vernal equinox remains in one 30-degree constellation.

Figure 12 shows the movement of the vernal equinox in relation to the zodiac constellations, covering a few of the Great Months of one Great Year. As this figure shows, in earliest Sumerian times the Sun was in Gemini. From about 4000 BC (Sumerian and Egyptian cultures), the point of the vernal equinox was in the constellation of Taurus; by the second millennium BC (the time of the Babylonian Empire, the rise of Greek civilisation, and of Jewish history) it had moved to Aries; then, around the time of the birth of Christ, the point of the vernal equinox moved from Aries to Pisces. The present point of the vernal equinox is about to enter the constellation of Aquarius, although modern opinions differ for a variety of reasons about precisely when this will be. Today we are therefore considered to be entering the Age of Aquarius.

The Jewish calendar

Although followers of the Jewish faith had contact with the Babylonians, they did not have much interest in astronomy and, consequently, made very little contribution to the subject. This is normally considered to be the result of the Ten Commandments, which specifically disapproved of the worship of celestial objects, a practice which, as discussed earlier, was very common in the Middle East. This disinterest in astronomy meant that their calendar was imperfect.

The Jewish civil day started in the evening. However, no evidence exists to show whether or not they divided the time between sunrise and sunset into twelve parts. It would appear that this custom was only followed from around the time of Christ's birth, when they began to follow the Greek example, although the Greeks themselves had imported this method of solar timekeeping from Babylon. For the hours of night, the Roman custom was followed, using the four night-watches, or *vigiliae*.

The Jews regulated the months and the festival calendar by the phases of the moon in the same way that the Babylonians had done for a long time. They also adopted the names of the months used by the Babylonians, first for civil and then for religious use. In their calendar, the year began with autumn at the time of a new moon, the seventh Babylonian month. In order to keep their lunar calendar in step with the season, it was necessary to add an intercalated month at the thirteenth moon. In later eras, the year began with the spring. According to *The History of Astronomy*, by Giorgio Abetti, it was only Babylonian Jews, supposedly the descendants of the ancient exiles who had migrated there with Nebuchadnezzar, who could carry out the 'calculations of the dates of festivals and the observance of rituals'.

The different roles of the Magi

The Magi played a variety of roles in the ancient world. They initiated an approach to mathematical astronomy that was to influence all later aspects of the subject. In this sense they were scientific innovators. Because they travelled a great deal, they assimilated the astronomical ideas of their neighbouring cultures and blended these ideas with their own. As a result, they were also synthesisers of knowledge of ancient astronomical cultures. In their travels they imparted what they knew to those people with whom they came into contact, and so were also the transmitters of the ancient wisdom of astronomy, astrology and the religious beliefs based on these subjects. Consequently, the Magi played an important part in preserving the most enduring aspects of ancient pre-scientific cultures, but by their own innovations and scholarship they laid the foundations of the first attempt at a grand unifying theory which could explain observed interrelationships between the cosmos and life on earth.

THREE

THE CELESTIAL MIRROR

It is not often realised to what extent symbolism and
languages have preserved concepts and terms of
Graeco-Roman astrology. Astronomers speak of
'conjunction' and 'opposition' of planets; one freely
discusses the 'aspects' of a problem. People thank their
'lucky stars' for escaping from danger. An unsuccessful
venture is 'ill-starred'. The 'stars' of the realm of arts, or
that of sports are those that rose to prominence in their
respective fields of endeavour
(F. H. Cramer,
Astrology in Roman Law & Politics)

In modern Western culture, astronomy and astrology are very separate areas of activity. Astronomy is an intellectual scientific discipline, totally acceptable as a valid subject for study and research in an academic environment. Astrology on the other hand is dismissed by some as nonsense: those scientists and scholars who take an interest in the history of the subject, or who try to investigate its claims, have to defend their interests and their work against hostility and prejudice, although this was not always the case.

What is astrology?

To understand the Magi, it is necessary to understand certain aspects of the astrology of their time. But what exactly is astrology? In *The Dictionary of Astrology*, Fred Gettings defined it as 'The study of the relationship between the Macrocosm and the Microcosm, which (in material terms) is often defined as the study of the influence of celestial bodies on the Earth and its inhabitants.'

Astrology began in the ancient world, and for the last 2500 years it has developed into a complex system of calculation and interpretation. Although there is some form of agreement over the main principles, disagreements do exist amongst astrologers of different schools, and much discussion takes place over some of the more subtle points of interpretation. Here, some of the basic ideas will be given, which will necessarily seem incomplete and oversimplified to some modern astrologers. But it is important to know about the kind of astrological thinking which formed part of the Magi's learning and gave a framework to many of the cultural ideas of Middle Eastern civilisation around the time of Christ's birth.

Many modern scientific and intellectual critics regard ancient astrology as mere superstition, which shows a basic misunderstanding of the matter. Astrology was the first attempt at a unification of scientific theory which would encompass human behaviour, meteorology, mundane affairs as well as the cosmos.

The earliest form of astrology was simply an association between human and terrestrial events and celestial phenomena of all sorts, including astronomical sightings and meteorological conditions. Its predictions came mainly from the assertion that when celestial phenomena were repeated, then associated events would recur on the earth. Such astrology existed in Assyria in about 800 BC. The Assyrians conquered the Babylonians, and, as a result, were influenced by the Babylonian astronomers, although they placed much greater emphasis on the astrological aspects of their work. The Assyrians also associated different countries with various constellations, compass directions and prosperity. The earliest type of astrology in Babylon and Assyria was naive and associated with their 'astral mythology'. The foundations of a more sophisticated 'celestial science' required a number of other factors before a systematic approach could begin.

Normally, when we talk about astrology in the West we have in mind horoscopic astrology. This form of astrology links personalities of individuals to the positions of the planets at their birth and tries to determine their destinies in terms of future movements of the planets. This type of astrology appeared fairly late in the ancient world, from about 500–200 BC. A system of constellations, a reasonable calendar and astronomical methods of timekeeping are necessary prerequisites for the development of horoscopic astrology. Another vital requirement was a method for calculating the position of all the known planets in the sky, even when they were not visible, because of their position above the horizon in the daytime.

The system of the constellations had many different roots which are not easy to pin down with any precision. However, our calendar and timekeeping are certainly of Egyptian origin. The method for calculating planetary positions was supplied by Babylonian arithmetical astronomy. The underlying philosophy and cosmology of the subject was provided by the work of Aristotle. The Pythagorean belief in the numerical basis of all nature provided a further quantitative basis for the work of the Magi.

The Magi at the time of Christ's birth were well-versed in the Greek understanding of the cosmos and the contribution that this civilisation had made to astrology. However, the Magi would also have had the additional knowledge of more ancient wisdoms: the different religious and cultural ideas of the Babylonian and Persian civilisations. At the end of the first century BC, the big cultural centres, such as Alexandria, were exciting, cosmopolitan places, with much interchange of ideas and beliefs. There were many schools of thought that included astrological knowledge, and the Magi would have known as much as anyone about all of them. Therefore, while having the knowledge about the scientific developments of the Greeks, the Magi also knew about the esoteric disciplines which went back to much earlier systems of thought. As a result, they would have had an impressive depth of understanding about astronomy and astrology, which should not simply be dismissed as irrelevant or naive and simplistic.

The astrological chart

The sky appears to circle above us each night: most of the stars appear to rise above the eastern horizon at nightfall, move across the sky and set in the west as the morning sun appears in the east. Polaris, however, remains stationary at the north point, in the northern hemisphere, and the circumpolar stars do not actually rise and set, but circle around it. If this nightly show is watched regularly, certain patterns become familiar. Additionally, one can see that the pattern of stars overhead each night varies as the year goes on, and one star group will always be overhead in December, for example, while another star group will always be overhead in April, another in June, and so on. These patterns have been observed since people began watching the movements in the night skies, and over time, have been divided into 'constellations', or groupings, and given names, as seen in chapter 1.

The apparent motion of the sun, moon and planets against the background stars serves to define the set of constellations known as the 'zodiac'. In order to cast a personal horoscope, it is necessary to know the positions of sun, moon and planets against the zodiacal constellations at the moment of birth. It is also necessary to know which particular constellation was rising above the eastern horizon at the same time. This means knowing the positions of planets even if they cannot be seen in the sky as a result of their rising with, just before, or just after the sun, or because the sky is clouded. It is also necessary to be able to *predict* the positions of the planets, sun and moon against the zodiac.

The moon and planets, which appear to make their own sets of movements in the sky, also move in front of the zodiacal constellations. It would seem that all societies of which we have any records looked at the sky and made these patterns out of the star positions. However, the groupings have not always been the same, and the names and associated ideas were different in each case. But what is particularly interesting is that the significance attached to the sun's progress through the zodiac does seem to be consistent within all cultures, however separated they may be in time or geography. The origins of astrology are clearly very old.

For purposes of astrology as it is understood today, this band of zodiacal stars is divided into twelve equal sections, and each is occupied by one constellation, or 'sign', of the zodiac: Aries, Taurus, Gemini, Cancer, Leo, Virgo, Libra, Scorpio, Sagittarius, Capricornus, Aquarius and Pisces. A horoscope gives a picture of a moment in time, and may be cast not only for the moment of birth of a human, but also for other significant events, for example the moment of the founding of Rome. Traditionally, astrologers would be asked to ascertain the 'auspicious' moment for such important occasions. A horoscope (in this case for sunset on 15 September 7 BC) is shown in figure 16.

The constellations of the zodiac are drawn in a circle with 30 degrees for each sign, in anticlockwise order. The circle is bisected by a line which represents earth's horizon, and the constellation which is rising above the eastern horizon at the moment of birth marks the 'ascendant' point, from which the rest of the chart is constructed. The sun, moon and planets are drawn on the chart at their exact positions within the constellations at the moment of birth. There is a four-way division of zodiacal constellations, accounting for the four elements of air, water, fire and earth. Besides the ascendant, other points are marked along the circle which represent the zodiac, including the descendant, the medium coeli and the imum coeli.

The descendant is the point on the opposite horizon and marks the sign that is setting at the time of birth. The medium coeli, which is sometimes called 'the midheaven', is the point at which the zodiacal circle crosses the meridian of the place at which the birth is taking place. The imum coeli is the point on the zodiacal circle which is diametrically opposed to the medium coeli. Within these placings, the sun, moon and planets are considered to symbolise particular 'traits' or possibilities.

Today astrology is normally used to provide information about the birth charts of individuals. 'Sun sign' astrology refers to the sign in which the sun is placed at the moment of birth. For example, someone with a birthday early in the new year is said to be a 'Capricornian' person, an 'earthy' person: ambitious, patient, conventional, perhaps pessimistic, with concerns about issues such as the importance of structure and rules. A 'fiery' personality, such as a Leo, may be a creative, generous, expansive person, perhaps showmanlike, but possibly also intolerant or conceited. This is of course ludicrously simplistic. Astrology, as it is usually portrayed in the media, which merely divides people into twelve simple groups, is far removed from the activities of serious astrologers. The position of planets on or near the ascendant, and the constellation on the ascendant, are often considered more significant than the position of the sun, and there are many other considerations to be taken into account, such as the placings and aspects of sun, moon and planets within the signs, houses and angles of the chart.

Finding the aspects is an important part of the process of constructing a chart. This is because the interrelationships of the various bodies with each other, with the ascendant, or with other angles, is considered highly significant in the interpretation of a horoscope. These angles, or aspects, are based on astronomical information, but relate to positions in the sky as seen from earth. For example, two bodies 180 degrees apart on the zodiacal circle of the chart are said to be in 'opposition'. Two bodies 90 degrees apart from each other on the chart are in 'square'. Two or more bodies which are very close to each other are said to be 'conjunct'. In the opinion of astrologers, these aspects are considered to be 'good' or 'bad', or 'strong' or 'weak', within certain contexts, but the particular ways in which they are interpreted may vary between different schools.

A question often asked in relation to the subject of aspects is: 'Do the 0 degree (conjunction), 90 degree (square) and 180 degree (opposition) have to be exact, or is some tolerance allowed? The answer is that tolerance *is* allowed, and this tolerance is called 'the orb' of the aspect. For all the aspects just mentioned, the orbs are between 8 and 9 degrees.

Only some of the terms used in relation to the history of astrology and the methods of constructing and interpreting a horoscope have been touched on here in order to make the ensuing discussion about the astrology of the Magi more simple. It is, however, important to remember that astrology is a very old and complex subject, and that even today, many different opinions exist among serious astrologers about how or what it should be doing or does do. But more than that, astrology in practice reflects the understanding and knowledge of its time. Today astrology is largely used in a psychological and personal way, often as an adjunct to personal development of the individual. This is because we view the world from a psychological standpoint and consider personal development to be very important. The astrology of the Magi's time had a different emphasis, and in discussing their use of astrology to seek and find a new messiah, it is important not to make claims which are coloured by our modern views.

A horoscope may also be divided into twelve 'houses', which are said to deal with ordinary, mundane matters. There are systems for deciding on the house placements, which do not necessarily correspond with either the zodiacal divisions or the main angles of the chart, although as with everything else, any house system begins from the point of the ascendant. Much controversy exists amongst astrologers about the different ways of calculating house positions. The house divisions, unlike other parts of the chart, do not bear a relation to the physical cosmos. They are not necessary in this investigation into the identity of the Star of Bethlehem, but it is interesting to note that some suggestions which have been made about Christ's birth do involve mention of house placements.

The messianic expectation
The 'official line' of the Jewish religion towards astrology has always been ambivalent:

> At that time the Lord charges me to teach you statutes and laws which you should observe in the land into which you are passing to occupy it.

On the day when the Lord spoke to you out of the fire on Horeb, you saw no figure of any kind; so take care not to fall into the degrading practice of making figures carved in relief, in the form of a man or woman, or of any animal on earth or bird that flies in the air, or of any reptile on the ground or fish in the waters under the earth. Nor must you raise your eyes to the heavens and look up to the sun, the moon, and the stars, all the host of heaven, and be led on to bow down to them and worship them; the Lord your God assigned these for the worship of the various peoples under heaven.

(Deuteronomy 4:14–21, New English Bible)

This passage is usually understood to mean that celestial objects are there for other people to worship, but not the people of Israel. In orthodox Jewish teaching very little attention was paid to astrology, and, in particular, Jewish teaching did not use the astrological principles which were linked to astronomical observations to find the time and place of the Messiah's birth. However, as David Hughes points out, 'Privately and in folklore, however, astrological speculation persisted from the earliest days of Israel's history.'

The Magi, as a group, were learned men from a Babylonian, Zoroastrian religious background. They were versed in hermetic studies and in ancient ideas about the great ages which made up the Great Year; they knew about the ideas of Pythagoras, and they were well informed about the newest Greek learning and the Platonic Great Year, based on precession of the equinoxes. They were well travelled and had international reputations for their wisdom and predictive skills. They would visit the cities of the Roman Empire and consort with the kings and political leaders of the different regions as well as with the priests.

The expectation of a messiah formed a part of many religious sects, including Zoroastrianism. Although the Magi were not themselves Jewish, they would have been aware of these people's expectation of a Jewish messiah. They would have known of the ancient biblical prophecies that at the End of the Days would come the Kingdom of God. For a deeper look at this notion of a specifically Jewish messianic expectation, see Hugh Schonfield's book, *The Passover Plot*, or *The Quest for the Historical Jesus* by Albert Schweitzer.

It is likely that some political leaders would have reluctantly respected, or even feared, these mysterious Magi. However, as men recognised to be of superior knowledge, they were consulted by Herod when the need arose. They used their depth of knowledge and the various arts at their disposal to give answers to any questions put to them. One of their arts was astrology, and they would therefore have made predictions based on astronomical knowledge, and interpreted celestial events in terms of the meanings ascribed by astrology.

The Magi were, of course, working before the birth of Christ. Consequently, no body of Christian doctrine existed which would need to be considered in their predictions about a messiah. In a highly controversial book about Jesus Christ entitled *The Passover Plot*, Dr Hugh Schonfield explains the expectations of the Jewish world into which Christ was born. He declares how crucial it is to proper understanding to remember that at the time of Jesus' birth, Christianity as we know it did not exist, and at the time of birth, Jesus did not represent a *new* religion. Schonfield also reiterates the fact that the word 'christ' is the Greek translation of the Hebrew term 'Messiah', meaning 'the Anointed One', and does not refer specifically to Jesus Christ.

Messianism was the religious belief that a saviour would come to rescue the Jews from their evil adversaries, namely the Romans. Several passages in the Old Testament were felt to be associated with the saving of Israel and the coming of a messiah. For example, in Genesis 49:10:

> The sceptre shall not pass from Judah, nor the staff from his descendants, so long as tribute is brought to him and the obedience of the nations is his.

And in Numbers 24:17:

> I see him, but not now; I behold him, but not near: a star shall come forth out of Jacob, a comet arise from Israel. He shall smite the squadrons of Moab, and beat down all the sons of strife.

Here the star is linked to the Messiah. The comet, which usually foretells doom and disaster, is the fiery sword which will smite and beat down the enemy.

In Micah 5:2:

> But you, Bethlehem in Ephrathah, small as you are to be among Judah clans, out of you shall come forth a governor for Israel, one whose roots are far back in the past, in days gone by.

85

This prophecy is recalled in John 7:40–42 in the New Testament:

> On hearing this some of the people said, 'This must certainly be the expected prophet.' Others said, 'This is the Messiah.' Others again, 'Surely the Messiah is not to come from Galilee? Does not Scripture say that the Messiah is to be of the family of David, from the village of Bethlehem?'

And in Isaiah 40:9–11:

> You who bring Zion good news, up with you to the mountain-top; lift up your voice and shout, you who bring good news to Jerusalem, lift it up fearlessly; cry to the cities of Judah, 'Your God is here'. Here is the Lord God coming in might, coming to rule with his right arm. His recompense comes with him, he carries his reward before him. He will tend his flock like a shepherd and gather them together with his arm. He will carry the lambs in his bosom and lead the ewes to water.

The Bible had predicted that in the Latter Days there would be a huge struggle between good and evil. This struggle would then be followed by a new age, a final age of peace and bliss, the Kingdom of God. The Jews at the time of Christ's birth felt a new and wonderful age was due and believed that Jesus was their saviour, a biblical prophecy, seemingly unconnected with Platonic ideas about a forthcoming new age. Therefore, in Daniel 9:24–27:

> Consider well the word, consider the vision: Seventy weeks are marked out for your people and your holy city; then rebellion shall be stopped, sin brought to an end, iniquity expiated, everlasting right ushered in, vision and prophecy sealed, and the Most Holy Place anointed. Know then and understand: from the time that the word went forth that Jerusalem should be restored and rebuilt, seven weeks shall pass till the appearance of one anointed, a prince; then for sixty-two weeks it shall remain restored, rebuilt with streets and conduits. At the critical time, after sixty-two weeks, one who is anointed shall be removed with no one to take his part; and the horde of an invading prince shall work havoc on city and sanctuary. The end of it shall be a deluge, inevitable war with all its horrors. He shall make a firm league with the mighty for one week; and, the week half spent, he shall put a stop to sacrifice and offering. And in the train of these abominations shall come an author of desolation; then, in the end, what has been decreed concerning the desolation will be poured out.

The Magi were a part of the culture which expected a messiah to herald in a new age at the end of the present time. The mythology underlying the Old Testament writings was shared by their religion and that of the Jews, although their interpretation of the biblical prophecies differed. The Magi predicted and sought to find a messiah because they believed a new prophet was about to appear on earth. However, Herod asked them to find out the birth place of the man who was to become the saviour sought by the Jews. Herod was ruled by Rome and therefore regarded as a serious threat the messianic Jews who would regularly stir up anti-Roman feelings. Herod needed information for his own purposes, which he hoped the Magi could provide for him.

The predictions made by St John the Baptist were perfectly understandable within this Jewish messianic framework. It was this religious environment into which Jesus was born. So is it therefore possible, as Schonfield suggests, that Jesus, being born and brought up within this framework, himself believed that he was the sought-for Jewish Messiah, and that the kingdom of God at that time was thought to be 'at hand' in a physical, material sense? The Jews were God's chosen people, and Israel was about to enter a new age where all Jews who had obeyed the religious Law of Moses would live in peace and bliss, while those who had not obeyed the Law would be damned. In this context, therefore, Christianity as meaning 'followers of Jesus Christ' had a somewhat different meaning: it was not a new religion, and not the religion it has since come to be.

This presents a challenge to Christians to reconsider the origins of their faith. It is vital to have the challenge of new thinking, and the challenge of rigorous historical research, however uncomfortable it might be for traditionally-held views. However, a fascinating situation within the whole interpretation of events is the fact that the Magi were not Jewish. They would have known of the biblical teachings, and were themselves a part of the religious environment which expected a messiah, but they would not have been bound to the prophecies and doctrine of the Law of Moses. Their religious motivations were different, they came from older Babylonian or Persian learning, combined with Greek ideas. They were wise in many things, and they did what Herod asked them to do, though with a very different motivation and a deeper understanding than that of Herod himself. Because they suspected his motives, they did not return to give him the information he required: the information which would tell him where Christ had been born.

The Church and astrology

In the early centuries after Jesus' crucifixion, the New Testament gospels were written down and as a result, Christian doctrine was slowly formalised. The history of Christianity is an enormous area of scholarship, fraught with problems. Recently, new information has come to light, and new ways of interpreting information have become accepted. These force us to question much of the orthodox history of Christianity and many dogmatic theological statements. Much has been published, and some of it is extremely challenging.

This book is not about Christian theology, and I do not wish to tackle the thorny problems of historical authenticity, which are being dealt with very thoroughly elsewhere. However, it is important to know what the Church has said or felt about astrology over the centuries, as the Church's ambivalent attitude towards this practice has often led to confusion and misunderstanding about who the Magi of Matthew's gospel really were and what they were setting out to achieve.

Religious ideas, both from Judaism and the religions of other countries within the expanding Christian empire, were at various times absorbed into Christian culture. The doctrine evolved by the priests and political leaders of Rome and other important Christian centres has frequently incorporated or 're-validated' the mythical ideas and religious beliefs of local cultures. Moreover, symbolism, particularly *astrological* symbolism, was a universal feature of myth and religion for the centuries before and following Christ's birth. While several groups argued and fought over their differences in religious belief, all learned men knew about astrology, and astrological symbolism was often used as a form of common language. The Christian Church made much use of astrological symbolism as a way to convey doctrine to the ordinary people.

In the Middle Ages, the Church is known to have encouraged and closely supervised the use of symbolism in prayer books and ecclesiastical decoration. Having lost touch with this language of symbolism, it is easy to forget that the impressive carvings in the great cathedrals of this period served a deeper purpose than that of mere decoration. They were designed to instruct and teach the ordinary, unlearned people about Christian doctrine, and they achieved this by using symbolism, which was frequently of an astrological nature. However, this *lingua franca* of symbolism was clearly the culmination of non-Christian and pre-Christian ideas. The Church was constantly fighting against heretical notions and attempting to ensure that the symbolism expressed was not the work of the devil; it was uncomfortable with any astrological implication that the cosmos could have a fatalistic influence on a Christian's destiny. At various times during its history, the Church has either tolerated astrological practice or been overtly hostile towards it. There was an ambivalence between the value of using rich and powerful astrological symbolism to convey Christian teaching and the wish to maintain the uniqueness and separateness of the Christian creed from other beliefs.

The debate about the nature of the Star of Bethlehem, its possible association with astrological charts and the interpretation of such charts, goes back to the very beginnings of the Christian Church. The eminent historian of science, Lynn Thorndike, made the point that:

> To an age whose sublimest science was star-gazing, it would seem fitting and almost inevitable that God should have announced the coming of the Prince of Peace in this manner, and the account in the Gospel of Matthew is in a sense an attempt to present the birth of Christ in a way to comply with the most searching tests of contemporary science.

In the fourth century AD, St John Chrysostom argued against seeing the Star of Bethlehem in astrological terms. Instead, he claimed it should be seen as a miraculous event. He was apparently an eloquent speaker, but his arguments were not very sound.

St Augustine who, in 601, became the first Archbishop of Canterbury, was a highly influential Christian theologist who attacked astrology on the grounds that it enslaved people to the notion of predestination and offered little hope of redemption. He used the example that a calf and a human baby born at the same moment did not have similar lives, though they would have the same birth chart. Unfortunately, this showed a total misunderstanding of the nature of astrology, but St Augustine was fighting a battle against a false view of Christian doctrine, and astrology did not help his case.

The debate about the Star and its relationship to astrology was revived in the high Middle Ages. Albertus Magnus (AD 1193–1280), a Christian scholar who taught St Thomas Aquinas, held moderate views about astrology. He attempted to rationalise the problem of predestination implicit in astrology with the Christian doctrine of free will. He stated that a properly trained astrologer might make predictions concerning the future life of an infant, but within constraints allowed by God, and was impressed by an extract from *The Greater Introduction to Astronomy* written by Albumasar of Baghdad, who died in AD 886.

Albumasar of Baghdad subdivided each of the twelve signs of the zodiac into decans, each decan being 10 degrees of the 30 degrees occupied by the zodiacal sign itself. Each of these decans was given its own image in addition to the images associated with the actual zodiacal signs.

In *Speculum Astronomiae*, which most people attribute to Albertus Magnus, Albumasar's book is described as an irreproachable work. However, Magnus also gives us a horoscope of Christ which shows the constellation of Virgo as just about to rise. In fact, the start of this constellation is just eight degrees below the horizon. This means that the ascendant lies within the first of the decans. Quite coincidently Albumasar had placed within this decan the following image:

A maiden fair and chaste and pure, with long hair, and a lovely face, having two ears of wheat in her hand, and she sits on a canopied throne and nourishes a child, giving him whereof to eat, dwelling in a place which is called Abrie; and a certain people call the name of this child Jesus.

Albertus Magnus assumed that there was some astronomical basis for this image, which led him to conclude that the birth of Christ was not only written in the stars, but also proclaimed by the Star of Bethlehem. He believed that the Star was a miraculous apparition in the sublunary sphere; i.e. not in the heavens but in the region of earth, the region of imperfection and corruptibility: 'Its place was not high in the firmanent; it occupied the space where the air is close around the earth.'

Magnus defends his viewpoint in the following way:

In this way he, who was not born in the course of nature, would be shown to be a real man of flesh. Not that the disposition of the stars was the cause why he was born; rather it was the sign that he should be born. Nay more; most true it is that he himself was the cause why the manner of his wonderful birth should be signified by the heavens.

St Thomas Aquinas (1225–74) was a supremely influential theologian whose arguments to prove the existence of God underpin Roman Catholic theory. He believed that the stars ruled both the passions and baser instincts of people, but in following the Christian task of conquering human passions, such astrological influences would be overcome. Thomas Aquinas followed Albertus Magnus in his beliefs about the Star of Bethlehem.

Three Christian scholars supported the concept that founders of great religions were most likely to be born at times of great conjunctions. These men were Pietro d'Abano, Cecce d'Ascoli and Pierre d'Ailly.

Pietro d'Abano (c. 1257–1315) was declared a heretic some years after his death when his bones were disinterred and burnt for a number of religious heresies. He had claimed that on the rare occasions of a great conjunction between Jupiter and Saturn in the constellation of Aries, a balanced individual would be born, but only one such birth would occur on each occasion. It was very likely that this person would become 'a prophet, introducing a new law or religion, and teaching sages and men'.

Other scholars who built on d'Abano's work claimed that such men were between angels and sages, and that Moses and Christ were to be numbered among them. Pietro d'Abano also suggested that astrological considerations could indicate how long such a personality's influence could last, and attempted to draw conclusions concerning the life of Christ. However, if he did draw up a horoscope for Christ, it has not survived. According to Thorndike, d'Abano carried his astrological interpretation of history even further back in time:

As he had divided man's life into seven ages, so he distributed periods of history among the seven planets ... When Mars governed the world, the flood occurred because of a greatest conjunction of the planets in the sign Pisces.

Cecco Ascoli (1269–1327) was burnt at the stake for religious heresies. There are indications that he produced a horoscope for Christ, since he deduced from a horoscope some facts about the life and death of Christ. Unfortunately, none of it has survived. Ascoli was a supporter of the doctrine of great conjunctions, but he was known to have embroidered this support with his own theories that certain types of demon resided at specific points in the sky associated with equinoxes and soltices, '. . . and that Christ and other religious figures were born under their influence [that of the demons] at times of great conjunctions' (from *Horoscopes and History* by J. D. North).

Pierre d'Ailly (1350–1420) was a more conservative churchman who ended his life as a cardinal. However, when Pope Urban VIII's inquisitor, Cesare Carena, issued a papal bull on 1 April 1632, specifically condemning the casting of horoscopes of Christ, d'Ailly was referred to and censured by name. D'Ailly was yet another supporter of the concept that great conjunctions played a role in the birth of religious leaders, but he objected to Roger Bacon's theory that Christianity was under the control of the planet Mercury. He also rejected the concept that the progress and development of the Christian Church was controlled by the stars, but did believe that the positions of the heavenly bodies at the births of Mary and Jesus did much to enhance their natural virtues. D'Ailly believed that in the horoscope of Christ, Libra was in the ascendant, and he criticised Albumasar and Albertus Magnus who had placed Virgo in the ascendant.

Some of these medieval horoscopes, as in older times, were not personal charts of Christ, but were charts relating to the origins of Christianity or to the year in which important events associated with the Church might have occurred. In medieval and later times, there was extensive debate about free will and predestination (i.e. whether we control our destiny or whether it is controlled by outside factors). This affected the ways in which natal charts of Christ were drawn up and understood, and it is therefore important that great care is taken today when attempting to interpret these charts.

J. D. North spoke of the medieval period when most conventional Christian teaching considered astrology to be sacreligious:

Some were wise enough to avoid the subject entirely; others spoke of the stars as a sign, or a foreshadowing, of Christ's birth; some separated the human character of Christ from the divine, and said that the former was subject to the same astrological determinants as were the characters of other men; while others avoided such debate entirely, and simply applied to Christ's nativity the rules they had learned from the standard astrological writers.

(from *Horoscopes and History*)

After the medieval period came the Renaissance, a time when vast amounts of new information swept into Europe. Newly discovered religious beliefs and ideas about the cosmos from the Near and Middle East were incorporated into the body of thought of the classical world. Although some of this ancient learning was transmitted to Europe in the Middle Ages via Arabic translations of great works of classical antiquity undertaken by Islamic scholars, it was in the Renaissance that the Italians tried to recapture the glories of Rome. According to Gombrich in *The Story of Art*, 'They were so convinced of the superior wisdom of the ancients that they believed these classical legends must contain some profound and mysterious truth.' Astrological ideas were to surface again, with renewed vigour, during this time.

Pope Leo X (who ruled from 1513 to 1521), received a book written by Tiberio Rossigliano Sisto of Calabria. In this work, Rossigliano raises the question of cosmic influences on the physical body of Christ. This book contains a number of horoscopes, some of which relate to the horoscope of the world when it was formed, and three relate to the birth of Christ. One of these horoscopes for the birth of Christ was his own, one was by Pierre d'Ailly, and the other was attributed to Albertus Magnus. They are all for 25 December 1 BC, the date which had been formally adopted as Christ's birthday. However, they are not identical. This is partly because they are drawn up for different times of the day, and partly because they used different tables for working backward in time. Rossigliano did not undertake to interpret these charts, as there was fierce debate taking place at the time on questions of determinism and free will; in particular, argument centred on how much of Christ's life and personality was determined by celestial influences.

Giovanni Pico della Mirandola (1463–1494) was an Italian scholar and Platonist philosopher who became one of the first Christians to introduce the Hebrew Kabbalistic doctrine into Christian theology. There is some evidence that he had an early interest in astrology, but in later life roundly attacked its basic ideas. To quote again from J. D. North, Pico claimed that 'The horoscope which is commonly said to be that of Jesus cannot be such, nor does it indicate either that he would die a violent death or be a great prophet.' Pico's comment, which might refer to each or any of these horoscopes as they were all for the same date and virtually the same moment, was perhaps simply an anxious attempt to avoid giving any credence to astrology.

Some astrologers believed that this horoscope did point to a violent end to the life of Christ, because the planet Mars was between 30 degrees and 60 degrees above the western horizon. In this period, this sector of the sky was called 'the house of death', and since Mars was associated with wars, blood and death, this was taken to indicate a violent death for Jesus. Pico obviously did not accept this argument.

Protestants have also looked at the nature of the Star. Martin Luther (1483–1546) returned to the attitude adopted by St John Chrysostom, dismissing the art of the Magi as 'a mixture of natural reason and the devil's aid'.

John Calvin (1509–1564) likewise dismissed the idea that the Star should be seen in astrological terms: 'It is very ridiculous to attribute to the order of nature what Scripture recounts as miraculous . . . This [star] must have been beyond nature, and consequently beyond the art of astrology.' Calvin was, however, willing to admit that astrology had a legitimate use in its application to calendar-making, weather forecasting and 'selecting the opportune moment for commencing a medical treatment such as bleeding or purgation'.

It is therefore clear that it was not unknown for churchmen to cast horoscopes for the birth of Christ. At certain times such practice was considered either reasonable and useful, or at least within bounds of the Christian doctrine, while at other times it was considered dangerous and/or heretical. The horoscope of Christ's birthday symbolised the highly sensitive issues which existed around the foundations of Christianity: it raised awkward questions about how pagan ideas could be reconciled with the true faith, and questions about the concept of free will against fatalism or predestination.

The fish and Christian symbolism

The story about the fish as a Christian symbol will be familiar to some from the teachings of the Church. The early Christians were persecuted by the Romans and had to keep their beliefs secret. The almond-shaped fish symbol therefore became a secret sign by which Christians could recognise each other without being recognised by the enemy. The Church has claimed this story for its own, claiming that Jesus was the 'Fisher-of-men' and that is how the symbol came to be used.

In the chapter 'Early Christian Art' in *Symbolism in the Bible and in the Church*, Gilbert Cope said:

> In early Christian art a Fish, in the first place, signifies the soul of the departed; secondly it signifies the eucharistic spiritual food; thirdly it signifies the presence of Christ himself, for very early it had been noticed that the letters of the Greek word for fish – I-Ch-Th-U-S – acrostically provided the initials for Jesus-Christ-of-God-Son-Saviour. The Fish, in early Christian centuries, was therefore a very powerful symbol indeed.

However, there is considerably more to this story, and the Church was clearly uncomfortable with the deeper significance of this fish symbol. When the Christian faith was first established it was necessary for the faithful to protect themselves from discovery, and the little fish symbol could well have been a simple and useful code to identify like-minded sympathisers. However, it does not follow, as the Church would like to hold, that the symbol of the Fish was a purely Christian symbol. In fact all the evidence shows that this was certainly not the case.

In *Christ and the Cosmos*, Gordon Strachan quotes certain comments made by Edward Hulme in his book *Symbolism in Christian Art*:

> It is somewhat curious that such a symbol (the fish) should have held its ground for so long, since it sprang merely from a verbal or rather a literal coincidence, and that too of a somewhat forced nature. It had nothing of the poetical feeling of that beautiful symbol, the Lamb, nor did it express like the Lion, anything of the royal majesty of the great King of Kings.

Strachan agrees with Hulme:

> The 'cold-blooded and apathetic creature of the waters' [here referring to further comments made by Hulme] symbolising the infinitely tender and exalted Saviour. How inappropriate! What have they in common? Surely nothing at all. I am so sympathetic to this position that I suggest that the whole thing is inexplicable unless we see in it the underlying reference to the Piscean age.

Herbert Whone in *Church, Monastery, Cathedral*, also comments on the Piscean symbol:

> The fish as a symbol is closely connected with Christ. In the early Church he is called Iesous Ichthus (Jesus the Fish) or sometimes 'the Great Fish'. This is because Christ's birth heralded the beginning of the zodiacal era of 2150 years, the Sign of Pisces (The Fishes).

Jesus Christ was therefore more than a representative of the Christian faith. He was the messiah who had been anticipated and heralded by pre-Christian peoples, the embodiment of the new Piscean age and a set of values and beliefs which was not only Christian. The symbol of the fish was far older than Christian symbolism, and had its roots in ancient astrology and sacred geometry.

It is easy to argue from the evidence that the symbol of the fish is an ancient symbol embodying ideas much older than Christianity, extending beyond Christian doctrine. The history of the Church is a history of debate about its origins. The Church has, as we have seen, struggled to assert its unique religious doctrine as the true faith. Naturally it has therefore had an ambivalent attitude towards astrology and the pagan symbolism which seemed to threaten such notions as free will. At times the Church tolerated free and natural expression of eternal truths; at other times symbols which embodied ideas beyond those of Christian doctrine were considered dangerous or heretical.

In using the fish symbol, what the early Christians were expressing went beyond theologically correct doctrine. The symbol of Christ as the fish could have been used to denote Christ the representative of the new Piscean age – a wonderful figure, long awaited, and significant in a more-than-Christian sense. On the other hand, the Church has often been the enemy of its own members as much as any outside enemy. Once the Church had accepted the symbol, it could be used as much in its deeper sense as in its orthodox sense: it could be used as a code, understandable to the initiated, but inoffensive to orthodoxy, to hide the esoteric knowledge that it was associated with astrology and the other ancient and sacred, but heretical ideas.

It must be true that the Magi would have understood the symbolic significance of Pisces in its ancient, pagan and astrological sense. They did not need a miraculous order from

God to instruct them to set out on a journey to find the Messiah, following a star to Bethlehem. They possessed the highest learning and intellectual skills of their time, and used astronomical and astrological knowledge to establish that Christ was about to be born. He was the new Messiah, as all their learning indicated, the representative of the coming new age.

Astrology, astronomy and the days of the week

The naming of the days of the week is a complex mixture of astronomical and astrological ideas. Several elements contribute to these names: the Greek way of ordering the planets in decreasing distances from the earth; the Egyptian system of a 24-hour day; and the astrological belief that the sun, moon and planets ruled over different hours of the day.

On the basis of their cosmology, the Greeks placed the 'wanderers', i.e. the sun, the moon and the five planets, Saturn, Jupiter, Mars, Venus and Mercury, in decreasing distances from earth. Saturn was considered to be furthest away, then came Jupiter, Mars, the sun, Venus and Mercury, with the moon the closest. Astrologers accepted the Egyptian division of the day and night into 24 hours, but believed that each hour of each day was ruled over by one of the wanderers. Therefore, Saturn ruled over the first hour of the first day of the week, which was Saturday (Saturn's Day). It is important to note that this was also the Jewish sabbath day, and Saturn came to be known as 'protector of the Jews'.

The second hour of Saturday would be ruled by Jupiter, the third by Mars, the fourth by the sun, the fifth by Venus, the sixth by Mercury, the seventh by the moon, and the eighth again by Saturn. Saturn would also rule the fifteenth and twenty-second hours of Saturday, which meant that Mars would rule the last hour of this day, and the sun would rule over the first hour of Sunday (Sun's Day). Following this sequence through to Friday, the moon rules over the first hour of Monday (Moon's Day), Mars over the first hour of Tuesday (after Tyr's Day, Tyr being the Teutonic equivalent of Mars), Mercury over the first hour of Wednesday (Day of Mercury – late Latin translation of the Old Norse 'Day of Odin'), Jupiter over the first hour of Thursday (again late Latin – Jupiter's Day) and Venus over the first hour of Friday (Germanic translation of late Latin: Day of the Planet Venus – Veneris Dies). This is shown in table 1.

Table 1:	The days of the week						
Hours	Saturday	Sunday	Monday	Tuesday	Wednesday	Thursday	Friday
1	SATURN	Sun	Moon	Mars	Mercury	Jupiter	Venus
2	Jupiter	Venus	SATURN	Sun	Moon	Mars	Mercury
3	Mars	Mercury	Jupiter	Venus	SATURN	Sun	Moon
4	Sun	Moon	Mars	Mercury	Jupiter	Venus	SATURN
5	Venus	SATURN	Sun	Moon	Mars	Mercury	Jupiter
6	Mercury	Jupiter	Venus	SATURN	Sun	Moon	Mars
7	Moon	Mars	Mercury	Jupiter	Venus	SATURN	Sun
8	SATURN	Sun	Moon	Mars	Mercury	Jupiter	Venus
9	Jupiter	Venus	SATURN	Sun	Moon	Mars	Mercury
10	Mars	Mercury	Jupiter	Venus	SATURN	Sun	Moon
11	Sun	Moon	Mars	Mercury	Jupiter	Venus	SATURN
12	Venus	SATURN	Sun	Moon	Mars	Mercury	Jupiter
13	Mercury	Jupiter	Venus	SATURN	Sun	Moon	Marsd
14	Moon	Mars	Mercury	Jupiter	Venus	SATURN	Sun
15	SATURN	Sun	Moon	Mars	Mercury	Jupiter	Venus
16	Jupiter	Venus	SATURN	Sun	Moon	Mars	Mercury
17	Mars	Mercury	Jupiter	Venus	SATURN	Sun	Moon
18	Sun	Moon	Mars	Mercury	Jupiter	Venus	SATURN
19	Venus	SATURN	Sun	Moon	Mars	Mercury	Jupiter
20	Mercury	Jupiter	Venus	SATURN	Sun	Moon	Mars
21	Moon	Mars	Mercury	Jupiter	Venus	SATURN	Sun
22	SATURN	Sun	Moon	Mars	Mercury	Jupiter	Venus
23	Jupiter	Venus	SATURN	Sun	Moon	Mars	Mercury
24	Mars	Mercury	Jupiter	Venus	SATURN	Sun	Moon

It is obvious from the above that different cultural influences have contributed to the English names in use today. This is a consequence of our rich inheritance of different languages: Latin, Anglo Saxon and French. In other countries, such as Italy, France, Sweden or Germany, the day names stick more closely to the roots of each country's particular language. However, whether a day is called Thursday, jeudi or Donnerstag, in each case the name refers to that particular language's version of the same god or goddess, who in turn is a cultural personification of the planet in question.

We have seen how, since the beginnings of Christianity, Christians have experienced problems with regarding the Star of Bethlehem from an astrological point of view because of the serious implications which that viewpoint has for Christian doctrine. But to understand what sort of people the Magi were, and to appreciate the meaning of their activities as described by St Matthew, it is vital to put ourselves into their world, to understand what they understood when they sought signs in the sky. The next two chapters will look more closely at various suggestions for physical events which could have been the Star of Bethlehem, as well as the set of circumstances which provide the date for Christ's birth. It will then become clear how the Star could have foretold the Magi the birth of the Saviour of the world, and we will follow them to Bethlehem.

FOUR

SIGNS IN THE SKY

Ye country comets, that portend
No war, nor prince's funeral
Shining unto no higher end
Than to presage the grasses' fall.
(Andrew Marvell,
The Mower to the Glow-worms)

In the New English Bible translation of the gospel of St Matthew, the Magi are described as astrologers. Astrology was an integral part of both their learning and the world they inhabited, and it shaped their view of the world. It is interesting to see that this translation of the Bible reflects modern Christian theological acceptance of this fact, as it is difficult to imagine what alternative interpretations the Magi could have given to their studies of the night sky other than an astrological one.

The Church however, as seen in chapter 3, was extremely uncomfortable with astrology as a result of its clashes with traditionally accepted doctrine. With the interpretation of historical events, the Church preferred to either ignore them or try to rationalise any relevant astrological opinions and ideas. As seen in chapter 3, churchmen either proclaimed the Star to be a miraculous occurrence or simply refused to get involved in discussions about it. Other claims have, however, been made by non-theologians about the Star, which do not rest on an astrological interpretation. Yet further claims have been made which do rest on an astrological framework, though not the one portrayed in this book. So to what extent do these ideas stand up as candidates for the real identity of the Star of Bethlehem?

The suggestions made fall into four main categories: a comet; a nova or supernova (an exploding star); an occultation of a star or planet by another body; or a conjunction of planets. All these possibilities have their supporters, but I will demonstrate that it was a conjunction which caused the Magi to predict the coming of the Messiah, and led them to travel to Bethlehem in search of him. There are several occurrences of conjunctions, and there are several views about which one it might have been. It will, nevertheless, become clear that the Star was a specific conjunction which would have been interpreted by the Magi astrologically. Astronomically speaking, this particular event was unique, certainly within the time of recorded history, and from an astrological point of view it had astounding significance.

The comet theory

Aristotle's cosmology was the dominant world-view for many centuries. In the same way, his views on comets were considered extremely important for more than a millennium. He believed that everything about the sphere of the moon – the supralunar sphere – was perfect. Because the Milky Way and comets were amorphous in appearance, and because they seemed not to have any regularity in their occurrence, Aristotle concluded that they must have existed in the imperfect area below the moon. Comets were included in his work on meteorology, and he gave not only his own ideas about them, but also those of other scholars.

According to Aristotle, the sphere below the moon was made of earth, water, air and fire. The fire was confined to a sphere immediately below the moon, and the airy sphere was to be found just below this. The sun or planets had the ability to cause warm and dry exhalations from earth to rise upwards, and at the border with the fiery sphere, the friction caused by their motion would cause them to ignite. This ignition created the comet which was then carried around the earth by the circular motion of the heavens. This view was predominant for centuries.

The idea that a comet might have been the Star of Bethlehem goes back a long way, and was immortalised by di Bondone Giotto, the Italian painter, who saw a comet in 1310 and incorporated it into his painting *The Adoration of the Magi*. This comet was later named Halley's comet when it returned to the skies in 1682. In 1577 another comet appeared in the skies. The Danish astronomer, Tycho Brahe, teamed up with others to find out how far the comet was from earth. This was done with the use of the parallax method, an easy concept to demonstrate. Hold a pencil upright about 6 cm from the end of your nose. First look at it with your right eye closed and then with your left eye closed. You will notice that the pencil seems to shift with respect to the background. If you were to put the pencil at arm's length and repeat the procedure, the pencil would again seem to shift, but the degree of shifting would be less. This illustrates the basic principle of parallax. Surveyors use this method to measure distances on earth, and astronomers use it to measure distances to objects within the solar system as well as distances to nearby stars.

If the position of the moon with respect to the more distant stars were measured from two different places on the surface of the earth, it would be obvious that the two positions were of measurably different distances. Brahe reasoned that if the comet of 1577 was below the sphere of the moon (as Aristotelian cosmology required), then it should change its positions by a greater angle than the moon itself. However, if it were a very long way from us, this angle should be very small indeed. The angle turned out to be too small to be measured by the instruments available, so Brahe concluded that the comet must be a great distance away, and consequently, above the moon's sphere.

This was the beginning of the end of Aristotelian cosmology. Following the scientific revolution during the sixteenth and seventeenth centuries, when Copernicus put forward the theory of a sun-centred rather than earth-centred universe, many astronomers worked to discover more about comets. Edmund Halley (1656–1742) showed that the comet which appeared in 1682 orbited the sun, and the comet was named after him. This was the same comet seen by Giotto three centuries earlier.

In 1985, Halley's comet appeared once more, reviving the theory that this may have been the phenomenon described as the Star of Bethlehem in Matthew's gospel. This hypothesis found particular support from Mr Fleming, a lecturer in Historical Geography and Archaeology at Jerusalem's Hebrew University. Reports on his work appeared in many national newspapers and on television. Mr Fleming had discovered evidence that there had been a census in 12 BC, and that Halley's comet had also appeared in the same year. He concluded that, since Mary and Joseph had gone to Bethlehem to take part in a census and the comet had appeared in the year of a census, this must be the Star of Bethlehem.

So what are the problems with this hypothesis? Firstly, Fleming does not explain *why* the ancients would have connected the appearance of the comet with the coming of a messiah. Comets under an Aristotelian Ptolemaic scheme were invariably associated with doom, death and disasters; they were never associated with good things happening on earth. Why, therefore, would the Magi have made an exception in this case? There is the slight possibility that one of Ptolemy's 'rules' about comets might be connected with the birth of a messiah. It said, 'An appearance in a succeeding house implied prosperity for the kingdom's treasury, but the governor would change.' This might have been interpreted as meaning that, since Jesus was born to be King of the Jews, he would eventually offer some challenge to the governor. However, the appearance of the comet would not suggest that it was only a King of the Jews who would offer this future challenge. Consequently, this particular astronomical phenomenon would not have had any relevance to an important aspect of the Magi's prediction.

Secondly, at this time in history it was not known that comets returned on a regular basis. Astrology was based on predictable events in the heavens which could be used to predict the destinies of kings, countries and individuals. Because comets appeared to be single, arbitrary occurrences, they were not considered to be a very important part of the astrologers' schemes.

The third problem with this theory is that it is not possible to use a comet to fix a position on earth or at sea, and therefore there was no way in which the comet itself could have led the Magi to Palestine or to Bethlehem.

The nova and supernova theories

As will be seen later in this section, some astronomers have argued that the Star of Bethlehem could have been a nova or a supernova. But what exactly are these astronomical phenomena?

Novae

The *Shorter Oxford English Dictionary* defines a nova as 'A new star or nebula'. Unfortunately, this is wrong. A nova is not a new star; it is one which has been in existence for a long time, but which suddenly and unexpectedly increases its brightness by a factor of 10,000 to 100,000 over a period of days. After several weeks or months it will come close to returning to its original brightness. Because stars which do this are often quite faint and unspectacular, people used to believe that such an occurrence is actually a new star.

The modern theory regarding novae is based on the fact that all such stars are members of double star, or binary, systems. It is now thought that the smaller and more compact member of the pair gathers matter from the other until it is surrounded by a shell of material which gets hot enough for nuclear reactions to occur. When this takes place, it suddenly increases its brightness to form a nova. Although some material may be ejected into space, only part of the star is disrupted, unlike in supernova explosions. Some novae are recurrent, i.e. the process may be repeated, but this does not happen on a periodic basis and astronomers cannot predict when such a recurrence will take place.

Supernovae

There are two types of supernova. In one respect Type I is similar to a nova owing to the fact that one member of a binary system explodes. However, the scale of the resulting explosion is much greater than for a nova. Typically, a supernova can increase its brightness by a factor of about 1000 times the brightness increase of a nova. This is because the amount of material gathered from its companion is so great that the resulting nuclear explosion is enough to completely disrupt the growing star.

A Type II supernova is caused by the disruptive explosion of a very large star. A famous example of a supernova is the Crab Nebula in the zodiacal constellation of Taurus. The expanding gas cloud from this explosion has a remnant near its centre which is a rapidly rotating neutron star. In 1968 astronomers detected the radio waves and light pulses emitted by this Crab Nebula pulsar.

In December 1987, *The Times* carried an article which revived the nova hypothesis for the Star of Bethlehem. It was based on an article by Dr Richard Stephenson which had appeared in the December issue of *Physics Bulletin*. Stephenson proposed that the Star was a supernova explosion, since his own research into the astronomy of the Far East showed that two such events had been recorded by Chinese astronomers in 4 BC and 5 BC.

A letter of mine, stating my objections to Stephenson's proposal, was published in *Physics Bulletin*, March 1988. The problems I found with this theory were as follows:

1. Stephenson's point regarding the Jupiter–Saturn conjunction of 7 BC is a red herring. He claimed that this event was not spectacular, since Jupiter and Saturn were always more than one degree apart, and therefore would not be considered as

important. The gospel of St Matthew does not say that the Star was spectacular, nor that it came as a surprise to the Magi. The event was indeed unimpressive enough to be missed by Herod's advisors, but significant enough for the Magi to take it very seriously. The significance and influence that astrology had on the world-view of antiquity is a fact which must not be ignored.

2. The Jupiter–Saturn conjunction was important to these astrologers because it occurred three times in 7 BC. Such an event in the constellation of Pisces (also important to the astrologers) only occurs once every 900 years. The Star was not simply an association of a celestial event with the birth of Christ by the people of the place in which he was born: it was significant enough to cause three of the wisest men of the age to journey to Bethlehem in search of a messiah.

3. The nova hypothesis ignores the world-view of antiquity. In ancient times the sphere of the stars was considered to be the region of perfection, and according to this view, stars did not vary their brightness with time: this concept did not exist. Consequently, there are hardly any recordings of novae, and this is why Stephenson and his colleagues had to search Chinese and Korean records to find one. Even several centuries later, the nova of the Crab Nebula was still not recorded in the West. It was only in 1572, with Tycho Brahe's discovery of a supernova, that the Aristotelian world-view was finally shattered.

The occultation theory

A recent theory regarding the Star of Bethlehem is that it was an occultation of Jupiter by the moon. An occultation occurs when a larger body completely or partially obscures a smaller one. The most frequent examples of occultations have occurred when the moon moves in front of a star or planet. However, occultations of a star by a planet are not infrequent and have been very useful in giving information about sizes of planets and the presence and nature of planetary atmospheres. The rings of Uranus and Neptune were first discovered with the use of terrestrially-based telescopes, when these two planets occulted stars. The nature of these rings was further investigated using photographs taken by space probes.

The theory proposing that the Star of the Magi might have been an occultation of Jupiter by the moon was first put forward by M. R. Molnar from the Department of Physics and Astronomy of Tutgers University, in the June 1995 issue of *The Quarterly Journal Of The Royal Astronomical Society*. Molnar produces powerful arguments in favour of seeing the Star in astrological terms:

> Chaldaean astrology [in Babylon astrologers were called Chaldaeans] not only predicted celestial positions; what is more important, it purported to forecast omens which led people to believe that they could control their fate . . . Augustus Caesar had publicised that his horoscope predicted a fate to rule the world . . . After he had defeated the last of his major opponents, Antony and Cleopatra . . . Roman society was convinced of the predictive power of astrology. For the next two centuries people's horoscopes would be scrutinized for imperial aspects which would either advance their lives or lead to their demise . . .

Molnar also suggests why the star was missed by Herod's advisors:

> The likely reason why no one around Herod understood the celestial event is that Chaldaean astrology was not practised among devout Jews . . . Further evidence that the Magi were referring to an astrological event rather than a visible astronomical one, is that Herod and his people did not know that a special star existed. This had to be an obscure, subtle event that was discernible only to those who were knowledgeable about astrology.

Molnar is right to emphasise that the Magi were referring to an astrological event, rather than a highly visible, astronomical one. However, there are problems with Molnar's claim that the Star was an occultation of Jupiter by the moon.

Firstly, occultations of the moon by Jupiter are quite common; there is one every few years and there may be more than one in some years. Therefore, while an occultation is a comparatively 'subtle' event, probably only noticed by expert sky watchers, it is not a rare or special occurrence. If the Magi had gone in search of a messiah on the basis of a lunar occultation of Jupiter, they would have been travelling most of the time.

Molnar produces evidence that such occultations were

associated with regal births, and also claims that two occultations which occurred in 6 BC took place in the constellation of Aries, which he argues was the sign of the zodiac symbolising the Kingdom of Herod. Molnar quotes from Ptolemy who said that Aries ruled over 'Coele Syria, Palestine, Idumaea, and Judaea'. It is clear from a study of translated documents on ancient astrology, that links were made between signs of the zodiac and terrestrial locations. Unfortunately, the detailed reasoning behind this is unavailable, as is any empirical evidence on which it might be based. Such esoteric knowledge was never written down, instead it was passed down through generations of the initiated by word of mouth, no one really knowing the exact reasoning behind it. It is most likely that these astrological connections were related either to the horoscope of the ruler who founded an important city, or the horoscope which was cast for the city or area itself.

Although Ptolemy's great work on astrology, the *Tetrabiblos*, was written around AD 150, Molnar points out that:

> major portions of this work are based on the writings of Posidonius (*c.* 135–51 BC) who is largely responsible for spreading astrology throughout the Roman world. The countries given in the *Tetrabiblos* agree very well with a list that is distinctive of Posidonius; thus, the list in the *Tetrabiblos* has its origins in the first century BC.

Other scholars, however – notably d'Occhieppo, Hughes and Jung – have argued that the area around Bethlehem was associated with the zodiacal constellation of Pisces. Furthermore, as seen earlier, the point of the vernal equinox had moved from Aries to Pisces about one hundred years before the birth of Christ. It is not possible to be more specific than this because the boundaries assigned by modern astronomy to different constellations are not exactly the same as those used by the ancients. But even without exact dates, it is possible to assume from available evidence that Pisces had in a sense 'replaced' Aries, and could be seen to be associated with a new age. I don't think Molnar takes this sufficiently into account.

A further problem arises from the nature of the two occultations singled out by Molnar for association with the birth of Christ. The first occurred on 20 March 6 BC and the second on 17 April 6 BC. As Molar points out, the first occurred one minute after sunset and the second occurred just after noon, when the sun was still in the sky. As Molnar says, 'Thus, the second occultation could only be detected through the mathematics of astrologers.' In fact, even the first occultation would have been difficult to see under normal circumstances. This is because the moon and Jupiter would have been very close to the setting sun, whose glow would have made it extremely unlikely that these two bodies could have been seen one minute after sunset. Molnar therefore overestimates the ability of the Chaldaean astronomers in this respect.

Conjunctions of slow moving bodies, such as Jupiter and Saturn, can be calculated with reasonable accuracy, even at the time of Christ's birth. However, calculating occultations of planets and stars by the moon was a much more difficult task. The moon moves against the background stars much more quickly than the planets, so calculations of its position with respect to other bodies require a highly developed theory of the moon's motion. Such a theory only became possible some decades after the establishment of the Royal Observatory at Greenwich in 1675. The lunar theory of the Babylonians was not really capable of such a task, and as a result, errors crept in very quickly. It would have been much more simple to calculate lunar conjunctions with other bodies than to calculate lunar occultations. This therefore rules out an occultation as a candidate for the Star of Bethlehem.

The planetary conjunction theory

Most scholars consider it far more likely that the Star of Bethlehem was a phenomenon called a planetary conjunction. I agree with this, since conjunctions would have been of far greater significance in the context of Christ's birth than the other possibilities mentioned above. But what exactly is a conjunction? Which planets would be involved? And why should such a conjunction be so meaningful for the Magi?

Different locations on the earth's surface can be referred to in terms of their latitude and longitude. Latitude is the location's angular distance from the equator, whilst longitude is the angular distance from the line of longitude which passes through Greenwich; this is known as the 'Prime Meridian'.

Astronomers use a similar reference system to describe the positions of objects in the sky. Those who are mainly interested in the planets use celestial latitude and longitude. Celestial latitude is measured in degrees from the ecliptic, the apparent pathway of the sun against the background stars, while celestial longitude is measured along the ecliptic from the point of the vernal equinox.

For both astronomers and astrologers, any two or more planets (or the sun or moon and any planets) are said to be in conjunction if they have the same longitude – it does not matter if their latitudes differ by a few degrees. This is why astrologers use two-dimensional charts which show the relative longitudes of various bodies but contain no information about latitudes. A triple conjunction occurs when any two or more planets appear to come together in the sky three times in one year.

Apart from conjunctions, astrologers consider other planetary configurations as being of particular importance; among these are oppositions and quadratures (squares).

Oppositions occur when two bodies are in exactly opposite parts of the sky, i.e. their longitudes are separated by 180 degrees. This means that one body is on one side of the earth and the second body is on the other. Quadrature occurs when two bodies are separated by 90 degrees of longitude in the sky, as seen from earth.

For centuries, astrologers have claimed that the effect on the earth and its inhabitants by the sun, moon and planets is enhanced when certain planets are in particular configurations with each other. Ancient cosmology referred to both the sun and the moon as planets, and for the purposes of astrology, this chapter will do the same.

The effects of two planets are enhanced when they are in conjunction, opposition or quadrature. It is clear that a variety of planetary conjunctions and other phenomena took place in the skies, so which planets could have been conjunct around the time of Jesus' birth, making them possible candidates for the Star? There are a variety of opinions which claim to answer this question, not only as to which planets were involved, but also as to how the Magi would have interpreted the information. One possibility, although not very likely, is that the Star of Bethlehem was a conjunction of Jupiter and Venus. Another, more likely, possibility is that it was a conjunction of Jupiter and Saturn.

Jupiter–Venus conjunctions
In the December 1986 issue of *Sky and Telescope*, Roger Sinnott supported the idea that 17 June 2 BC was Christ's birthday,

because of the Jupiter–Venus conjunction which took place that night.

In the past this suggestion had been ruled out because Herod had been thought to have died in 4 BC, and as a result, Christ could not have been born two centuries later. The original estimate of Herod's death was based on a recording that it was preceded by an eclipse of the moon. This particular eclipse was thought to be that of 12–13 March 4 BC. However, Sinnott argued that it may have been the eclipse which took place on 9–10 January 1 BC. The Jupiter–Venus conjunction of 2 BC therefore became a candidate for the Star.

There are definite objections to this argument. It is important to remember that the Star of Bethlehem was an unusual event, and one of great significance to the Magi. Jupiter–Venus conjunctions are frequent occurrences which take place roughly every one to three years. However, Sinnott claimed that this conjunction was more significant because the approach of the planets was remarkably close on this occasion. But here Sinnott is talking as an astronomer, not as an astrologer. The two planets Jupiter and Venus were particularly close in celestial latitude, but celestial latitude is not related to the astrological concept of a conjunction. In astrological terms, the 'influence' of a conjunction is not weakened if the latitudes of the bodies in question differ by a few degrees. Therefore, the degree of closeness which, according to Sinnott, is what makes the Jupiter–Venus conjunction of 2 BC special, is not of significance to astrological interpretation.

In support of his belief Sinnott claimed the following:

> But our modern calculations show that the Jupiter–Venus event did occur squarely between the lion's feet . . . Furthermore, I recently came across this picture of an amulet, or religious chart-stone, in *Jewish Symbols In The Greco-Roman Period*, Vol. 3, by E. R. Goodenough (New York, 1953). No definite association with the nativity can be claimed, yet the star symbol, placed just where the Jupiter–Venus event occurred in Leo, is certainly startling.

Unfortunately, no definite link exists between this symbol and the birth of Christ, nor is there clear evidence that the star symbol represents the Jupiter–Venus conjunction. It is somewhat surprising that Sinnott's drawing of the picture on the amulet had a crescent moon just above Leo, yet in his calculated chart of the event there is no sign of the moon in this constellation. My own calculations show that on 17 June 2 BC the moon was in a completely different part of the sky.

An examination of a similar artistic representation of Leo shows clearly how much care must be taken when examining artistic symbolism. In *Astronomy: A Popular History* by J. Dorschner, C. Friedemann, S. Marx and W. Pfau, a photograph is shown of a relief monument which stood on the mountain of Nimrud Dag, beside the river Euphrates in Turkey. The monument, they suggest, represents the horoscope of the coronation of King Antiochus I of Commagene (as this area was known), which took place on 7 July 62 BC.

The authors claim that on this day the sun was in the constellation of Leo. However, simple calculations show that on this day the sun was actually in the constellation of Cancer. They also claim that 'On the breast of the beast there can be seen the crescent of the Moon, enclosing Regulus, the brightest star in the constellation of the Lion.'

Again, calculations show that on this day the crescent moon did not 'enclose' Regulus, but did appear close to the conjunction of Mars and Mercury which was taking place on this day. It is possible that the monument was referring to the conjunction of these two planets rather than to the star Regulus, and that some artistic licence was used on this occasion, as indeed it was used in other representations of astronomical facts.

The Jupiter–Venus conjunction, which Sinnott claims to be the Star, offers no explanation for why the Magi should have linked the event with the birth of a King of the Jews. Neither does it explain why Pisces became a part of Christian Symbolism, nor shed any light on the enigma of the Virgin birth. Furthermore, the conjunction does not give any clues as to why the Wise Men should have interpreted from its prediction a need to journey from their own country in search of Jesus, nor does it give any astrological symbolism about which direction to take to set about finding him. It is a naive, associative kind of theory which is mute on these important questions.

Dr Ernest L. Martin, an American biblical scholar, has also opted for a Jupiter–Venus conjunction, despite the difficulties. In 1978 he published *The Birth of Christ Recalculated*. However, it is in his more recent book, *The Star That Astonished The World*, that he develops his support for the Jupiter–Venus conjunction.

Two conjunctions of Jupiter and Venus occurred between 10 BC and 1 BC. The first was on 12 August 3 BC, the second on 17 June 2 BC. Martin believes that the second conjunction was the Star:

> It was the early evening of June 17, 2 BC. All the cities around Babylon in Mesopotamia were aglow with talk about a spectacular astronomical event in the western sky . . .
> The astronomical drama being enacted in the western part of the sky showed the collision of the two brightest planets in the heavens.

This argument is wrong in many ways. To begin with, conjunctions do not look like a 'collision'. People who do not observe them have often thought that a conjunction means that two bright objects come together to make one brighter object. This is not the case. When astronomers and astrologers talk of conjunctions they mean that two or more planets are on the same line of celestial longitude. As a result, they do appear to be very close together from the earth, but they do not have to be touching. In fact, only when the sun or moon conjuncts a planet will they appear to touch, and of course a sun–planet conjunction would not be visible because of the very bright glow of the sun. It is possible that in some cases a moon–planet conjunction may be visible and look as if the moon was touching the planet. The two planets in the Jupiter–Venus conjunction to which Martin refers did appear to be very close on this occasion. However, their apparent closeness would not be of particular significance in any astronomical or astrological interpretations made.

This particular conjunction was also in the wrong place. According to chapter 2 of Matthew's gospel, the Magi asked, 'Where is the one who has been born to be king of the Jews? We saw his star in the east and have come to worship him.'

The Magi refer to the east, not to the west. Furthermore, 'Then Herod called the Magi secretly and found out from them the exact time the star had appeared.'

If the Star had been the spectacular object which Martin would like it to be, why did Herod need to enquire about the exact time the star had appeared? Surely it would have been as obvious to his advisors as to everyone else? Again, Martin chooses this event on grounds which have little to do with the understanding of the time. He does not give due credit to the fact that the Magi were astrologers, and that astrology was the received wisdom of the age.

The separation between Jupiter and Venus was 0.20 degrees on

12 August 3 BC and 0.05 degrees on 17 July 2 BC. Both conjunctions were therefore well within orb, i.e. they were close enough to a strict conjunction to be allowed by astrology. Why, therefore, was the second conjunction considered more important than the first? Martin resorts to historical evidence to answer this question. In fact he eventually chooses neither date as the day of Christ's birth, but instead claims that 'Jesus Was Born In A Stable In The Twilight Period Of September 11th, The Day of Trumpets, 3 BC.'

Martin chooses this date because by so doing he can say that Christ was born with the sun in Virgo, the Virgin. He has not understood the basic concepts of ancient astrology, but has constructed a symbolism of his own, very vaguely based on what he believes were accepted practices of the type of astrology prevalent at the time when Christ was born.

K. Ferrari d'Occhieppo was a professor at the Astronomical Institute of the University of Vienna, and he wrote a highly respected book entitled *Der Stern von Bethlehem* (1991). The following is his summary of the objections to Martin's explanation:

1. Saturn, not Venus, was considered to be the planet of the Jews.
2. Pisces, not Leo, was associated astro-geographically with Palestine.
3. In the Middle Ages Jewish astrologers linked expectations of a messiah with conjunctions of Jupiter and Saturn in Pisces.
4. The star Regulus was always, in Babylonian astrology, linked with the ruler of the homeland, which at that time was the Parthian king.
5. Conjunctions of Jupiter and Saturn are far less frequent than conjunctions of Jupiter and Venus, and are thus more significant.
6. In long-term predictions of Babylonian astronomy and astrology latitudes of planets were not considered at all. Thus it would have been possible neither to predict minimum distances between two planets at any expected conjunction nor to include this in astrological forecasting.

Professor d'Occhieppo's summary suggests why most scholars with an understanding of the history and culture of the period have tended to opt for a Saturn–Jupiter conjunction as the most likely candidate for the Star of Bethlehem.

Jupiter–Saturn conjunctions

These conjunctions take place once every twenty years. In the July of 26 BC, the Jupiter–Saturn conjunction took place in the constellation of Leo. However, triple conjunctions of these two planets are a rare occurrence which only takes place every 139 years. A triple conjunction of these two planets in a particular constellation is even more rare. For example, a triple conjunction of Jupiter and Saturn in the constellation of Pisces only takes place once every 900 years.

As d'Occhieppo explains in *Der Stern von Bethlehem*, Babylonian astrologers linked the area around Bethlehem with the constellation of Pisces. In addition, Jupiter has for centuries been seen as the planet of kings due to the claim of astrological tradition that it is commonly in the ascendant at the moment of royal births. A triple conjunction of Jupiter and Saturn in Pisces is, on any level, a very rare event, and for the astrologers of Christ's time, it would have carried enormous significance.

Johannes Kepler was well known for his discovery of the laws of planetary motion, which helped Newton to formulate the laws of motion and gravity. Kepler was, however, uncertain about the contribution that astrology could make to his work. But on 17 December 1603, he observed a Jupiter–Saturn conjunction in Scorpio from his observatory in Prague, which set him thinking. He knew about the Jewish idea that Jupiter–Saturn conjunctions in Pisces had particular significance for Israel. He therefore decided to work backwards to see if the conjunction he had seen in Scorpio could have had a similar counterpart in Pisces near the time of Christ's birth.

Kepler's calculations showed him that Jupiter and Saturn were conjunct three times in 7 BC. He had formulated his own brand of astrology in his attempt to rationalise the subject, and for him the moment of conception was more important than the moment of birth. Kepler therefore decided that the triple conjunction was significant in correlating with Christ's conception. As a result, his claim was that Christ was born in the following year, in 6 BC.

Professor d'Occhieppo took Kepler's suggestion much further. He combined modern methods of calculation with current knowledge about Babylonian astronomy and astrology. Because of his belief that the Magi were Babylonian astronomer-astrologers of the Zoroastrian religion, he claimed that the Star should be seen in the astrological terms discussed earlier.

In *The Star of Bethlehem Mystery*, David Hughes introduced Professor d'Occhieppo's work to the English-speaking world. In his book, he developed d'Occhieppo's theory and listed the most important events relating to the Jupiter–Saturn conjunction, which occurred in 7 BC.

The first conjunction of Jupiter and Saturn in the constellation of Pisces took place on 27 May 7 BC, the second on 6 October and the third on 1 December. Yet d'Occhieppo believed that the Magi were convinced that Christ was born on 15 September. Why? On this day, just as the sun was setting, Jupiter and Saturn were rising in the east. This rising is called an 'acronychal' rising. Planets like Jupiter and Saturn rise acronychally when they are in opposition to the sun. This means they rise at sunset and remain in the sky all night, reaching their highest point, fairly high above the south point, around midnight. Astrologers consider planetary influences to be at their greatest when conjunctions and oppositions are taking place.

In the astrological thinking of the Magi, this event, when combined with the particular significance of the planets involved, would have been linked to the concept of a Jewish king. The Magi would have seen the first conjunction of 27 May, but by using the sophisticated mathematical astronomy that they had already developed, they would have been able to predict that a further two conjunctions would take place that year. They would also have been in a position to predict the acronychal rising of Saturn on 15 September 7 BC.

As Hughes made clear, the Jewish people were unsure about the significance of astrology, as in orthodox teaching little attention was paid to it. He does, however, mention a Jewish work from 1497 by Don Isaac Abrabanel. This is the same work that was known to Kepler, and it explains the historical importance that the Jewish people attached to Jupiter–Saturn conjunctions, dividing them into five classes: small conjunctions which took place every 20 years; middle conjunctions which took place every 60 years; great conjunctions which took place every 139 years; large conjunctions which took place every 953 years; and, finally, mighty conjunctions, which took place roughly every 2860 years and were associated with the births of revealers of secrets, great prophets and the Messiah.

Abrabanel believed that mighty conjunctions would always take place in the conjunction of Pisces, which was associated with Israel. Pisces was a constellation of the element of water and, according to Abrabanel, astrological tradition made many connections between Moses, the patriarchs and water, and claimed that it was also the astrological house of Jupiter. Abrabanel believed that Moses was born in 1396 BC, so the next mighty conjunction should occur in 1465. He expected the Messiah and redeemer of Israel to be born in that year. However, he did not provide any explanation as to why the triple conjunction of Jupiter and Saturn in Pisces in 7 BC had not been considered a mighty conjunction, important enough to herald the Messiah.

In 1972 Roy A. Rosenberg wrote a paper called *The 'Star of the Messiah' Reconsidered*. He makes an interesting point about ancient mythology and the Jewish interpretation of the Jupiter–Saturn conjunction of 7 BC. The God of Israel, Yahweh, was the high father-god and was associated with Saturn, as was Kronos, the Greek version of the high father-god. Kronos was dethroned by his son Zeus, who was linked to Jupiter. Kronos gave Zeus 'all the measures of the whole creation' because he was 'the originator of times'. Rosenberg suggests a mythological interpretation of this important Jupiter–Saturn conjunction:

> In Jewish theology . . . Yahweh was still the universal ruler, and the transfer of powers symbolized by the periodic conjunction meant something different: Yahweh was giving to his Messiah a portion of his power and authority, so that he, the Messiah, might scatter the wicked principalities that hold sway over the earth, condemn them to punishment and exalt the righteous in his stead. The planet Saturn in this cosmic drama represents Yahweh, while the planet Jupiter, called Sedeh, represents his 'son', the Messiah.

Rosenberg therefore backs the Jupiter–Saturn conjunction of 7 BC as the Star of the Messiah. He says of Matthew's gospel:

> Though the Evangelist speaks only of the 'star' as having been observed by 'magi' from the east, it is likely that he reflects in his presentation what was essentially a Jewish astrological tradition. Bearing in mind Kepler's speculation as to the identity of the 'star' we find that there is indeed a Jewish astrological tradition linking the appearance of the Messiah, and other great events, with the conjunction of the planets Jupiter and Saturn.

116

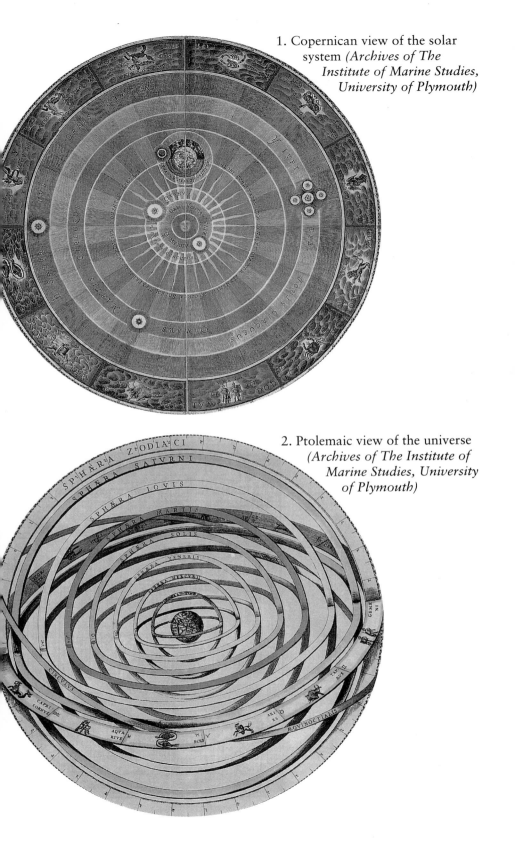

1. Copernican view of the solar system *(Archives of The Institute of Marine Studies, University of Plymouth)*

2. Ptolemaic view of the universe *(Archives of The Institute of Marine Studies, University of Plymouth)*

3a. The Milky Way galaxy as seen from the top

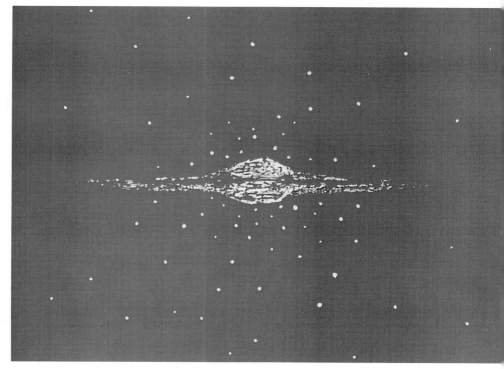

3b. The Milky Way galaxy as seen from the side

• IVPITER •

4. A mythological view of Jupiter from a 15th Century manuscript
(Archives of The Institute of Marine Studies, University of Plymouth)

SATVRNVS ✦

5. A mythological view of Saturn from a 15th Century manuscript
(Archives of The Institute of Marine Studies, University of Plymouth)

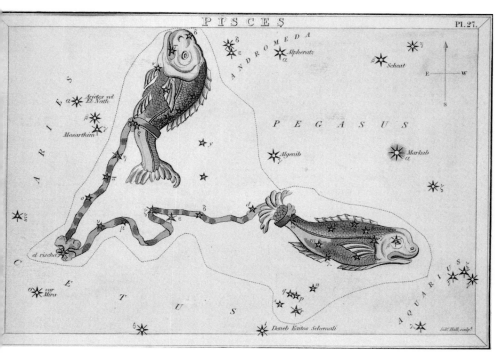

6a. A representation of the constellation of Pisces from Bloxam – *Urania's Mirror*
(Royal Astronomical Society)

6b. A representation of the constellation of Virgo from Bloxam – *Urania's Mirror*
(Royal Astronomical Society)

Left: 9. Dr Seymour, with orrery (model of the solar system). Painting by Robert Lenkiewicz

Below: 10. Dr Seymour, with orrery in the William Day Planetarium, Plymouth

p left: 7. *Adoration of Magi*, Giorgione *The National Gallery, ndon*)

ttom left: 8. *Adoration the Shepherds*, Reni *The National Gallery, ndon*)

11. A fantasy view of an aurora seen in Europe in the 15th Century
(Archives of The Institute of Marine Studies, University of Plymouth)

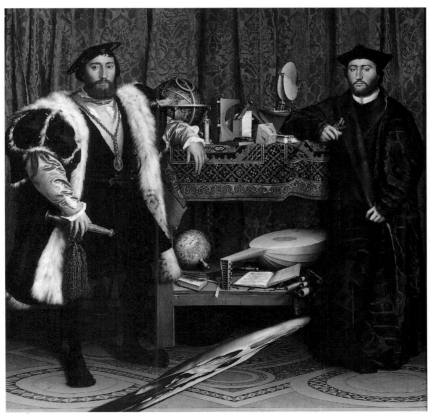

12. *The Ambassadors*, Hans Holbein (© *The National Gallery, London*)

Jewish sources therefore provide important evidence which supports the Jupiter–Saturn conjunction and its interpretation as the Star of Bethlehem. Rosenberg's emphasis on the meaning of the conjunction for the Jewish people strengthens the arguments that the Magi sought a King of the Jews, the Messiah, and then travelled to Jerusalem to find him. Although there is much evidence to support the birth of Christ as 15 September 7 BC, there are alternative, but much weaker, claims for other dates in 7 BC which should be mentioned.

Other dates in 7 BC

As explained in chapter 3, an astrological chart provides a two-dimensional picture of positions of the sun, moon and planets, in relation to the zodiac constellations, at a given moment. A natal chart is cast for the exact moment of birth of an individual. Some well-known modern astrologers have attempted to calculate a natal chart for Jesus. One of these astrologers was the late John Addey, who used a combination of historical and astrological evidence to arrive at a date and time for the birth of Christ.

Addey accepted the 7 BC triple conjunction of Jupiter and Saturn in Pisces, but then used historical evidence to calculate the time of year and the day of the week. Using historical arguments and common sense, Addey narrowed down the time of year to August, September or October of 7 BC. He argued that because so much is known about the life and character of Christ, it would be possible to use this knowledge to work backwards, construct an astrological chart suiting the known personality of Christ and therefore look for a chart like this in order to decide on his date of birth. Addey's research led him to the conclusion that Christ was born on Saturday 22 August 7 BC, just after sunset, as this chart had the sun and moon in Leo, and Aries in the ascendant (about to rise above the eastern horizon). According to Addey, these elements indicated the fiery and charismatic side of Jesus' personality as well as his qualities of leadership. He went on to say that Christ the Saviour and mystic came from the placing of Mars, which is associated with energy and drive, next to Neptune, which symbolises spirituality and transcendence.

It is very interesting to try to work backwards to a birth date from an individual's known characteristics, but there are problems with it. Addey gives far too much weight to the correlation between birth charts and personality. This is a modern emphasis and depends on psychological interpretation to a great extent. As a result, it is very different from the approach used by the wise men of Christ's time. Another problem is the extent to which we can really know about Christ's personality. Although Neptune is said to represent spirituality and transcendence and would therefore be expected to figure prominently in the chart of an individual like Jesus, the Magi did not actually have any knowledge about the existence of this planet, as it was only discovered in 1846. As a result, Neptune could not figure in their calculations. Whatever Addey's claims to deduce a horoscope 'appropriate' to Christ's personality, I do not feel he makes a strong case for the Star which would have been predicted by the Magi and used as justification for their journey to seek the Messiah.

Another astrologer, Penny Thornton, disagreed with John Addey and produced her own chart, which appeared in *The Weekend Guardian*, 17 December 1988. She used the same techniques as Addey, but said:

> However, I disagree with Addey's date since, to my mind, September 12, 7 BC – the night Jupiter and Saturn would have been at their most brilliant – is more truly a reflection of Christ as I perceive him . . . The fundamental theme of Christ is that through love in the form of sacrifice (Pisces) man is saved, and through his death and re-birth (Pluto) eternal life is a reality.

This too is a modern and psychological approach and shares the disadvantages of Addey's approach. Pluto was not known to the Magi as it was discovered this century in 1930. Thornton's date was just three days earlier than the date arrived at by d'Occhieppo in 1977.

David Hughes agreed with d'Occhieppo, and so do I. In fact, Jupiter and Saturn were in opposition to the sun on 15 September 7 BC. This means that they were closest to earth on that date, and therefore at their brightest. As will be seen later, this date is supported by statistical work of Gauquelin but also by my own theory that the magnetic influences of the conjunction will be enhanced when it is in opposition to the sun.

A new book has recently been published entitled *Magi – The Quest for a Secret Tradition* by Adrian Gilbert. Here, Gilbert uses

a variety of arguments to suggest that Christ was born on 29 July
7 BC. The main problem with Gilbert's proposal is the
astronomical inaccuracy of his description of the 7 BC conjunction:

> It seems likely that what the Magi saw, and what they had been
> anticipating, was a coming together of the two largest planets in
> the solar system, Jupiter and Saturn, so that their light was doubled
> and they could not be distinguished one from another ... On 29
> July, 7 BC the two planets Jupiter and Saturn would be in
> conjunction, forming one very bright star.

As described earlier on in this chapter, it is not true to say that a
conjunction of two planets has the appearance of one even
brighter object. At no time in 7 BC were Jupiter and Saturn so
close that they were indistinguishable from one another; they
were always at least one degree apart. The misunderstanding,
common amongst those who are neither astronomers nor
astrologers, arises because people are not accustomed to looking
at the night sky. On Gilbert's suggested date, the two planets were
about three degrees apart and there would have been a clearly
visible space between them.

The astronomical facts of the matter are as follows: the first
conjunction of Jupiter and Saturn in 7 BC occurred on 27 May,
when they appeared to be one degree apart against the
background stars. Then they appeared to separate slightly until
they were almost three degrees apart on and around 27 July. By
the end of August or beginning of September they had appeared
to move rapidly together. From mid-September to early December
they appeared to do a little 'dance' in the sky, due to the
complexity of their apparent motions, but they were about one
degree apart at all times. On 6 October they were one degree
apart and on 1 December they had a separation of 1.05 degrees.
Objects are conjunct when they are close together along a line of
celestial longitude, though they may not be close in terms of
celestial latitude. During the whole period of the triple
conjunction the planets were within orb, which means that from
the point of view of earth, they seem close enough together to be
considered conjunct (though astrologers differ as to the amount
of orb which is allowable). However, 15 September is the only
occasion on which Jupiter was in exact opposition to the sun.
Astrologically speaking, this makes the Jupiter position much

more powerful and therefore meaningful. Furthermore, as will be seen in chapters 6 and 7, when applied to the birth of great leaders, there are scientific grounds to support this claim about a sun–Jupiter opposition.

Gilbert was using many factors other than astrology, both to arrive at his suggested birth date for Christ and to support his arguments about the motivations and purposes of the Magi. Some of his ideas are interesting, but in this case I find his line of reasoning generally unconvincing. I believe he has fundamentally misunderstood the astronomical and astrological skills of the Magi.

So, to recap:

1. On 15 September 7 BC the sun was exactly in opposition to Jupiter, and Saturn was one degree from Jupiter.
2. Both bodies were in the constellation of Pisces, as they were for most of that year – this being part of the triple conjunction.
3. This was the first time in 900 years that a triple conjunction of these planets had occurred in this constellation, but it was also the first time in recorded history that the vernal equinox was in Pisces.
4. The sun on this day was in Virgo, the Virgin.

So how could the Magi have used the Star of Bethlehem to find Jesus?

CHAPTER

FIVE

How the Magi found Jesus

A star, not seen before in heaven appearing
Guided the wisemen thither from the east,
To honour them with incense, myrrh, and gold,
By whose bright course led on they found the place,
Affirming it thy star new-graven in heaven,
By which they knew thee King of Israel born.
(John Milton, *Paradise Regained*)

How did the Magi find Jesus? On what day was he born? A careful reading of Matthew 2 (New English Bible version) provides some very important information: 'Jesus was born at Bethlehem in Judaea during the reign of Herod. After his birth astrologers from the east arrived in Jerusalem, asking, "Where is the child who is born to be king of the Jews?" '

A footnote provides an alternative translation for the Magi's question: 'Where is the king of the Jews who has just been born?' We have the information about when and where Jesus was born: in Bethlehem during Herod's reign. We infer that the Magi have come from lands to the east of Judaea, that they seek a King of the Jews, and that they believe he has recently been born.

They evidently seek a very important person: 'We observed his star, and we have come to pay him homage.'

> King Herod was greatly perturbed when he heard this; and so was the whole of Jerusalem. He called a meeting of the chief priests and lawyers of the Jewish people, and put before them the question: 'Where is it that the Messiah is to be born?'

The implications of this passage are clear: Herod and the people of Jerusalem had not noticed anything unusual in the sky. They were concerned, not with anything they might see themselves, but instead by what the astrologers had said. Therefore, the Star was something which was not obviously visible, but instead was of astrological significance.

'At Bethlehem in Judaea', they replied; and they referred him to the prophecy which reads: 'Bethlehem in the land of Judah, you are far from least in the eyes of the rulers of Judah; for out of you shall come a leader to be the shepherd of my people Israel.'

The Magi told Herod that the new-born child they sought was the Messiah who had been prophecied by the Bible text, and that they expected to move on to Bethlehem to find him.

Herod next called the astrologers to meet him in private, and ascertained from them the time when the star had appeared. He then sent them on to Bethlehem, and said, 'Go and make a careful inquiry for the child. When you have found him, report to me, so that I may go myself and pay him homage.'

It is clear that Herod was not an astrologer, and his only source of informaton about this important event was the knowledge of the Magi.

They set out at the king's bidding; and the star which they had seen at its rising went ahead of them until it stopped above the place where the child lay. At the sight of the star they were overjoyed. Entering the house they saw the child with Mary his mother, and bowed to the ground in homage to him; then they opened their treasures and offered him gifts: gold, frankincense, and myrrh. And being warned in a dream not to go back to Herod, they returned home another way.

There is a pictorial sense in which the Star could be said to have 'gone ahead' of the Magi and stopped 'over' Bethlehem. The latitude and longitude of Jerusalem are 31°47′ north and 35°10′ east respectively, and Bethlehem is 31°43′ north and 35°12′ east. Bethlehem is virtually on the same line of longitude as Jerusalem and a few miles to the south. Therefore the Jupiter–Saturn conjunction in Pisces would have been due south of Jerusalem for much of the evening. To travellers familiar with the night sky this planet would therefore appear, from ground level, to be 'ahead' of them as they travelled towards Bethlehem. Moreover, any such travellers who arrived in Bethlehem at midnight would now see the same star very high in the sky, and apparently stationary.

The main points in the argument that Jesus Christ, the Messiah, was born in Bethlehem on 15 September 7 BC are as follows:

1. The Magi sought a messiah, a King of the Jews. A messiah who would save Israel from her adversaries had long been expected by the Jews, as the Bible had foretold that he would come at the 'End of the Latter Days' and would herald a new age of peace, literally a kingdom of God on earth. The Magi were familiar with this messianic expectation. It is also probable that they were well-versed in hermetic disciplines and knew of the intellectual developments of Greece. Whatever their background, and whatever depths of learning they brought to the task, they worked within a culture which anticipated and sought to discover a very special messiah.

2. The Magi were astrologers, and astrological concepts informed their thinking. In the quest for a messiah they would use astrological principles to seek guidance from the stars and planets. There is evidence from different sources that the Magi would have been aware of the concept of the Platonic Great Year. For example, it seems that the ancient Egyptians knew about precession of the equinoxes long before the Greeks, the civilisation which is normally credited with the discovery of this phenomenon. As was seen in chapter 2, various studies suggest that ancient learning attributed definite significance to this phenomenon whereby the sun moves into a new constellation on the first day of spring. As a result of this, the astronomical knowledge, and the mythological and astrological significance attached to it, would have been known to the Magi. Because the event only takes place once in every 2000 years or so, its occurrence would be particularly significant. At the time around the birth of Christ, the sun at the point of the vernal equinox had just moved into the new constellation of Pisces: a new age was dawning.

3. In 7 BC a triple conjunction of Jupiter and Saturn took place. This in itself was a rare event (they only occur every 139 years), and astrologically speaking it signified something important. The planet Saturn was seen to be the 'protector of the Jews'; the planet Jupiter was associated with kings or great leaders; and Jupiter on the ascendant (i.e. just above the horizon at sunset) was associated with the births of such people. Furthermore, the conjunction was to take place in Pisces, the sign of the zodiac associated with Bethlehem. It

could reasonably be predicted, in confirmation of the biblical prophecy, that a King of the Jews was to be born in Judea. This planetary configuration was rare and therefore suggested a special, unusual kind of leader. However, it might not in itself foretell when this leader would arrive, except that it would be at a moment when Jupiter was on the ascendant. The Magi had the ability to work out the occurrence of the triple conjunction in advance, and they knew it would last a year, but could they do more than simply notice that the planetary positions probably confirmed the old prophecies?

4. They could. This already important conjunction was to take place in Pisces. A triple conjunction of Jupiter–Saturn in Pisces only occurs once every 900 years or so, making it even more special. In additon to this, the sun had just entered Pisces at the vernal equinox, and a new age was beginning. This event, observed and proclaimed by the Magi, had never occurred before in the recorded history of humankind. As a result, it was not simply special, it was historically unique. This starry symbolism therefore meant that the Messiah was coming: the child who was to be the Saviour, not only of the Jews, but of the whole world. Such information would be more than enough for the Magi to justify setting off on a long journey to Jerusalem in order to worship the coming Messiah. But when would he be born? The two planets would be closely conjunct on three occasions during that year. Did it portend that he would be born on one of these dates, and if so which one?

5. Oppositions (when two bodies are 180 degrees apart against the background stars) are considered very significant in astrology. When the sun is in opposition to another body, this is particularly important. The conjunction of Jupiter and Saturn was in exact opposition to the sun on 15 September 5 BC, when the sun was in the sign of Virgo, the Virgin. It is difficult to conceive of any pattern which could have held more sigificance for the Magi.

On the evening of 15 September 7 BC, as the sun was setting in Virgo in the western part of the sky, Jupiter and Saturn, in the constellation of Pisces, were rising above the eastern horizon. All the planets that the ancients had knowledge of were visible on

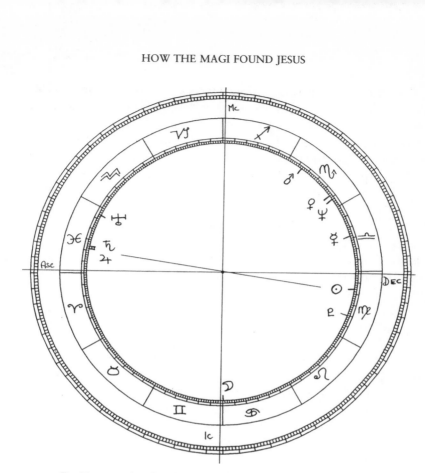

Positions and main relevant aspects

Ascendant: 28°42′ Pisces

Sun:	21°57′ Virgo	Jupiter:	19°11′ Pisces
Moon:	0°6′ Cancer	Saturn:	18°28′ Pisces
Mercury:	15°58′ Libra	Uranus:	3°10′ Pisces
Venus:	6°17′ Scorpio	Neptune:	3°37′ Scorpio
Mars:	22°51′ Scorpio	Pluto:	10°22′ Virgo

Jupiter conjunct Saturn in Pisces
Jupiter/Saturn opposition Sun in Virgo

FIGURE 16. HOROSCOPE FOR SUNSET AT BETHLEHEM, 15 SEPTEMBER 7 BC

that night, perhaps making it seem as if the whole heavenly sphere wished to partake in the presentation of this symbol to people on earth. Every aspect of this event was meaningful, and it had never happened before in the history of humankind. The computer-generated diagrams shown in **figures 17a, b** and **c** are printouts of the sky over Bethlehem for this date, while **figure 16** is a representation of the horoscope for this particular moment in history.

The Bible implies that neither Herod nor his advisors could *see* the Star. However, as an astrological event, this is not surprising. Herod was anxious that the Wise Men should identify the person sought as the Messiah. He was under the control of the Romans, who were encountering problems with the messianic Jews, whose beliefs were so strong that they were threatening Roman order. The Magi accordingly set off, but they obviously understood Herod's motivations and used the guidance of a dream to return home not via Jerusalem and Herod, but a different way.

But how did the Wise Men know *exactly* where to look for the baby? This is not as difficult as it might seem, given the specific information they had at their disposal. The Magi sought a male baby, who had been born in Bethlehem (due to its association with Pisces) on 15 September 7 BC as the Jupiter–Saturn conjunction rose above the horizon in opposition to the sun at sunset.

The birth-rate figures for Bethlehem at the time would also have given them guidance, as a comparison of present-day statistics will make clear. For example, in a city the size of Plymouth, UK, today, with a population of about 250,000 people, the average number of births per day is approximately 24. This means that on average one baby is born every hour, and roughly half are likely to be male. The population of Bethlehem at the time of Christ's birth could not possibly have been greater than it is today, i.e. about 17,000. Therefore, even if we allow for the possibility that modern averages like the Plymouth birth rate might be low, it is very unlikely that there would have been as many as one birth per hour in Bethlehem at the time of Christ's birth.

It is also known that a census was in progress at this time, and this explains why Joseph and Mary went to Bethlehem in the first place. It is likely that the Magi enlisted the help of census organisers in their search for Jesus, though in the face of the skills demonstrated above, it is tempting to think that they did not need such mundane help!

The Virgin birth

To continue with the astronomical and astrological significance of the sky on the night of 15 September 7 BC, the sun was in the constellation of Virgo on that evening. As anyone who looks at newspaper horoscopes knows, people are grouped according to

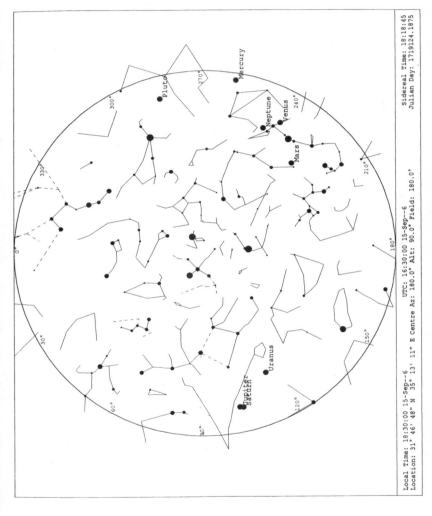

FIGURE 17A. THE SKY OVER BETHLEHEM, 15 SEPTEMBER 7 BC (whole sky)

Local Time: 18:30:00 15-Sep--6   UTC: 16:30:00 15-Sep--6   Sidereal Time: 18:18:45
Location: 31° 46' 48" N 35° 13' 11" E Centre Az: 180.0° Alt: 90.0° Field: 180.0°   Julian Day: 1719124.1875

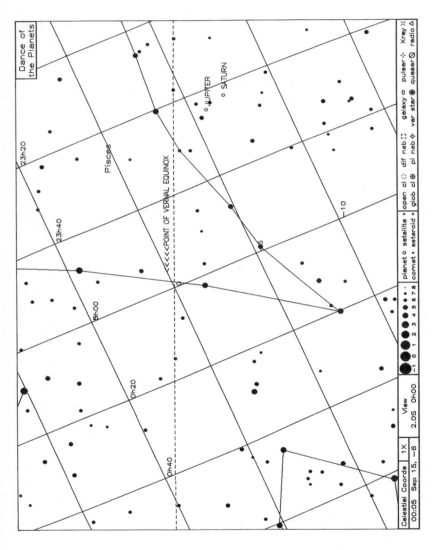

FIGURE 17B. THE SKY OVER BETHLEHEM, 15 SEPTEMBER 7 BC (DETAIL OF JUPITER/SATURN CONJUNCTION IN PISCES)

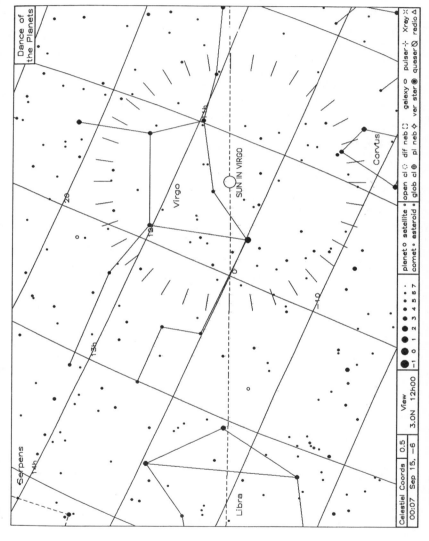

FIGURE 17C. THE SKY OVER BETHLEHEM, 15 SEPTEMBER 7 BC (DETAIL OF THE SUN IN VIRGO)

their sun signs, i.e. the part of the zodiac in which the sun was on the day of birth. If Jesus was born on 15 September 7 BC he would, according to this simplistic aspect of astrology, come under the sign of Virgo, the Virgin. In other words, he would be described as having the 'sun in Virgo' or being a 'son of Virgo'. John Addey, who tried to work backwards to calculate an astrological birth chart for Christ, said:

> The symbolism of the Pisces–Virgo polarity is so intimately involved with the life of Jesus and his religion (not only have we the Virgin birth but the word Bethlehem means 'house of bread' – the sixth house, Virgo, the Virgin with the ear of corn), that we must certainly expect these signs to be strong.

To talk of a Pisces–Virgo polarity is an astrological way of saying that the two constellations are diametrically opposed along the zodiac. Some art historians have drawn attention to the use of this polarity in religious art.

The German art historian, Erich von Beckerath, in *Secret Messages in Pictures* has discussed two examples of the use of Virgo in art as well as the Virgo–Pisces polarity. His first example is *The Virgin of Brauweiler* which was carved out of stone by an unknown artist in the eleventh century. Beckerath identified this female figure as Virgo because of its inclusion with a series of portraits representing the twelve signs of the zodiac. These works of art were displayed in the former Brauweiler Benedictine Monastery, near the city of Cologne. Attention is drawn to the fact that the figure is holding a lily in her left hand, the symbol of purity and innocence. It is also interesting to note that this symbolic use of the lily has been found in the oldest hymns of the Syrians and Persians, thus it was used in the early days of Christianity. Von Beckerath then goes on to reveal that the symbol continues to be of use in Judaism. He adds:

> In order to emphasize clearly the astrological nature of this stone figure as a symbol of the zodiac sign Virgo the astrologically competent stone mason has given the girl a bridal bouquet in her right hand, round which she has wound the end of her beautiful plait for the unbelieving and ignorant observer.

After discussing the many ways in which Mary has been presented in Christian art, Beckerath goes on to discuss a rare representation, a woodcut by a south German from the middle of the fifteenth century, which portrays Mary in reaper's clothing. 'The picture shows that Mary, expecting Jesus, will present the bread of the Eucharist.' In this woodcut Mary is holding a single ear of corn in her hand. Because bread is made from corn, the ear of corn is symbolic of feeding, which has a direct relationship to the zodiacal sign of Virgo. He then points out that the glyph associated with Virgo takes the form: ♍ pointing out that the three perpendicular strokes represent the corn, and the curved stroke the sickle. When are the cut ears of corn collected? At harvest time, in September, when the sun is in Virgo. Further on, he says:

> From the relevant literature about the symbolism of the Middle Ages one can deduce that many sculptures on city fountains, cathedrals, town halls, public buildings, monuments, etc., and their ornamentation very often have hidden meanings, which were well known to the initiated city and cathedral masons, town councillors, city astrologers, etc.

An interesting example of such decoration on a fountain can be found on the Justitia Fountain at the lawcourts in Frankfurt. Here, four mermaids sit below the figure of Justitia, the muse of Justice. Their heads are turned towards the column, and water flows from their breasts into the trough of the fountain. Von Beckerath claims that a great deal of other work on the use of mermaids in symbolic art shows that mermaids are supposed to represent the Virgo–Pisces polarity. As pointed out by Otto Neugebauer in *Astronomy and History: Selected Essays*, 1983: 'The history of art and philosophy of the Renaissance has gained immensely from the researches carried out by the Warburg Institute [of the University of London] on the astrology of the preceding periods.'

This work points very clearly to the extensive use of astrological imagery in many works of art from classical times and also in more modern works inspired by classical learning and philosophy. The signs of the zodiac are clearly associated with terrestrial tasks (known as the Labours of the Month) which are undertaken during the various months of the year when the sun is said to be 'in' a particular sign. In some cases signs were paired with their diametrical (and symbolical) opposite on the zodiac circle, and thus we have the Virgo–Pisces polarity mentioned by von Beckerath. Opposition of signs is important in astrology and is considered to influence a horoscope, even more so if the pair of signs in question is significantly positioned.

A fascinating addition to this line of argument which relates to the Justitia can be found in Lersner's Chronicle of the city of Frankfurt. Here, it is revealed that on 18 August 1542 at seven o'clock in the evening water started to flow from this fountain for the first time: at this time and on this date Pisces rose in the east and the sun was in Virgo.

The language of astrology

The language of astrology is the language of symbolism. In an astrological context, to describe Jesus as 'son of the virgin' is to say that he was born with the sun in Virgo. Hans Sandauer, former vice-president of the Viennese Astrological Society, also discussed this matter in his book, *History Controlled by the Stars*. Here, he suggests (working on a birth date for Christ as 17 September 7 BC) that because Christ was born with the sun in Virgo, the story that Jesus was the son of a virgin may have originated from this fact. It is, however, important to note that choosing 17 September as the birth date for Christ puts the sun in Virgo, but does not encompass the direct opposition of 15 September which seems so important for a strong astrological interpretation, enhancing the Virgo–Pisces polarity.

Mythology also sheds light on the description of Christ as the Son of the Virgin. Joseph Campbell, in his extremely important four-volume work entitled *The Masks of God*, makes it very clear that the religious concept of a 'son of God born of a virgin' is far older than Christianity itself. Many religious themes and motifs from both the Greek classics and the Bible can be demonstrated as having their roots in ancestral ideas as old as the Bronze Age civilisation of Mesopotamia (*c.* 2000 BC). Concepts such as the virgin birth of a son of God, along with many other themes which include the deluge, departure from God's garden, and trees of life and knowledge, originate in much more ancient cultures than the Hellenistic world of the Magi and Jesus.

Campbell cites a legend considered to stem from Egypt of the third century BC where a human virgin priestess gives birth to Pharoahs, the sons of Ra the sun-god. References are also made to two other stories, one from classical Greece and the other from the Bible. In the Greek myth the maiden goddess Persephone gives birth to Dionysus, the god of bread and wine, and son of the great god Zeus. Dionysus was born in a cave, he was torn to death as a babe and was then resurrected. In the Christian story, the Virgin Mary conceived God's son, Christ, who was born in a cave, died, and was resurrected. For Christians bread and wine symbolise the body and blood of Christ.

In Christian theology the story of Mary's miraculous conception of Jesus is considered to be a unique, historical fact, verified by biblical texts. It is regarded as being very different from the mythological stories of Greece which were never considered historically factual, although the origins of the stories may have had a basis in a historical event. It is also considered different from older mythologies where such stories may well have been believed to be factual.

In earlier times, the suggestion that Jesus was not miraculously conceived by Mary would have been considered heretical, and for some people it still is. In history, those who questioned orthodoxy were burnt at the stake. However, since the nineteenth century, which Campbell calls 'That epochal century of almost unbelievable spiritual and technological transformations', it has become necessary to look at the sources of religious ideas in a new way. Studies in archaeology and the development of language have made it clear that the meaning of a theme such as a virgin birth may be deeper than the specific value given by a specific doctrine.

Today, Christianity embodies differing sects with differing interpretations of theology, and the Church as a whole is finding its teaching seriously challenged from many quarters. Yet modern Christians, such as the former Bishop of Durham, who have questioned traditional assumptions and doubted the historical veracity of such stories as the Virgin birth, have been subjected to a torrent of abuse. For some Christians, to doubt the historical truth of the Bible is to be unchristian, while for others it is possible to recognise this story as a reflection of ancient pre-Christian themes which represent deeply important psychological or spiritual insights. It is also possible to see that for the early Christians trying to establish a foundation of doctrine, these legendary stories were utilised to give form to this hugely significant new expression of faith called Christianity.

Whether one regards the Christian story as a matter of fact, or as something which possesses a somewhat different value and significance, for the Magi and the people who expected a messiah, Christianity as the term is understood today did not exist. The prophets foretold a saviour, and the Hebrews considered the coming messiah to be the King of the Jews; they believed that he would deliver Israel from her enemies and prepare for the golden age which was approaching. At this point in history, the new religion of Christianity was not known as a religion which would be based on the birth, death and resurrection of the historical man named Jesus.

The Magi and Jesus

The scenario for the events described in the gospel of St Matthew is sufficiently interesting in itself to 'explain' the Magi's journey and the phenomenon which is called the Star of Bethlehem. However, other suggestions have been made regarding the Magi's purpose in seeking a messiah.

Morton Smith, Professor of Ancient History at Columbia University, wrote a book entitled *Jesus the Magician*. He has some interesting comments on the story of the Magi, which he sees as having been inspired by a similar story relating the visit of Tiridates and his retinue to the Roman Emperor Nero (AD 54–68), which ended with him being revered as a god:

> Matthew's tale belongs to a body of material that attributes to Jesus titles and claims characteristic of the emperors and their cult. People said that Tiridates and his magi had initiated Nero in their mysteries and secret meals; the gospel story implies that Jesus needed no initiation: he was the predestined ruler of the magi, as well as of the Jews; but unlike the ignorant Jews, the magi knew this. They understood the star that signaled his coming and came themselves to meet him, make their submission, and offer their gifts due to their ruler. Moral: all magicians should do the same; Jesus is the supreme magus and master of the art.

Smith's attitude to this story is ambivalent: he strongly implies that it is not factual, but instead was related by Matthew for specific purposes:

> Matthew also used the story for other purposes: to reconcile the biblical prophecy that the Messiah should be born in Bethlehem with the known fact that Jesus came from Nazareth, and to explain away the report that Jesus went to Egypt and learned magic there ... the magi's coming occasioned Herod's plot, which occasions the flight into Egypt.

Smith's credentials with regard to theological scholarship and biblical history are impeccable and he, like others, is making fundamentally important points about the way biblical texts should be interpreted. He is not alone in questioning the historical 'truth' of the Bible, but my only comment at this point is that he has not taken sufficient account of the influence and use of astrology in the world into which Christ was born. The Magi's learning could not fail to include astrology, whatever else they knew of magic and forms of divination.

Some authors, such as Adrian Gilbert, have suggested that the Wise Men were initiates of an ancient sect which has its roots in ancient Egyptian civilisation, and continues a secret but unbroken tradition to this day. I find most of these arguments unconvincing, being a mixture of circumstantial evidence and wishful thinking. It seems unlikely that even the most secret, esoteric discipline would have the ability to travel down through several millennia in one single, unbroken tradition, mainly because this is not how the history of ideas works. Thinkers of any time are inevitably altered by contemporary experience: ideas alter, opinion changes, human thought encompasses new structures, and doctrine is modified. Most cults which claim historical consistency for their beliefs are fictionalising history to fit in with current ideology, and this applies to Christianity as much as to any other human cult group. As shown earlier, theologists argued about what could or could not be said about historical events in order to maintain an 'acceptable version' of Christian history. Those who see the Magi of Matthew's gospel as a part of a long-standing secret 'brotherhood' also tend to choose supporting evidence selectively to support their own opinions.

Theologians tend to interpret history without always under-standing the dynamics of the ages in question. It *is* vital to question established orthodoxy, but it is unfortunate that many academic scholars often seem hidebound and limited, unable to contribute much towards enlightenment about their own subjects. However, some of the depth of knowledge and caution of the academics is necessary if a reasonable understanding of history is to be arrived at. An oversimplistic interpretation of evidence, or straightforward mistakes of fact, detract from the credibility of the argument.

There is perhaps a longing for 'mysterious truth' which can no longer be found in religion; the present surge of renewed interest in ancient history and archaeology may partly be a longing to return to a deep, abiding sense of the meaningfulness of human experience. Today's world is ruled by science and technology, yet science can to some people seem dry and unreal in its apparent denial of mystery. Science is arid, but there is no alternative; religious doctrines no longer possess any real power to persuade. Is there a feeling that we may be able to rediscover what we have lost – that which the ancients knew – if only we can interpret the secrets? And if we can interpret the secrets, is there a hope that we will rediscover the value of our lives?

The shepherds and the 'heavenly host'
According to Luke 2:8–14:

> Now in the same district there were shepherds out in the fields, keeping watch through the night over their flock, when suddenly there stood before them an angel of the Lord, and the splendour of the Lord shone round them. They were terror-stricken, but the angel said, 'Do not be afraid; I have good news for you: there is a great joy coming to the whole people. Today in the city of David a deliverer has been born to you – the Messiah, the Lord. And this is your sign: you will find a baby lying wrapped in swaddling clothes, in a manger.' All at once there was with the angel a great company of the heavenly host, singing the praises of God: Glory to God in highest heaven, and on earth his peace for men on whom his favour rests.

It is often assumed that whatever the shepherds saw out in the fields was the same astronomical event which led the Magi to Jesus. However, if one believes that the Star was a conjunction, this is highly unlikely. It is true that almost any shepherd would be able to tell the time at night using the stars, as recognised by Thomas Hardy in *Far From the Madding Crowd*, when the shepherd Gabriel Oak looks at the sky:

> The Dog-star and Aldebaran, pointing to the restless Pleiades, were half way up the Southern sky, and between them hung Orion, which gorgeous constellation never burnt more vividly than now, as it soared forth above the rim of the landscape. Castor and Pollux with their quiet shine were almost on the meridian: the barren and gloomy Square of Pegasus was creeping around to the north west; far away through the plantation Vega sparkled like a

lamp suspended amid the leafless tree, and Cassiopeia's chair stood daintily poised on the uppermost boughs. 'One o'clock,' said Gabriel.

It is, however, unlikely that the shepherds of Christ's time would have had much interest in the planets, or would have understood the complexities of planetary motion. Even if they had recognised some of the planets, they would not have been well-versed in concepts of astronomy or astrology to any great extent, and been unable to impart significant meaning to these objects.

If the shepherds were not seeing the same astronomical phenomenon that the Magi were seeing, then what was it that made them 'terror-stricken'? The description that 'the splendour of the Lord shone round them' seems to suggest that it was something which covered the whole sky. Could it have been a display of the northern lights, the aurora borealis? Initially, this seems highly unlikely, partly because it is normally only seen in more northerly latitudes. But if this suggestion is examined more closely, some interesting issues arise.

Under normal conditions, the northern lights (and the southern equivalent, the aurora australis) are only seen on the periphery of an oval shaped area around the magnetic poles, known as the 'auroral ovals'. As can be seen in Appendix I, aurorae are the result of solar wind particles crashing into gas particles within the auroral oval in the upper atmosphere. However, it is known that when solar activity is high, solar wind particles are more energetic and the overall width of the auroral oval is larger than normal. It also moves closer to the magnetic equator of earth. Consequently, at these times the northern and southern lights may be seen in latitudes far closer to the equator. Auroral activity is a consequence of sunspot activity, and high sunspot activity is more likely when particular alignments of the planets occur.

In South Devon, the northern lights have been seen on two occasions over the last nineteen years: the aurora borealis was seen in 1979 and again in 1989. On both occasions sitings were linked to spectacular alignments of the planets as seen from the sun. On the first occasion there was an alignment between Jupiter, earth and Mars, and on the second between Neptune, Uranus, Saturn and Mars. Also on the second occasion, the northern lights in South Devon were not only seen in the northern sky but also in the southern sky. Calculations showed it was highly likely that they would have been seen in North Africa, and there were also some sitings in the Bay of Mexico.

As a result of the alignment of the planets Saturn, Jupiter and earth at the time of Christ's birth, the right conditions existed for strong solar activity which could well have given rise to a much more extensive auroral oval. It is likely that this was the phenomenon seen by the shepherds, and because it would have been unfamiliar to them, it is unsurprising that they might have been 'terror-stricken'.

There is plenty of literary and illustrative evidence to prove that people have been frightened by auroral activity over the centuries. In their book *The Northern Lights*, A. Brekke and A. Egeland claim:

> From time immemorial people have stopped in their tracks and become lost in thought when the northern lights have thrown their manifold flames into the sky. Fluttering draperies of innumerable spectral colours have often led the mind to wander into the realm of dancing spirits and fighting hordes . . . It is only natural that any tribe or group of people would seek an understanding of this phenomenon in terms of familiar events of their immediate neighbour and everyday life.

A host of examples is provided to illustrate these points. In Greenland the Eskimos thought aurorae were an indication that dead relatives were anxious to contact surviving relatives, while to some North American Indians the northern lights were believed to be their gods dancing across the firmament. The Norwegians and Swedes sought omens for huge herring runs and schools of fish in the oceans; they believed that the northern lights were reflections in the sky of these fish as they swam in shoals, close to the surface of the sea. The Finns saw the northern lights as fighting angels bearing torches. Some scholars have claimed that the Valkyries of Norse literature (warrior handmaidens of the god, Odin, who rode over the battlefields to claim the dead heroes) are also connected with the northern lights: the lights are explained as reflections from the shields of these beautiful women.

Brekke and Egeland quote the following extract from a Bohemian text which they believe is a description of the northern lights:

> On the 12th of January 1570 in Bohemia an unusual omen was seen in the sky between the clouds. It lasted for four hours . . . The

nightwatch rang his alarm to awake the people so they could see this miraculous omen from God . . . There, dear Christians, take this awful sign into your hearts and pray that God might ease our punishment.

Fanciful drawings of the northern lights seen in Europe in the seventeenth century are a fascinating addition to the wealth of knowledge about this phenomenon. One illustation shows armies locked in battle, and the northern lights represent the streams of blood from the battleground. This was apparently based on an occurrence seen in Hungary in 1663. Another illustration also shows a clash between two armies, although this battle takes place in Austria over the Danube on 10 February 1681.

When the northern lights are seen at low latitudes they tend to be predominantly red in colour. In Rome in AD 37, during the reign of Emperor Tiberius (AD 14–37), a red aurora was observed. Thinking that the village of Ostia was on fire, Tiberius ordered a troop of soldiers to go to its rescue and put out the flames. In London, on 15 September 1839, red lights were seen in the north causing the dispatch of engines from the fire stations in Baker Street, Farringdon Street, Watling Street and Waterloo Road to the 'scene' of the fire.

On 6 March 1716 Edmund Halley, who later became the second Astronomer Royal, observed auroral activity in London. He read a paper on his sighting to the Royal Society in which he proposed that the phenomenon was connected with the magnetic field of the earth. Halley was correct in making this connection, though as Appendix I shows, the link between aurorae and magnetism is not quite as Halley had imagined.

In some mythologies, such as the Slavonic legends, the sun was said to have two daughters who accompanied their father across the sky. The first daughter, Zorya Utrennyaya (the Aurora of the Morning), opened the gates of the celestial palace when the sun set forth on his daily voyage across the sky, while Zorya Vechernyaya (the Aurora of the Evening), closed them again when the sun came home.

'The Ambassadors'

It is most likely that the Wise Men would have had a knowledge and insight even deeper than the traditionally-held views of their time. They would have known as much as anyone about the ancient learning behind the biblical prophecies, and would have assimilated ideas from Babylon, Egypt and Greece, as well as from Israel. They may even have been similar to the Ambassadors, the men in the famous painting of that name by Hans Holbein the Younger (see plate 12).

The Ambassadors is of interest because there is an analogy to be drawn between the ambassadors of Holbein's painting and the Magi who travelled to honour the birth of Christ. In a sense the Magi were ambassadors: they certainly would have been diplomats, practised in talking to the great men of the day, with a wide knowledge of the cultures and politics of their time. If this Renaissance painting of The Ambassadors is looked at from the revised interpretation, it provides a unique insight into understanding exactly how the Magi stood in relation to their time.

The Ambassadors is an impressive example of painterly skill and, as is now known as a result of improved research, is a highly interesting historical artefact. Recent restoration, together with some fascinating detective work carried out by the distinguished historian Mary Hervey, has enabled people to look at the picture in a more informed way and to discover much from the visual references. The painting, which is dated 1553, has, like so much else, been reinterpreted with a fresh approach and a different understanding of contemporary history, with a better appreciation of the symbols or emblems commonly used by painters and recognised by their audiences. The painting symbolises the religious and intellectual crisis of Renaissance Europe in the early sixteenth century. More specifically, it portrays two French diplomats, and seems to refer to the momentous events of 1533, when Henry VIII divorced himself from Catherine of Aragon, and the Church in England from the Roman Catholic Church of Rome.

Renaissance Europe would have been an extraordinary place in which to be a diplomat: both exciting and dangerous. There had been amazing voyages of discovery to the New World, and vast wealth gained. The Church of Rome considered itelf the spiritual centre of the world, and the Pope had divided the globe into two halves, giving one half to Spain for conquest, and the other half to Portugal.

The Roman Catholic Church was vastly rich. However, the traditional medieval world in which the Church of Rome had

140

grown to such enormous power was being turned upside down by the rediscovery of ancient learning from Greece, Rome and the Middle East. Humanistic ideas, celebrating the validity and value of individual human experience, threatened the religious doctrine which emphasised the authority of the Pope, and these new ideas spread, helped by the development of printing. Many people were critical of the lax behaviour of the clergy and were unable to accept the strict, dogmatic rule of the Church any longer. The Pope himself seemed to be under the secular power of Emperor Charles of Spain, weakening the moral strength of the Church even further, while Martin Luther was challenging what he and many others saw as a corrupt papacy. There was also much political unrest: at the time at which *The Ambassadors* was painted, Luther and others were seeking reform of the Catholic Church rather than complete separation from it, but events in England at this time helped to bring about the development of Protestantism.

Henry VIII had married his brother's wife, Catherine of Aragon, and had needed the Pope's approval to countenance what would otherwise have been considered an adulterous relationship. The Church had granted approval, but Henry wanted an heir, which Catherine could not give him. In 1533, when Holbein painted his picture, Henry's mistress, Anne Boleyn, was four months pregnant. Henry now wanted to divorce Catherine and marry Anne in haste, so that her child, who he felt certain was to be his heir, would be born legitimately. Henry therefore decided that his marriage to Catherine had been illegal, and as a result he could claim that he had never been married and could legally marry Anne Boleyn. Needless to say, the Church took a dim view of this, particularly when Henry challenged the authority of Rome in dictating what an English king could do.

Henry was not seeking to promote Protestantism, but was determined that he should be allowed to do as he pleased, claiming this in the name of dubious historical precedent that the King of England must be the supreme spiritual authority in England, above Rome. He succeeded because he played upon his subjects' hatred of the clergy, who were seen as corrupt, and he also got support from the King of France, who found the enmity between England and Spain very useful.

Henry did not want Protestantism; in separating the Church of England from Rome he intended to maintain Catholic doctrine within the new Anglican Church. But in divorcing Catherine he divorced Rome, and so his activities, carried out entirely for his own ends, contributed much to the development of the Protestant faith. It was in this volatile and risky political situation that Holbein's painting was commissioned.

The two men in the painting are French Catholic diplomats, and the painting sets the scene in London, on a very specific occasion. The man on the left is Jean de Dinteville, who was in London at the request of the French king to observe and report on Henry's machinations. He is quite young, his age (29) is given on the golden sheath of his dagger; ages and dates were often displayed in this way in pictures. The other man is Georges de Selve, a bishop and diplomat. Again, his age (25) is given, visible on the book under his elbow. Between the two men, and central to the painting, are various objects, ranging from astronomical instruments of various kinds to mathematical and prayer books, and musical instruments. Some have said these objects were put into the picture merely to represent the wide learning of these cultured men, as was the practice of that time. The objects certainly do illustrate that, but as Mary Hervey and others have shown, they can also be seen to represent significantly more.

On the upper shelf are astronomical instruments and devices for telling time: a celestial globe; sundials; quadrants used to measure heights of celestial bodies; and another astronomical instrument called a 'torquetum'. These represent the foremost scientific developments and discoveries of the day. On the lower shelf is a globe indicating the recently discovered new route to America. There is also a newly published arithmetic book, set-square, dividers, a German translation of a hymn book, a lute and a case of flutes. The two men stand on a floor decorated like the floor of Westminster Abbey, while in the top left-hand corner, glimpsed behind a curtain, is a crucifix. Finally, at the bottom of the picture, centrally placed, is a peculiar slanting shape which turns out on careful scrutiny to be a skull, distorted by perspective unless looked at from a certain angle.

The picture displays two learned and politically astute international figures represented by the globes, the instruments and the books. The faces are real and the objects are carefully and accurately depicted, even though there are one or two small irregularities here and there, to suggest that perhaps not all is perfect. National Gallery archivists suggest a fairly cautious interpretation of the picture. They point out certain irregularities about the instruments; they suggest that the objects on the top shelf may be said to represent the cosmos, and allude to the passing of time. The objects may therefore symbolise a world of chaos and of the times which were 'out of joint'.

The objects on the lower shelf represent more earthly matters, such as music, geometry and arithmetic. But the lute, which was recognised as a symbol of harmony, has a broken string. This can only symbolise *disharmony*. Moreover, the Lutheran hymnal was, as the authors state, 'a highly contentious book', and would only appear in the painting by quite deliberate design. These men were living at a time of enormous change; they were loyal to France and good Catholics. Dinteville is known to have been unhappy in England at this time, and de Selve is known to have been a passionate supporter of reform of the Church in a peaceful and harmonious way, to accommodate Luther's ideals and avoid bloody conflict.

> The whole painting then may be read as a meditation on Dinteville's melancholy and misery, and on de Selve's despair at the condition of Europe. Standing on a floor which may allude to the cosmos, and placed between objects ... perhaps arranged to simulate heaven and earth, and which certainly allude to a world of chaos, both men think of the brevity of life and their end, but also the hope of the life to come (represented by the crucifix as the symbol of the resurrection).

Whatever the significance of the other objects in the painting, the scar-like shape of the skull seems to cut across the materialistic realism of the picture. Once noticed, this strange shape dominates the picture. To be recognised properly, the skull must be viewed from a different point of view; perhaps the whole scene should be understood from a different point of view.

Richard Foster and Pamela Tudor-Craig wrote *The Secret Life of Paintings* to accompany a BBC television programme in 1986, and they give much more weight to the symbolic side of the painting. Firstly, the scientific instruments and mathematical precision, which are so clearly celebrated in this painting, were products *not* of the Italian Renaissance, but of the Reformation movement in Germany:

> Techniques of engraving sheet metal with precise scales for the manufacture of instruments ... contributed to the invention of

printing. In its turn, printing fuelled further scientific developments. It was no coincidence that Augsburg and Nuremberg
became the great centres for both printing and instrument making.
Holbein had spent his childhood in Augsburg, and Nuremburg,
where much of Apian's work was published, is prominently
marked on the terrestrial globe of 'The Ambassadors'. The
mentality of the picture is firmly rooted in the scientific and
humanist traditions.

Richard Foster and Pamela Tudor-Craig suggest that the painting
represents a fairly precise moment in time as indicated by the
various astronomical instruments: between 9.30 and 10.30 on the
morning of 11 April 1533.

> Now in the year of our painting, 11 April was a Friday. To be
> precise, it was Good Friday and Easter 1533 wasn't just any Easter
> – it proved to be a turning point not only in the history of England,
> but in the delicate balance of power in Europe. This was the very
> weekend that Henry VIII had set as the deadline for the resolution
> of 'the King's great matter' – his divorce from Catherine of
> Aragon.

This is what had brought these two diplomats to London. France
mediated between Henry and the Pope, but it also suited the
French king to have English support against the power of the
Holy Roman Emperor, Charles V, who happened to be the
nephew of Catherine of Aragon. France needed to play a careful
game, protecting her interests as a Catholic country, while also
fostering dissension between Henry and Rome. Dinteville and de
Selve were among the most highly respected and cultured men of
their day, and they were at the centre of the 'biggest political
storm of the century' (Foster/Tudor-Craig, 1986). Henry's actions
were to 'open the door' to the English Reformation. These two
ambassadors were therefore observers and heralds of dramatic
political, cultural and spiritual changes in the history of the
Christian world.

The lute was used as an emblem of harmony and alliance
between different factions, and so here the broken string
symbolises discord. Moreover, the arithmetic book on the same
shelf is open at the page on 'division'. The Lutheran hymnal is
another discordant note: the book, which is open at the Ten
Commandments, was clearly included in the painting with
deliberate intent, and it is possible that it may have been de Selve's

own copy. He was of the more tolerant, liberal Catholic faction, and longed to achieve the reunification of the Church. But perhaps this painting shows that these two diplomats, who are realists, know that peace is not a likely outcome of the events of this day.

Ambassadors must be discreet, and as has perhaps been suggested in this painting:

> the Lutheran hymn book, a lute with its broken string and the page of arithmetical division present a plea for reform, but reform without rupture. Now, however, all hope of peaceful reform had been prejudiced by the king of England's public defiance, not only of Rome, but of one of the Ten Commandments themselves: 'Thou shalt not commit adultery.'
>
> (Foster/Tudor-Craig, 1986)

The skull suddenly shakes the viewer out of the realism of the painting, and to recognise what it is, it is necessary to look sideways at the picture. From this angle (halfway up the right-hand side) the rest of the picture is unreadable, but the skull is now clearly in perspective: this is called 'anamorphism'. It is possible that this may be a reference to the 'dance of death', reminding the viewer that all must die. The flooring has set out a philosophical statement of Creation, and its end. The revelation of the skull is Holbein's indication that his celebration of human knowledge is shadowed by pessimism: 'Knowledge, like the rules of perspective, can distort as well as reveal the truth. The artist's perspective produces an illusion of reality; the scholar's learning the illusion of enlightenment.'

Finally, the crucifix, glimpsed behind the curtain, is the emblem of true spiritual wisdom. Faith was ultimately a simple matter, nothing to do with great learning; earthly power and learning is mere vanity. The sixteenth century was a time of turmoil and uncertainty:

> The condemnation of all vanities was the common cry of reformers, Protestant and Catholic alike. There was but one bulkhead against the swell of pessimism ... The inevitability of Death could be ameliorated only by the hope of Resurrection. The road to real understanding and ultimate truth was through faith: all else was 'vanitas'.

So *The Ambassadors* contains double meanings, which symbolise the intellectual crisis of the Renaissance: 'The Ambassadors,

145

Janus-like, look forward to the expanding horizons of the modern scientific world with one face, and backwards to the comfortable security of the medieval world picture with the other.'

Until fairly recently, the two men in this painting were mysterious figures. Yet much more is known about them than can possibly be known about the Magi who travelled to honour the birth of the new Messiah, Jesus Christ. But they too were ambassadors, and undoubtedly, like the diplomats of Holbein's painting, the Magi had need of discretion and diplomacy. They had to mediate with political leaders, like Herod; they had to avoid stirring up conflict and hostilities, yet as intellectual and cultural figures they also had to do justice to the new discoveries, the new insights. As cultural ambassadors from the East travelling in Herod's kingdom it was inevitable that they would go to Jerusalem to meet Herod, to do him his honour as political leader. However, as spiritual ambassadors and heralds of the coming Messiah, they would then move on to Bethlehem, to pay their respects to the New King of the Jews.

In ushering Christ into the world, the Magi were also ushering in a radically new reform to the Jewish faith that would give rise to a completely new and separate faith: Christianity. Like Holbein's diplomats, the Magi would have been well aware of the religious and political implications of all that was happening. They did not tell Herod everything; they returned another way to avoid difficulties. Ambassadors find themselves operating at important transitions in human history. They are observers and they are peacemakers, but they are also agents of change. Like the sixteenth-century ambassadors, the Magi too were 'Janus-like' – they possessed the understanding of the past, and they also proclaimed the future.

SIX

COSMIC BIOLOGY

*To a questing mind without an inkling of the processes
by which heredity and environment shape a man's
character, astrology . . . was the most obvious means of
relating the individual to the universal whole . . . by
establishing an intimate sympathy and correspondence
between microcosmos and macrocosmos.*
(Arthur Koestler, *The Sleepwalkers*)

For the next couple of chapters, the world of the Magi will be left behind as we move forwards in time to the modern world of science and technology.

For many people today, and certainly for most of those who put their intellectual faith in scientific 'reality', astrology is not considered to be factual. Moreover, it seems impossible that it could be relied on to provide real answers in the same way that scientific method can be relied on to provide real, factual answers. To many people astrology is merely a bit of fun and not to be taken seriously. Others believe it might contain intuitive or psychological truths, and at worst it is regarded as a superstitious and even dangerous practice.

Is there anything in the astrology which the Magi would have used to find Christ which could be said to be 'factual' in our modern, scientifically oriented sense of what that means? The very idea is anathema to scientific orthodoxy, and yet scientific developments over the last 150 years or so have led to some very interesting conclusions. As a result, it is no longer sensible for science simply to deny the possibility of a planet's influence upon another object. As we all know from our school days, a magnet causes a pin or other metal object to move by means of magnetic attraction. The region of influence of the magnet is called its magnetic field. The sun, earth and other planets each have a magnetic field, and research into these fields demonstrates that the fields of these bodies can affect each other. The influence of the sun's magnetic field upon the earth or another planet is well established, but the potential influence of a planet, for example, Jupiter, upon the sun or earth is much more complex. Yet it is science itself which is demonstrating that such an influence can and does exist.

On the other hand, astrologers in modern times have often felt a need to 'defend' their discipline, although some astrologers do not feel this need. For them astrology has been, and remains, an art which does not need to be justified in irrelevant or narrow scientific terms. Others, however, have at least questioned whether there might be a demonstrable correlation between the art of astrology and the science of modern astronomy. In particular, a psychologist named Michel Gauquelin sought to bring together fascinating discoveries about the influence of the planets on human births. His work showed that many claims made by astrology were without scientific basis, but in the course of his work he discovered some very interesting evidence about the effects caused by certain planetary configurations. He demonstrated, amongst other things, that people who become great leaders were statistically likely to have been born with Jupiter in the ascendant at the moment of birth.

I am an astronomer and astrophysicist, and my own area of expertise is magnetism. Once I became aware of the new discoveries about the earth's magnetic field, the possibility that certain planets could influence human life and development occupied me greatly. Could the planets be said to have an 'influence' as astrologers have always claimed, but in the modern, scientific sense of effects transmitted via the various 'fields' of a planet? So what exactly is the evidence which shows that gravitational and magnetic fields cause certain effects between the sun and the planets, and indirectly between the planets and earth? Interestingly, these concepts in some ways resemble the ancient astrological ideas about influences.

Following directly from my own theoretical work in magnetism, and taking Michel Gauquelin's studies as a focal point, I have developed a theory which provides scientific support to one small aspect of astrology. I have suggested a way in which Gauquelin's evidence for a link between great leaders and the planet Jupiter's position at their birth could be explained in terms of known physical forces.

There is a lot of science involved in understanding how planets might influence human behaviour, and the chain of argument is

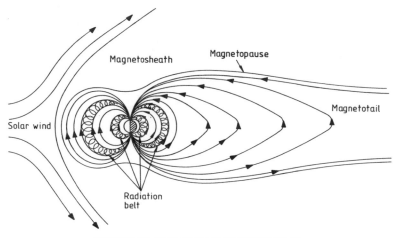

FIGURE 18. THE GEOMAGNETIC FIELD

complex. The background science behind the argument has therefore been put into Appendix I, to keep the story comprehensive. However, some readers may prefer to turn to Appendix I at this stage, before continuing with the main body of the book. The rest of this chapter summarises the evidence, without going into too much detail about the science underlying it.

Magnetism and everyday life
Magnetism plays a vital part in modern life – from simple applications, such as fridge magnets, to very sophisticated uses in computers. The electricity used in homes is generated by spinning enormous coils of wire within magnetic fields in the hearts of the generators in our power stations. The electric motors in our washing machines, freezers and hairdryers use the dynamic interactions which exist between electric currents and magnetic fields to spin drums, compressors and fans to wash, freeze and dry. In a television set the picture is built up by the rapid scanning of a thin beam of electrons (the carriers of electricity) across the inside of a fluorescent screen. This scanning is done by magnetic fields created by electric currents which flow through wires.

Audio tapes, video tapes and computer discs all carry information in coded form, which takes the form of the alignment of small magnetic particles within the tapes and discs. Magnetism is therefore woven into modern life in a variety of different ways.

So how does magnetism affect the earth and life on earth? What do we know about magnetism? The space age has provided a great deal of information which helps the understanding of how the earth is linked to the sun and the other planets, and how those interrelationships affect the inhabitants of earth.

Earth is surrounded by a magnetic field called the 'geomagnetic field' (see figure 18), in which life on earth is perfectly comfortable. Many living organisms appear to have 'biological compasses and clocks' which are closely linked to their environments. More details about this field are provided in Appendix I.

Earth and the other planets orbit the sun (see plate 1). The sun also has a magnetic field which surrounds it. Periodically, this field has violent storms, and every eleven years or so the number of 'sunspots' (or magnetic storm centres) rises to a maximum, and then dies down again. This sunspot activity causes a number of effects upon earth. For example, when sunspot activity is high, variations of the compass needle are much more erratic than at other times. Mariners and aviators know this and take account of it. Radio reception is also affected, and noticing this led to some interesting discoveries.

The aurora borealis, or northern lights, is an impressive light display in areas around the North Pole. The waving bands of coloured light in the sky are a visual indication of the state of the earth's magnetic field. When sunspot activity is high the geomagnetic field is affected, and the auroral patterns spread more widely. In 1989 (one of the sunspot 'maxima'), sunspot activity was quite violent, and had such a severe impact on regions near the Poles that it tripped the high-voltage regulators on the electric grid system in Quebec, and for nine hours the city was without electricity. It is interesting that this event corresponded to a particular alignment of the planets as seen from the sun. As will be seen in the next chapter, this was more than mere coincidence. It is therefore clear that there is a definite correspondence between the magnetic activity on the sun and the behaviour of the earth's own field.

Another phenomenon associated with the sun is the solar wind. This is a stream of very fast-moving fragments of atoms which constantly flows out from the sun. The solar wind gusts more violently during high sunspot activity, and therefore contributes to increased storm conditions in the earth's magnetic field when the sun's field is stormily active.

The pull of gravity

The tides in the earth's oceans are mainly due to the gravitational pull of the moon on the waters. However, the sun also makes a small contribution. When a new moon appears, the moon and sun are in conjunction and therefore pull in the same direction. But during a full moon, where they are in opposition, they pull in opposite directions. At both these times, higher oceanic tides occur: the spring tides. During the first and last quarters of the moon, the sun and moon are square, i.e. they are pulling at right angles to each other. When this takes place, the lowest tides of the lunar month occur: the neap tides (see Appendix I).

The terms 'conjunction', 'opposition' and 'square' arose earlier in relation to planetary positions in astrology. They also have significance beyond the effect upon earth's oceans.

But just as there are tides in the waters of the earth, there are also tides in the earth's magnetic field. The moon has an effect on earth's magnetism which is called the 'lunar daily magnetic variation'. This is explained in Appendix I, but put simply it means that the moon causes peaks and troughs in the earth's magnetism, which are linked to the moon's position, just as the ocean tides are linked to the moon's position.

Gravity and magnetism are not the same thing, as explained in Appendix I. However, magnetic fields usually contain particles of matter, and all particles from atoms to boulders, from planets to suns, are attracted by gravity. So sometimes the gravitational field of a body, for example, the sun, moon or a planet, can seem to exert a 'pull' on a magnetic field, like the magnetic field of the sun or the magnetic field of earth. This takes place because gravity can pull at the particles which then distort the shape of the magnetic field. It is important to understand this to see how a planet like Jupiter could possibly have any sort of physical influence on earth.

The geomagnetic field and life

In 1995 two scientists working in Germany, Drs Roswitha and Wolfgang Wiltschko, wrote a book called *Magnetic Orientation in Animals*, and in the preface they say:

> Biological effects of magnetic fields have been studied in many animals and plants . . . Effects on the cellular level, on biochemical processes, growth and development, interactions with physiology,

sensory input, rhythm control, to name just a few have been reported. Numerous magnetically induced changes have also been described. Recently, the amount of literature covering biological effects of magnetic fields has been rapidly increasing.

The Wiltschkos pointed out that many scientists were initially reluctant to enter this field of research, and suggested three reasons why this may have been the case. Firstly, it requires a great deal of technical effort to define and control magnetic conditions of an experiment; secondly, many biologists had a limited understanding of the more subtle properties of the geomagnetic field; and thirdly, because humans do not have the ability to directly sense the field, researchers believed that such biological effects could not possibly exist. However, much of this was changed by a young biologist, Richard Blakemore, who made an important discovery in 1975.

Blakemore, who was working at the University of New Hampshire, was studying the behaviour of a certain type of bacteria taken from marine sediments from the east coast of North America. Under the microscope, these bacteria always seemed to be swarming across the slide in the same direction. At first he thought that they were swarming to the light under which he was working, but he soon showed that this was wrong by repeating the experiment in a darkened room in which the only illumination came from the microscope's own light just below the slide. It then dawned on him that they were always swarming towards the direction of north, and he realised that they might be responding to the earth's magnetic field. To test this idea he placed a small bar magnet close to the microscope slide: he found that when the north end was close to the slide the bacteria swarmed towards this, but when the south end was placed near the slide they swarmed away from it. His hypothesis was therefore confirmed. Further experiments showed that the bacteria were attempting to swim north because they were actually trying to move *downwards*, away from the higher concentration of oxygen near the surface (these were anaerobic bacteria, i.e. they did not use oxygen for respiration).

In the northern hemisphere the earth's magnetic field not only points almost exactly north, it also dips downwards to the earth's surface. Therefore, by following the magnetic 'lines of force' of the earth's field, the bacteria would not only move north, but would also move downward. This was confirmed by an experiment in which the bacteria were taken to the southern hemisphere. Here they swam south, once again because they wanted to move downward towards the sediments and away from the surface of the water where the concentration of oxygen, which is toxic to them, is much higher. Following these results, the bacteria were studied under a powerful electron microscope, and it was observed that they contained a string of metallic 'beads', each bead consisting of a magnetic substance called 'magnetite' – the principal ingredient of lodestone, which is naturally magnetic. So Blakemore's idea that organisms might make use of the geomagnetic field had found solid support.

Blakemore's work provided a possible explanation for a completely different series of experiments, also on a type of marine life. These experiments were concerned with the effect of long-term reversals of the earth's magnetic field on microscopic marine life. Fossilised remains of these organisms have been found in sediments laid down thousands of years ago, and have been examined in great detail to see when these fossilised forms of life became extinct, and whether their extinction coincided with any particular periods in the past. Biologists have shown that there had indeed been some extinctions in the past which seemed to correlate with reversals in the geomagnetic field.

This work was carried out before Blakemore made his discoveries about magnetic bacteria, and it had already been suggested that extinctions could be connected in some way with the magnetic field of earth. Blakemore suggested that if these organisms (known as 'radiolaria') had indeed been influenced by the geomagnetic field, as his own studies on other bacteria showed, then a reversal of the field would have led them to higher levels in the water and this would have tended to shorten their life spans, because the higher levels contained more oxygen, which to them was toxic.

A pioneer of this field in the Western world was the late Professor Brown of Northwestern University in America. He set up an experiment with a horizontal magnetic field which was very close in strength to the geomagnetic field, and discovered that mud snails responded to altered directions in this field. But more than that, their responses were shown to relate to the time of day, the phases of the moon, and the relationships between the times of the tides and the times of day. Brown added: 'These last were quite what one would expect if the magnetic fields were, indeed, affecting daily and tidal rhythms of the organisms.'

After a lifetime of research, Professor Brown concluded that the ability of many animals to respond to the time of day, the phases of the moon and the time of year could not all be understood simply in terms of light cues, as was the orthodox view. Many of his experiments pointed to the daily lunar magnetic variation as an important alternative synchroniser of internal biological clocks. The daily lunar magnetic variation causes peaks and troughs in the geomagnetic field, and Brown showed that the internal biological clock of particular species was 'tuned' into these peaks or troughs, and that this tuning in turn affected the behaviour of the species. Professor Brown made a radical claim: he said that the logical conclusion of all his work was that *all living organisms necessarily had their own magnetic fields, this being demonstrated by the electrical activity present in the organisms.* These fields, said Brown, become coupled to the geomagnetic field. Therefore, in a sense many organisms were actually 'riding' the field. Their own internal rhythmic activity was coupled to specific periodic fluctuations of the geomagnetic field via a phenomenon known as resonance. When an opera singer hits a certain note and a wine glass shatters, this is as a result of resonance. When the frequency of an object matches exactly the frequency of an external force, resonance effects can occur. For example, a radio is 'tuned' so that it picks up certain broadcast signals and no others. In the case of fields of living organisms, Brown is suggesting that the fields of the organism are 'tuned' or are resonant with specific fluctuations of the earth's magnetic field. This then contributes to the particular behaviour patterns of organisms.

A biologist called Karl von Frisch demonstrated that bees also have internal biological clocks. He trained a group of bees to forage for food at a particular time of day in Paris, and then his student, Max Renner, flew the bees across the Atlantic Ocean to New York. The bees foraged according to Paris daylight hours and did not change to New York daylight hours, even though New York is about five hours behind. Von Frisch therefore concluded that the bees had some kind of internally governed biological clock.

It was von Frisch who discovered the dance of the bees. When bees find a source of food they communicate its direction to other bees by performing a dance in the hive. The dance takes the form of a figure of eight, and the direction of the central part of the figure indicates the direction where food may be found. However, von Frisch observed that, from the point of view of the experimenter, the bees seem to get the dance direction wrong by a few degrees. He noticed that this 'humanly perceived error' would change in the course of the day, but the pattern would be very similar from one day to the next. The problem was eventually solved by Martin Lindauer, a student of von Frisch. He tried an experiment, using an electric current to create a magnetic field just strong enough to cancel out the influence of earth's magnetic field. When he did this, the apparent error in direction vanished. He also found that when the bees acted naturally, the exact magnitude of the directional errors was related to daily fluctuations of the geomagnetic field. From these two situations he concluded that bees were indeed responding to influences of the geomagnetic field, and moreover they were able to detect extremely small fluctuations of the geomagnetic field called 'the solar daily magnetic variation'.

Following on from the discovery that bees had internal clocks, Professor James Gould, then of Princeton University, did some different experiments. He showed that the internal clocks of bees could be reset, over longer periods of time than those used by Renner, using variations in the earth's field. Gould also initially trained bees to forage at a given time of day, and he also noted the daily changes in earth's field near the hive. Later on he 'recreated' this record of magnetic daily changes for the bees, but this artificially recreated field was shifted in time from that of the real field. After a while the bees conducted their foraging using the new magnetic time rather than real time.

A number of experiments have been carried out to try to discover how birds can navigate when they migrate at night. The evidence seems to indicate that, most of the time, birds use the stars as navigational aids. Birds which are released under clear skies tend to fly in the direction in which they want to migrate. Yet if the birds are released under cloudy skies they tend to fly in random directions. However, one series of experiments seems to show that, if necessary, birds can also use the magnetic field of earth.

In a further experiment, a sample of birds was divided into three groups. The first group was fitted with contact lenses which allowed normal light levels through to their eyes, but blotted out the faint light of the stars. These birds were also fitted with magnetised rings on their feet. The second group had contact lenses but no magnetised rings and the third group had neither lenses nor rings. The aim was to see if the birds set off on their migration, or if they failed to start and returned to base, and for those birds which did return, how long they took to arrive back at the base. The birds of the first group never returned home; those in the third group did return home; and those in the second group also returned home, but took longer than the third group. This series of experiments seemed to indicate that migrating birds flying at night can either use the stars or the geomagnetic field for navigation, although they prefer to use the stars.

Appendix I shows that when an electric conductor moves across magnetic lines of force, then currents are generated in the conducting material. This discovery can be related to organic life. For example, when a fish is swimming across the lines of force of earth's field, it is generating small electric currents within its body, just like the coils of wire of a dynamo. However, when the fish happens to be swimming along the lines of force, no such currents will flow. If this fish is sensitive enough to electricity to pick up any currents induced in its body, then this response could allow it to use the geomagnetic field for directional guidance. Researchers have tested several marine organisms, and they have detected electric sensors sensitive enough to respond to these induced currents. Therefore, evidence exists that many marine organisms do indeed use these sensors as navigational aids.

Humans and the geomagnetic field

In the years of preparation before NASA undertook manned space flights they sponsored a series of experiments to find out what effects shielding people from the geomagnetic field might have. Because astronauts would be separated from the geomagnetic field on a flight to the moon, they needed to know if such effects might occur. The results of some very simple experiments indicated that shielding from the geomagnetic field did indeed influence certain responses of the human nervous system. For example, the time it took to adapt to seeing in the dark (dark adaption time) was slightly increased; certain reaction times were slowed down; and the frequency at which a rapidly fluctuating light source appeared to be a constant source of light (the flicker-fusion threshold) was decreased.

It seems to be true that humans also have a subconscious ability to find direction using the geomagnetic field, although this ability varies tremendously from one person to another. The first experiments in this area were carried out by Dr Robin Baker, a zoologist from Manchester University. In one of his early investigations, he drove blindfolded students via winding routes to distances of up to 50 km from the university. He found that students gave good estimates of the direction of the university while still blindfolded, but when the blindfolds were removed they became disorientated. This suggested that while they were blindfolded they were responding to some unseen field, but when they were able to see, visual clues conflicted with the information coming from this field.

Baker then tried an experiment using a group of schoolchildren on a bus journey. They were divided into two groups: one group had bar magnets attached to their heads, while the second group had unmagnetised pieces of metal, similar in shape and size to the bar magnets, attached to their heads. Baker discovered that the second group was much better at finding the direction of north than the first group. This suggested that the 'field' in the first series of experiments was the magnetic field, and that the second group were also responding to this field. However, the magnets attached to the heads of the first group interfered with their magnetic 'receiving' mechanism and they were therefore unable to respond to the geomagnetic field.

Baker's work was taken a stage further by Dr R. Gai Murphy, who carried out work on children and young people. Murphy found that the ability of children aged between four and eleven to find direction using earth's field was very weak. Further experiments showed that for teenage boys the ability increased only marginally. However, for teenage girls the ability increased noticeably after the age of nine and reached a plateau of performance at eighteen. These experiments established a clear correlation between 'magnetic detection abilities' and maturity.

In 1991 Dr Mary Campion carried out her own investigations at Keele University. She also concluded that humans have the ability to find direction using earth's field, although this ability is only measurable using large samples. She concluded that it is a latent ability, and one which may be developed. She believes this because the ability to find direction proved better on later experiments than on earlier ones with the same group, suggesting that the group was able to 'rediscover' this ability.

Neural networks

If organisms do have an ability to respond to magnetic influences, what allows them to do so? While it is still highly controversial to claim that life forms on earth can and do respond to the geomagnetic field, it is accepted that *if* such influences exist, they will be working upon the nervous system of the creature concerned.

In higher organisms, such as mammals, there is a complex central nervous system within which information is conducted by neurons. Neurons are the basic building blocks of the central nervous system and are often described in terms of electrical circuits. The genetic code of the organism carries information on how neurons of the nervous system should be structured. To use the electric circuit analogy, the genetic code organises how the nervous system is 'wired up'. Obviously the 'wiring diagram' of a particular species is recognisable in each individual member of the species, but just as the DNA code of any individual within the species is unique to that individual, so the finely tuned wiring may also be unique in specific ways. This wiring-up not only determines the basic character traits of the individual, it also regulates the internal biological clocks of that particular, unique individual.

Therefore, just as electrical circuits can be influenced by fluctuating magnetic fields, so can the neurons of a central nervous system. When a bacterium moves in response to magnetic forces, the field is acting directly on a string of the magnetic lodestone beads within the organism. Indeed, even a dead bacterium will align itself with the field, so in the northern hemisphere a live one simply uses its motor mechanism to move along the lines. When a bird finds direction apparently using magnetic information, this is conveyed through the nervous system to the bird's brain. When a human being is observed to respond to a magnetic influence, this response is a result of magnetically altered neural activity in the central nervous system of the person.

Having looked at gravitational and magnetic links between the sun, moon and earth, it is clear that there is established evidence to show that magnetic fields can and do influence organic life in certain ways, and that new discoveries are being made all the time. But what, if anything, does science have to say about *planetary* influences upon earth? Is there any evidence that the planets might influence organisms, and if so, how could this happen?

There are two completely separate approaches to the question about evidence for planetary influence: one comes from mainstream physics, the other from Michel Gauquelin's statistical studies of astrology.

Planetary alignments and sunspot activity

In 1845, George Biddell Airy, then Astronomer Royal at the Royal Observatory Greenwich, wondered why big tides (spring tides) should occur when the moon was at its first and last quarters, rather than when it was either full or new, as was the case in ocean tides. He calculated a rigorous mathematical theory to explain his thinking. He suggested that if a circular canal could be built around the earth parallel to the equator, then by choosing the dimensions of this canal carefully it would be possible within such a canal to have spring tides at first and last quarters of the moon rather than at full and new moon. (This corresponds to square positions for the sun and moon as seen from earth.)

But what does this mean, and why is it significant? Airy was using resonance in his argument. Such a canal would greatly amplify the weak tides associated with the open oceans, and he explained this by physics. According to Airy, if a rock were dropped into this canal, a wave would occur which would travel at a given speed. This is called 'the speed of the free wave', and its value depends on the cross-sectional dimensions of the canal. If the dimensions were chosen so that the speed of this wave was faster than the speed with which the point immediately below the moon travelled across the face of earth, but slower than the speed with which the point immediately below the sun travelled across the earth, resonance would have a strongly amplifying effect. Therefore, spring tides would occur at the first and last quarters of the moon, rather than a new and full moon.

In the 1940s it was noticed that planetary alignments coincided with the disruption of radio communications. A radio engineer named John Nelson worked for the Radio Corporation of America. He discovered that when Venus, earth, Mars, Jupiter and Saturn were in a straight line with the sun, or when they made 90 degrees with each other, radio reception was particularly bad. He also noticed that conditions for radio reception were good when the angles between these planets were 30 degrees, 60 degrees, 120 degrees, or 150 degrees.

As explained earlier, alignments of sun and moon with respect to earth have a definite effect upon the tides. In the same way, Nelson's discoveries seemed to suggest that alignments of planets with respect to the sun also had an effect upon earth. These angles seem to coincide with astrological aspects:

opposition	180°
quincunx	150°
trine	120°
square	90°
sextile	60°
semi-sextile	30°

In traditional astrology, the opposition, square and trine aspects are considered to be very powerful, the other aspects less powerful. However, for later reference, it is important to know that an astrological horoscope is calculated using positions as seen from *earth*, and not from the sun.

Eventually, Nelson's work was largely discredited, but in the process much further work was done to investigate links between planetary configurations and magnetic activity on the sun. The US Air Force and NASA were interested in this subject, as it had been recognised that severe sunspot activity had been causing damage to communication satellites. One scientist, J. B. Blizard, was particularly puzzled that some of the violent sunspot activity correlated with the square (90 degrees) position of the planets as seen from the sun. It seemed to Blizard that all the planets must be involved, not just those with the strongest gravitational pull on the sun. Blizard suggested that, just as the moon and sun raise tides upon earth, so planets could raise tides in the sun's gases. This could explain the violent events that correlated with conjunctions and oppositions, but it was unable to explain the squared positions, which were also observed. Blizard could find no satisfactory scientific explanation for this phenomenon.

The possible effects on the sun by the planets evoked a response from *The Times* on 5 December 1970, following a report in the science journal *Nature*. The *Nature* paper had drawn attention to certain correlations between solar activity and planetary alignments, and *The Times* article pointed out that this type of alignment was exactly the relationship studied by astrologers. The report ended with these words:

> The radiation from the sun is one of the prime hazards to manned space flight, so we may find the curious anomaly that the dates of future space flights might be chosen using the textbook astrological techniques of Kepler to predict low sunspot activity.

Airy used the concept of resonance to explain certain features of tidal activity upon earth. Can Airy's theory be used to explain surprising features of magnetic activity on the sun? Surely the idea of canals on the sun is as fanciful as the now debunked idea of canals on the planet Mars? Surprisingly, this is a very fruitful idea. By studying the geometry of magnetic fields in sunspots, and the loops of hot gases that link pairs of sunspots together, it is clear that just below the surface of the sun, in the build-up to sunspot maximum, canal-like magnetic structures exist. These canals tend to become increasingly parallel to the equator as activity increases, while the strength of the magnetic field in these structures also increases. This strength affects the speed with which a magnetic wave will travel along one of these magnetic canals.

The speeds at which planets travel with respect to material on the spinning sun varies from one planet to the next. This means that as the speed in a magnetic canal increases (with increasing field strength), the magnetic tidal waves will be tuned to each planet in turn, starting with Mercury. Furthermore, if the tuning lies between the different tidal frequencies associated with two planets, a square of these planets will give rise to larger tides on the sun. At other times conjunctions and oppositions will have the same effect.

Astrologers believe that the geocentric aspects (as seen from earth) of conjunction, opposition and squares are important, whereas the scientific evidence points to these heliocentric aspects (as seen from the Sun) as being important. How did this astrological idea arise in the ancient world? This is discussed in more detail in Appendix II.

The advent of radio introduced many new concepts and phrases into our language. The phrase 'being on the same wavelength' is often used, as is 'tuning into someone's thoughts' or 'picking up their vibrations'. Underneath the functioning of all radio and television communications is the very important concept of resonance.

Resonance is a phenomenon which is sometimes ignored by 'pure' scientists, although it is much more widely recognised and understood by practical people like wireless technicians or engineers. Resonance is the phenomenon which makes it possible for a radio telescope to tune into the specific vibrations of hydrogen atoms in the Andromeda galaxy, fourteen million million million miles away; it is what enables us to communicate with friends and family using mobile phones. It is through resonance that the moon's gravitational pull on earth shifts a hundred billion tonnes of water out of the Bay of Fundy in Canada twice a day. In the biological world many animals respond selectively to sounds made by their own species; the ability of a robin to distinguish another robin's song in the musical din of a dawn chorus is a result of the robin 'tuning in' to the robin frequency – a result of resonance.

This important phenomenon of resonance, as explained earlier, is not fully understood by many scientists who ought to know better. In particular, the detailed calculations which are supposed to demonstrate conclusively that the sun, moon and planets cannot possibly affect life on earth have ignored the possibility of resonant interactions. Yet the existence of the phenomenon of resonance is indisputable. Moreover, there is plenty of evidence that resonance has a profound and amplifying influence on interactions.

Statistical research into astrology
Michel Gauquelin was a statistician and psychologist who conducted a series of statistical investigations over many years into the validity of certain astrological claims.

Gauquelin's first experiments were in the field of sun-sign astrology. Using the rigorous statistical methods in which he was trained, he found that there was no evidence for sun-sign astrology, the type of astrology which appears in newspaper columns. However, in the course of this work some interesting statistical results began to appear. The first positive results came when he looked at the birth data of 576 members of the French Academy of Medicine. Theoretically these people should have been born, quite randomly, at any time of day. Yet Gauquelin found that of those doctors who had attained distinction in their profession, there was a statistical likelihood of their being born when either Mars or Saturn was in the ascendant, or had reached the highest point in the sky.

Further studies showed that Saturn was generally associated with a higher than average number of scientists and physicians, but a lower than average number of actors, journalists, writers and painters. Few scientists and physicians were born under Jupiter, but a much higher number of political and military leaders, top executives and playwrights were born with this sign at an important angle. For Mars the high frequency was associated with sportsmen and sportswomen, and the low frequency with painters, musicians and writers, while the moon was statistically associated with births of great writers.

In his book, *Cosmic Influences on Human Behaviour*, Michel Gauquelin used the example of Louis XIV to describe someone who fulfils the expectation of this effect:

> When the future Louis the Great uttered his first cry on September 5, 1638, at eleven minutes past eleven in the morning, the planet Jupiter was just rising on the horizon at the Saint-Germain castle ... In short, the future Louis XIV was born at an hour favourable for those who are to participate in the leadership of state affairs.

Louis XIV, also sometimes known as the Sun King, had a powerful effect on the role of the monarchy in France. Before 1661, France was really ruled by the chief minister Jules Mazarin, but after this Louis XIV assumed absolute power, declaring that 'I am the State.' Almost throughout the whole of his reign, Louis involved his country in wars which were an attempt to expand his kingdom, although most of them did not bring him what he hoped for. He was not only a great patron of the arts, but also a supporter of science. One of his most enduring contributions to astronomy was establishing the Paris Observatory. The main aim of this establishment was to find a method of calculating longitude by using the moons of Jupiter: they believed that this would improve their knowledge of the shape of earth and allow better maps to be drawn of France. The Paris Observatory was to have a lasting effect on the history of astronomy. It could be argued that in many ways Louis XIV's influence on France was not always beneficial, but there can be little doubt that he was a great leader who inspired many people in his country.

As was seen earlier, when looking at the Star of Bethlehem, at sunset on 15 September 7 BC, Jupiter was also in the ascendant position.

Gauquelin's studies demonstrated that this particular planetary effect existed for the moon, Mars, Jupiter and Saturn. None of the other planets, Mercury, Venus, Uranus and Neptune, were strongly associated with any successful group of people.

Gauquelin also discovered what he called the 'planetary heredity' effect. The idea that people tend to be born when planetary alignments as seen from earth are similar to those when their parents were born has run through astrology for almost 2000 years, ever since the time of Ptolemy. Kepler had also believed in this concept: 'There is one perfectly clear argument beyond all exception in favour of the authenticity of astrology. This is the common horoscopic connection between parents and children.'

Gauquelin decided to use modern statistical methods to test this hypothesis. Initially he found that parents and children showed little or no tendency to be born at the same time of year. However, further investigations revealed a very interesting result. If one or other parent was born with a given planet just about to rise or at the highest point of the sky, then there was a significant tendency for their children to be born with the same planet in one of these positions. This tendency was further increased if both parents were born with the same planet in one of these two sectors of the sky. As pointed out by psychologist Professor Hans Eysenck, the increase was in keeping with known statistical laws of heredity. This planetary heredity effect was shown to be most marked for the moon, Venus and Mars, followed by Jupiter and Saturn, but was absent for the sun, Mercury and the other planets.

These results were taken from a more general sample, i.e. a sample which was not confined only to eminent individuals, as with his previous work. This later work of Gauquelin was therefore based more soundly on objectively measurable quantities, such as birth times and planetary positions; it did not depend on relatively subjective criteria such as what might constitute 'eminence' in a given profession.

In a later repeat of this experiment he divided his sample into two categories, according to whether births were induced or not. He found that the effect only applied to natural, uninduced births. This is an astonishing result, seeming to suggest that the planets may in some way 'influence' the natural timing of birth, so that a person with a certain type of inherited characteristic is more likely to be born in 'response' to particular 'signals' from a specific planet. But Gauquelin took the experiment forward another stage. In a further replication of this experiment he divided his sample of natural births into two groups: one group born on days when the geomagnetic field was highly disturbed; the other group born on magnetically quiet days. Amazingly, the planetary heredity effect was statistically greater for the first group than for the second.

This was the very first indication that a physical agency might be involved in these apparent planetary correlations. It was also an extraordinary extension of the idea that the geomagnetic field had an effect on living organisms. In France, where Gauquelin worked, birth data includes time of birth, which is an important factor. Unfortunately this information is not automatically recorded in Britain, although many parents do in fact note the time of a child's birth.

Replication of the planetary-success effect

Gauquelin's first experiments were restricted to data collected from France. Because it was possible (although unlikely) that the data reflected a peculiarity of native French people, he decided to extend his studies to Germany, Italy, Holland and Belgium.

In Belgium, the Committee for the Scientific Investigation of Alleged Paranormal Phenomena decided to see whether Gauquelin's results could be replicated. This committee, called the Committee Para for short, consisted of a team of 30 astronomers, demographers, statisticians and other scientists. They tested for links between the planet Mars and sports champions. Using a new group of 535 sports champions from France and Belgium, they came up with the same statistical results as Gauquelin had found. Yet they decided not to publish their results, and they issued the following statement: 'The Committee Para cannot accept the conclusions of the research of M Gauquelin based on hypotheses in which the committee has found inexactitudes.'

If the committee felt that Gauquelin's research methods

contained 'inexactitudes', why did they spend time and money replicating the tests at all? Why did they not refine the tests to get rid of the 'inexactitudes'? It seems that officials were not ready to acknowledge as a serious possibility the notion that planetary influence could be a factor in births of sports champions.

The same thing happened in America with a group called the US Committee for the Scientific Investigations of Claims of the Paranormal or CSICOP. The story is told in the foreword, written by Brian Inglis, to *The Message of Astrology* by Professor Peter Roberts (a physicist, systems scientist and active researcher into astrology):

> So scrupulously objective had the Gauquelins' work been – as Peter Roberts shows – that it was possible to repeat it in the United States in exactly the same form, and in 1977 the Humanist reported that the results revealed that there was no need to take the Gauquelins seriously. Only gradually did it begin to emerge that in fact the American results confirmed the Gauquelins', as six years later Kurtz and his fellow workers in CSICOP had to confess ... Yet in their embarrassment at finding their preconceptions upset, they had permitted what was in effect a smear on the Gauquelins, by pretending that their work had been discredited.

Professor Suitbert Ertel, a German psychologist from the University of Göttingen, decided to find out for himself what was going on. He thoroughly investigated Gauquelin's Mars-successful sports people effect, and replicated the experiment. Ertel confirmed the results, therefore four separate research experiments have brought up the same statistical findings: that there is a correlation between the position of Mars with the birth of sports champions. Ertel has demonstrated that the criticisms of 'orthodox' scientists are ill founded. His most recent work on the subject appears in his book *Tenacious Mars Effect*, which was published in 1995. In his review of this book Professor Hans Eysenck has acknowledged that the Mars effect is now so well established, as a result of Ertel's work, that one should treat it as scientific fact.

Is there not an extraordinary anomaly here? Well-trained, orthodox scientists have replicated Gauquelin's work, and come up with the same results. These people undoubtedly pride themselves on their objectivity and careful research methods, and would wish to be trusted not to let prejudice influence them. Yet these same people are so extremely reluctant to acknowledge their own findings, that they prefer to ignore the results. They are even willing to say that the methods they themselves adopted contain 'inexactitudes' – anything but admit that there could possibly be any factual basis for planetary influence. It is difficult to respect a scientific orthodoxy which is so fundamentally unscientific in its dealings. There is no future in an attitude which is so afraid of awkward possibilities that they must be suppressed, even at the expense of scientific credibility. Scientists who allow their emotional reactions to astrology to override rational enquiry are behaving like the worst defenders of the Christian Church in the Middle Ages. They do not deserve the trust placed in them, and unfortunately they open the door to further misunderstanding and prejudice.

Genetics and behavioural characteristics
One further question of relevance is whether behavioural traits can be genetically transmitted. The work of Gauquelin seems to indicate that this is the case, but is there any additional evidence to support this? It is a complex area of research because it involves trying to separate the relative roles of inherited characteristics from those that may be acquired from training and environmental factors. It is also a matter of controversy, on which various views have been expressed over many centuries.

A contribution to this debate can be found in the New Testament in the parable of the sower. St Matthew, Chapter 13:

> Behold a sower went out to sow; And when he sowed, some seed fell by the way side, and the fowls came and devoured them up: Some seed fell upon stony places, where they had not much earth: And forthwith they came up, because they had no deepness of earth: And when the sun was up, they were scorched, and because they had root, they withered away. And some fell among thorns; and the thorns came up and choked them: But some fell into good ground, and brought forth fruit, some an hundredfold, some sixtyfold, some thirtyfold.

Seeds contain the basic genetic code of the species, and as the parable implies, in all kinds of environment, seeds readily spring up into plants, if given the chance. However, the environment, whatever it is like, cannot alter the basic programming of a seed: a sunflower seed will develop only into a sunflower; the seed of a potato will not bring forth a rose. The environment may foster or hinder development of the seed into a plant, therefore the innate qualities of the species are held within the particular type of seed, but the successful development of that seed depends very much on its environment.

An enormous amount of work has been done in genetic research, which might amaze or horrify us. An understanding of genetics has enabled the fight against killer diseases and the selective breeding of plants and animals for our own benefit. We may feel very glad about such things, but less comfortable with the implications of modern genetic engineering, or with the political use of such factors. But even today, when vegetables are genetically altered and sheep cloned, it is not really known how far human abilities and personality characteristics are genetically determined, or to what extent complex environmental factors are responsible for the development of human beings.

This area is an extremely difficult one to investigate, and not only because of ethical problems. Even leaving aside questions of morality, it can be difficult to know exactly what we are testing, even in rigorously controlled experiments. What is meant, for example, when we talk of 'personality'? Are we talking about conscious behaviour only, or should we include involuntary mood swings as well as organised, self-consciously directed activity? Even if we do manage to clearly define exactly what we want to test, how do we tackle testing whether a particular personality or behavioural trait is a consequence of our genetic make-up? How do we measure our own or another's experience of pain, or joy? Can we be sure our perceptions of what is going on are objective? These are questions which are handled in different ways by different kinds of scientific discipline.

To some extent it has been possible to test genetic influence on behaviour in animals. For example, breeders of dogs and horses have used an understanding of genetic principles to breed certain characteristics into animals which they require for different purposes. Therefore, the sheepdog is selectively bred for those characteristics which make it suitable for herding sheep; racehorses are selectively bred for speed; carthorses for strength for heavy work. Although such characteristics, chosen to make a breed suitable for a specific purpose, are physical qualities, they also involve behavioural traits. For example, it is not enough for the sheepdog to be good at rounding up sheep, it must also be responsive and lack another canine capacity to worry them.

These kinds of experimental testing are not done on human beings. But there are some ways to investigate genetic transmission of human character traits. The relative importance of heredity or environmental factors has been investigated in twins. Identical twins are monozygotic (MZ) which means they are formed from one fertilised egg which splits into two. Non-identical twins are dizygotic (DZ) where two eggs are separately fertilised at the same time. Certain tests have been conducted to investigate whether IQ scores are very similar in twins. Three different groups were tested: DZ twins reared together; MZ twins reared together; and MZ twins reared apart. Results for the similarity of IQs in the three groups were all different: the correlation (statistical significance) for DZ twins reared together was 0.53 – not particularly high; for MZ twins reared together the correlation was much higher, at 0.87; and for those reared apart the correlation was 0.75. This indicates that genetic factors do indeed play a major role in determining intelligence, although environmental factors also play a significant part.

It is often noted that excellence in a subject is passed down through families. Johann Sebastian Bach (1685–1750) is the best known of an outstanding musical family. His four sons were also musically outstanding. He had two sons by his first wife, Maria Barbara: Wilhelm Friedemann (1710–1784) and Carl Philipp Emanuel (1714–1788). He then fathered two more sons by his second wife, Anna Magdalena: Johann Christoph Friedrich (1732–1795) and Johann Christian Bach (1735–1782). The musical success of this family may suggest that musical talent could have been inherited by both sets of sons from the father. But nothing very scientific can be stated here. Naturally, the children grew up in an atmosphere of music, and it is impossible to say to what extent, if at all, any genetic inheritance factor outweighs the environmental one.

The study of genetics and human behaviour is an enormous field which is being explored by people from many different disciplines. It takes us right to the edge of what we can say we know. It is not just difficult to test human behaviour objectively, it is also difficult to define what a good test might be. We recoil from intrusive testing of human subjects, but such testing may not be very useful anyway. For all that, we are a part of the biological world and share a genetic history with all living organisms, but we are also a different kind of organism from any other on earth. We have self-consciousness, we have language, we have musical and numerical ability, and we have the capacity for self-reflection. We can contemplate our own humanity in a way in which no other organism can do. These characteristics separate us from other organisms. However, we are also limited by our humanity: we cannot 'get outside' ourselves in order to look objectively at what we are.

It is recognised at the most fundamental level of physics that there are areas where a scientific question cannot be asked without affecting the answer to that question. The observer, in the very act of studying a particle, changes the behaviour of that particle. There is nothing the observer can do to avoid this happening. Similarly, at some levels in the study of human behaviour, it may be that we simply cannot frame sensible scientific questions about human activity, because no answer could be given which would count as scientifically useful. In *Men of Ideas*, philosopher Noam Chomsky, well known for his work on language, pointed out:

> We can reach some understanding of the principles that make it possible for us to behave in a normal creative fashion, but as soon as questions of will, or decision, or reasons, or choice of action, arise, human science is pretty much at a loss. It has little to say about these matters, as far as I can see. These questions remain in the obscurity that has enveloped them since classical antiquity.

This does not mean that there is no more to learn, as this is a very active area of human intellectual effort. In the third edition of their book *Behavioural Genetics* (published in 1997), Plomin, DeFries, McClearn and Rutter say:

> One of the most dramatic developments in psychology during the past few decades is the increasing recognition and appreciation of the important contribution of genetic factors. Genetics is not a neighbor chatting over the fence with some helpful hint – it is central to psychology and other behavioral sciences. In fact, genetics is central to all the life sciences. Genetics bridges the biological and behavioral sciences and helps to give psychology, the science of behavior, a place in the biological sciences.

Behavioural Genetics is a thorough overview of the majority of the important areas in this field of research. It is not only restricted to human behaviour, but also considers certain aspects of animal behaviour. It reviews not only the genetic transmission of general cognitive ability (the mental act or process by which knowledge is acquired), but also the transmission of cognitive disabilities and certain mental diseases. In the last section of the book, on 'Nature and Nurture', they say:

> The controversy that swirled around behavioral genetics research in psychology during the 1970s has largely faded. One of the many signs of the increasing acceptance of genetics is that behavioral genetics was identified by the American Psychological Association at its centennial celebrations in 1992 as one of the two themes that best represent the future of psychological research. This is one of the most dramatic shifts in the history of modern psychology.

They end their book with these words:

> The basic message of behavioral genetics is that each one of us is an individual. Recognition of, and proper respect for, individual differences is essential to the ethic of individual worth. Proper attention to individual needs, including provision of the environmental circumstances that will optimize the development of each person, is a utopian ideal and no more attainable than other utopias. Nevertheless, we can approach this ideal more closely if we recognise, rather than ignore, individuality. Acquiring the requisite knowledge warrants a high priority because human individuality is the fundamental natural resource of our species.

Conclusion

It cannot be doubted any longer that gravitational and magnetic fields have an influence on terrestrial life. Astrologers have always claimed that such influences do exist, although they did not understand the nature and details of these unseen cosmic forces. While many astrological statements do not stand up to a scientific criterion of validity, certain claims, as we have seen, do appear to correlate with evidence which has been obtained using scientific method. Michel Gauquelin's work has given results which are statistically valid. Statistical 'proofs' are perfectly acceptable, and very useful, but what science really wants is an explanation in terms of the known forces and fields, which is testable using rigorous scientific criteria. I have developed a theory which brings together evidence from a wide variety of different areas of research, including solar physics, planetary astronomy, solar-terrestrial relationships, geophysics, investigations on the biological effects of the geomagnetic field, as well as artificially produced magnetic fields and statistical research on selected aspects of astrology. It provides a scientific explanation of how planetary influence may affect the birth of a human individual. The full physical theory is published in a monograph (ISBN 0 9508 6161 8 – November 1986) and is stated in technical terms which are beyond the scope of this book. However, in the next chapter we will explain the fascinating evidence which links planetary position with the moment of birth of an individual.

SEVEN

WRITTEN IN THE STARS?

*When the pioneer in science sends forth the groping
fingers of his thoughts, he must have a vivid, intuitive
imagination, for new ideas are not generated by
deduction, but by an artistically creative imagination.*
(Max Planck)

Many different theories involving radiation, gravitation or
magnetism have been proposed to account for possible cosmic
effects on our environment and life on earth. Scientists have
shown that the forces associated with these factors are far too
weak to have any measurable effects of the kind claimed by
astrologers or revealed by statistical investigations. As a result of
this, some people have made the unscientific presumption that all
possibilities have been exhausted, and therefore any freshly
offered suggestion is rejected out of hand. This is to mistake the
proper task of theoretical physics. Scientists can be arrogant –
they can assume they have 'thought of everything' – yet new
people continue to come along with new solutions to old
problems, and therefore science proceeds.

What is a scientific theory?
A scientific theory attempts to provide an explanation which does
not yet exist for observed data. The observed data usually consist
of events or measurements which are accepted as factual.
However, it may also include statistical results, as well as
evidence that may be rejected by some scientists because it does
not fit into the currently accepted framework. For example,
Newton's observed fact was an apple falling from a tree to the
ground. There were endless numbers of apples (and other objects)
falling to the ground, but neither mathematics nor physics
explained why this should be the case. It was also known in
Newton's time that the moon orbits the earth and that the planets
orbit the sun, but it was Newton who saw a link between the
apples falling from the tree and the planets orbiting the sun. His

genius lay in taking established information which everybody knew about, and coming up with a convincing reason why this should be the case. A theory is considered to be scientific if it manages to provide a convincing new explanation within the already existing and accepted body of knowledge about fields and forces.

However, as is stated in Appendix I, Newton's theory stepped outside the established knowledge of the time. He put forward the concept of gravity, something that was not a known force. Some of Newton's sceptical peers therefore considered his theory to be weak, simply because it had to resort to 'occult' forces. 'Occult' means 'unseen', and in this context 'unheard of', and consequently it is not recognised as a proper, scientifically demonstrable force.

The practice of science is mostly a conservative, sceptical and reductionist activity which seeks to establish what exactly can be said regarding the knowledge we have about the world. It is separate from what we would like to say, what we want to be true, and what we strongly feel 'ought' to be true. A good scientist regards the liberal use of doubt to be the best tool for achieving good scientific method. Scientific method does not care how much we long for something to be true, or how personally convinced we are that it *is* true. For science, truth only includes what cannot be proved to be wrong.

However, scientific advances are not actually made in such a pleasingly objective and simple way. The continuing progress of science has produced a great deal of evidence that is consistent with Newtonian mechanics; or, more accurately, Newton's concept of gravity formed a basis for enormous amounts of new scientific and technological understanding and discovery. This continued until the limitations of Newton's thinking galvanised other thinkers to formulate new theories. Einstein's concepts of relativity demonstrate two things: they show the limits of Newtonian science (which does, however, remain extremely useful at several levels) and describe a new kind of conceptual thinking which replaces the previously accepted Newtonian science. It is important to bear in mind that Einstein, like any other scientist, started from the point where his predecessors left off, and without the body of existing information, it would have been impossible even for an Einstein to formulate his advanced theories. But it is also necessary to realise that Einstein, too, had to step outside the limits of current scientific orthodoxy to create his new theories.

Scientific theories are creative. They have to step beyond what is known and put forward a new way of looking at familiar events. The creator of the theory has to take a step which is not scientific, in the narrow sense described above, but daringly speculative. He or she must suggest a new scenario which may well reassess evidence and challenge scientific doctrine, but which does not flout any established scientific criteria.

Once a theory is published, it is then available to be doubted, challenged, tested and retested. Most new theories are regarded with scepticism by scientists, and it is in the nature of the discipline that this should be the case. This sometimes very hostile approach to new ideas is both science's greatest asset and its greatest weakness. Scientists who dare to speculate are sometimes scorned and derided by their conservative peers. For example, when Kepler and Newton put forward their radical suggestions, they risked the savage hostility of other scientists. They did not *know* that they were making valuable contributions to scientific understanding; they could not see into the future and be confident that history would vindicate their activities. They had to face the doubt of their contemporaries with nothing but the unscientific conviction that their creative thinking did have value and relevance to general scientific undertaking.

Michel Gauquelin was, as seen earlier, a modern scientist who worked with the relatively modern tools of statistics and followed the scientific method of his discipline. He wondered about astrology's claims that planets influence people, and proposed a hypothesis that the planetary position at birth has the ability to affect human personality. He collected evidence using the recognised methods of statistical enquiry and then made a careful assessment of the results. Gauquelin concluded that there *was* evidence, and published his results so that his work could be replicated and tested by others. Unfortunately, Gauquelin also suffered the derision and scorn of scientists who could not, and would not, take his research seriously: research which seriously proposed the possibility that astrology could indeed contain certain elements of truth. The reaction of scientific orthodoxy to emotive words like 'astrology' is sometimes astonishingly irrational and unscientific.

The following theory attempts to give a causal mechanism for

175

this observed correlation. The observed agreement is strictly limited and neither Gauquelin nor I make any broad claim for the scientific validity of astrology.

My theory makes extensive use of the concept of resonance – resonance between the tidal pull (caused by gravity) of the planets on the very hot gases trapped in the magnetic fields of the sun and earth, and resonance between the resulting fluctuations of earth's magnetic field and the electrical activity of the neural network of the foetus.

The aim is to point out that a certain type of correlation does exist. It also asks why the correlation exists and suggests a mechanism – which is testable – which can explain the correlation in terms of known forces.

Magnetic–tidal resonance between the sun, earth and planets
We should start with what we can say we know:

1. It has been observed that violent magnetic storms on the sun coincide with certain planetary configurations. These violent events take place when planets are in conjunction with, in opposition to, or square to the sun (as seen from the sun). It therefore appears that the planets have a gravitional effect upon the sun's magnetic field. This seems inexplicable because:
   (a) gravity does not affect a body's magnetic field, so no planet's gravitational field could affect the sun's magnetic field;
   (b) the gravitational pull from a planet would be so weak compared with the sun's own gravitational field, that it could not possibly affect the sun in any way.
2. However, we also know that:
   (a) the sun's magnetic field has particles associated with it which can be subject to gravitational pull;
   (b) via the phenomenon of resonance, canals in the magnetic field of the sun can channel the field and particles within them, and can therefore greatly amplify the relatively weak force of gravitational pull, to the extent that the gravitational pull of a planet can have a measurable effect.

Hence there is a mechanism by which a planet's gravitational field may have an effect on the sun's magnetic field.

3. Both the sun and the moon exert a gravitational pull on the earth. This gravitational pull can influence the geomagnetic field via the charged particles which are known to exist in this field high above the atmosphere. In particular, the fluctuations in the moon's gravitational field, at a specific location on earth, follow a pattern of peaks and troughs which has an observable counterpart in the geomagnetic field (known as 'the lunar daily magnetic variation').

4. Violent sunspot activity is known to correlate with increased activity in the magnetic field of earth. This is as a result of changes in the solar wind, which constantly pours out from the sun, but which increases in intensity during high sunspot activity.

5. Organic life on earth has been shown to respond to the variations in earth's magnetic field. This applies not only to simple life forms, but has also been measured in human beings.

As a result, a mechanism already exists whereby a planet could in principle evoke a response in a human being in some way. Organisms (including humans) can therefore be affected by the geomagnetic field; in turn, the geomagnetic field is affected by sunspot activity, and sunspot activity is triggered by the gravitational pull of planets when they are in certain alignments to the sun.

6. Magneto-tidal resonance also occurs directly between certain planets and the geomagnetic field. Certain frequencies in the field match those of planetary tides and become locked in the same phase as these tides. The direct effect of planetary conjunctions on the sun's magnetic field enhance the solar wind, and, consequently, the effects upon the geomagnetic field are amplified.

There are three further points that we can say we know, perhaps with less certainty:

7. The influence of magnetism upon a simple organism is explained in terms of the beads of magnetite within the organism. Higher organisms possess nervous systems which are like electrical networks, and electrical networks

respond to magnetic fluctuation. The structure of the nervous system is organised by the genetic code. Some organisms have been shown to have 'locked into' their genetic make-up a response to specific fluctuations of the geomagnetic field.

8. Human biological dispositions and abilities may be described, up to a point, in terms of how their nervous systems are structured by the genetic code. This is not to claim that all human personality is genetically based, but some qualities, e.g. physical abilities or inherited psychological traits, may be demonstrated to be genetically based. This area of biological research is known as 'behavioural genetics', and is an expanding area with more to be discovered.

9. Shortly before birth, the foetus in the womb possesses the normal five senses (sight, hearing, taste, touch and smell), and can respond to events outside the womb, as well as events which affect the mother, such as noises or shock. Its genetically organised nervous system is fully functional, so a foetus may also respond to its magnetic environment.

It is therefore clear that there is a growing body of knowledge about the links between genetic structures of organisms and the ways in which organisms respond to magnetism. We now come to Gauquelin's statistical findings.

10. Statistical evidence shows that a particular planet is likely to be in the ascendant or at its highest point in the sky when a certain type of individual is born. This suggests that any mechanism, by which a planet might evoke a response in a human being, would apply to the moment of birth.

11. The incidence of planetary positions at birth being the same in parent and child is enhanced on magnetically disturbed days. This is explained in point 6 above.

So far, the observed effects have been organised into a sequence. From all of the above, it can be stated that there is a certain chain of events which may be said to associate planetary positions with the moment of birth of a human being. The associative links are statistically significant, although at the moment there is no explanation for the type of physical mechanism involved except that it involves magnetic fields. The following is a suggested extension of the mechanism whereby a planet may influence human activity within a prescribed limit:

12. As we know, the nervous system of a human being may be described as a 'wiring system' which determines basic character traits and the biological clocks of the individual. These have been linked to the geomagnetic field, and I am suggesting that the neural activity of an individual responds to fluctuations of the geomagnetic field in a very specific way:

    (a) neural activity responds only to certain magnetic fluctuations, not all fluctuations, and this can be explained as a phenomenon of resonance. The neural activity of a human being is wired up so that it responds to certain kinds of magnetic fluctuation which are too minute in themselves to have a measurable influence, but are resonantly magnified to a clearly measurable degree;

    (b) an individual possesses a particular kind of biological clock which schedules the timing of birth at a resonantly appropriate moment, a moment which is 'locked in phase' with the tidal magnetic influence of a particular planet. As a result, there is a correlation between the moment of birth and significant planetary positions.

I have put together information collected by other people, set it out in a systematic way, and developed it by adding speculation of my own. This speculation is that the phenomenon of resonance can be brought in to explain results for which at present no other scientific explanation exists. A scientific hypothesis has therefore been constructed, which is now available to be tested to prove whether or not the suggestion works. My theory is speculative, although it rests firmly on known physical forces and observed statistical correlations, and suggests a way in which a planetary influence on certain human behaviour might occur. The point of a scientific theory is to frame questions in terms of already known facts, so that work may be carried out to test that theory, and that is how science progresses.

So how exactly can the moment of birth of a human being be linked with a planet's position in the sky? I believe that the genetic code of a foetus carries a particular set of inherited characteristics, and that these particular abilities enable the foetus to respond to its magnetic environment in a subtle way. They constitute a kind of biological clock which is 'in phase' with a certain set of magnetic circumstances. In a natural birth (not in a birth which has been induced), there is an interaction between the foetus' biological clock and the fluctuating geomagnetic field via the neural activity within the foetus. This interaction can give a 'suitable time' for the moment of birth. The suitability of the timing is the result of inherited characteristics, and can therefore be influenced by similar timing mechanisms present in the parents of the foetus.

The magnetic circumstances, which foster the suitable birth moment, are a result of fluctuations in the geomagnetic field. These fluctuations are consequences of direct and indirect influences upon the field, the indirect influences of which include the planetary influence as described above and in the previous chapter. Contrary to some scientific opinion, the effect of such influence is not minimal but is amplified by the phenomenon of resonance. This is not an argument to say that the cosmos 'makes us what we are' in any deterministic sense; what it says (in a strictly limited context) is that the neural activity of certain individual personality types is associated with certain particular planetary positions.

The argument that an unborn baby can be affected by planetary influence makes use of known scientific forces, and rests upon evidence gathered from a wide variety of sources. It is highly controversial and it is speculative, but it is entirely scientific in its formulation and in its ability to be tested.

The aim of a scientific theory is to attempt to provide an explanation for difficulties or anomalies within existing doctrine. My theory meets this criterion because it provides an explanation for difficulties in several areas.

Firstly, it provides a causal mechanism for observed statistical findings, namely that there is a correlation between certain planetary positions and the births of scientists, writers or great leaders. It also explains why the planetary heredity effect noticed by Gauquelin is enhanced on the days when earth's magnetic field is disturbed. Additionally, it answers a question posed by John Addey in his book *Harmonics in Astrology*:

Of all the astrological problems which beckon to us from the future there is one which must excite the thoughtful astrologer more than any other . . . This is the queston of how astrology and genetics are to be related and, specifically perhaps, how the genetic code is expressed astrologically.

Addey further clarifies what he means by this:

We know that there are laws of heredity by which natural characteristics are transmitted from generation to generation; we also know that the natural characteristics of each person are described by the horoscope calculated for his date, time and place of birth. It therefore follows . . . that the astrological code, by which the horoscope is interpreted, must be in agreement with the genetic code by which natural traits are transmitted from one generation to the next.

As more is understood about exactly what is or is not contained in the genetic code, it becomes much simpler to measure how the genetic code relates to, or interacts with, its surrounding environment.

The Mars effect

The suggested correlation of the position of Mars with the births of great sportspeople is called the 'Mars effect' and has been a focus of criticism for many of those opposed to Gauquelin's work. J. Dommanget is a member of the Committee Para (the Belgian Committee for the Scientific Investigations of Alleged Paranormal Phenomena) which looked at Gauquelin's work 21 years ago. Recently he has tried to justify the work of this Committee in more modern terms. In the *Journal of Scientific Exploration* he says:

It is the position of the Committee PARA that, while some of Gauquelin's astronomical and statistical computations appeared perfectly correct, the theoretical principles proposed by Gauquelin to support his research have to be rejected because they do not take correctly into account the fundamentals of the problem – the secular and diurnal socio-demographic factors.

Jan Willem Nienhuys, a mathematician from the Netherlands, has also recently launched a renewed attack on Gauquelin's work. Writing in the *Skeptical Inquirer* he says: 'The so-called Mars effect has haunted science for forty years now, but there's light at the end of the tunnel. It most likely has been an illusion after all.'

Nienhuys is basically claiming that Gauquelin was biased in his selection of what constituted an outstanding sportsperson, and that he did so, perhaps subconciously, to strengthen his case.

I was well aware of these controversies when I began to formulate my theory about how certain planets and the moon might be linked to individual personalities. This is why, in my book *Astrology: The Evidence of Science*, I wrote the following:

> These particular results of Gauquelin's [his work on the planetary heredity effect] are the most important of all his findings, as far as my theory is concerned ... They are based on objectively measurable quantities, like planetary positions and birth times, but they also indicate quite clearly that a physical agency is involved, and that this agency is the magnetic field of Earth ... The theory itself ... shows that Gauquelin's finding supports more of the basic ideas and concepts of astrology than he himself thought it did, and ... other parts of astrology not immediately evident from Gauquelin's results.

Professor Suitbert Ertel (Professor of Psychology at the University of Göttingen) is a firm supporter of Gauquelin's work. Both Ertel and Gauquelin's further work on the planetary hereditary effect are discussed in my book *The Scientific Basis of Astrology*.

By focusing on the Mars effect, both the Committee Para and Nienhuys have missed the larger context of Gauquelin's findings. Gauquelin's work showed the same pattern of planetary heredity for the planets Venus, Mars, Jupiter, Saturn and the moon, but not for the other planets. His methodology therefore revealed not only positive results for some planets but also negative ones for others. Even if the criticisms of Dommanget and Nienhuys were soundly based, there is still something very puzzling about the work of Gauquelin on planetary eminence. The same pattern emerges for Mars, Jupiter, Saturn and the moon. That is to say, two large peaks emerge (one at rising and another at the planet's highest point in the sky) as well as two smaller ones (one at setting and one when the planet is directly overhead on the other side of earth). Still more intriguing is the fact that the lunar pattern is the pattern one would expect if the lunar type personality was responding to the lunar daily magnetic variation.

Although my work started with the Gauquelin findings, it incorporates a much larger database from a variety of other disciplines. On page 5 of my monograph *A Causal Mechanism for*

Gauquelin's Planetary Effect, the type of data needed to test my mathematical theory of this effect is discussed. I also made the following statement in an interview with Dava Sobel, author of *Longitude*: 'What I need to do now is to take Gauquelin's data and marry them up with a spectral analysis [a mathematical search for specific periodicities] of the records from magnetic observatories.'

Jupiter and politicians

Anecdotal evidence does not constitute scientific evidence; nevertheless, it can sometimes yield interesting results. In April 1997, just before the last general election in the UK, I took part in a local television programme about astrology and politics. On this programme I pointed out that for political leaders, Jupiter was the important planet. I then cast the natal chart for the leaders of the three main parties: Paddy Ashdown was born on 27 February 1941 at 04.30 (local time) in New Delhi; Tony Blair was born in Edinburgh on 5 May 1953 at 06.10 (BST); and John Major was born in London on 29 March 1943 between 02.00 and 04.30 (BST). Where was planet Jupiter when these men were born? Blair was born with Jupiter just about to rise, Major was born with Jupiter just about to set and Ashdown was born with Jupiter overhead on the other side of earth! Leadership of any effective political party indicates a tendency towards political eminence. Tony Blair fits into the strongest of the Gauquelin sectors; both the other leaders fit into two of the other three sectors.

More about the planets of success

Having demonstrated that individuals who had achieved outstanding success in certain professions were born under specific planets Gauquelin decided to investigate character traits considered typical of these professions. His aim was to identify the traits associated with particular planets, and he did this by studying biographical dictionaries of the various areas of excellence and other published biographies. In his book *Cosmic Influences on Human Behaviour*, he looks at birth data for individuals whose outstanding qualities could clearly be identified with specific planets. Obviously, since he did this work in France the examples quoted are French. However, a few English examples which relate to the findings of his studies will be added further on.

In the field of sports, Gauquelin quotes two examples: the first is Yvon Goujon, a French internatinal football player who was born just as Mars was rising and who characterised himself in the following way: 'I would have made a poor sailor. I would have been bored on a boat, I loathe being still and waiting. I am not a dreamer, I love life and action.'

For the second example of someone born 'under' Mars – this time with Mars at its highest point in the sky – he chose the cyclist Eddy Merckx, who won the Tour de France on more than one occasion. Apparently Merckx's fame was so great that American reporters were stationed along the entire route of the race solely to cover his performance.

Examples of people who excelled in different ways included Louis Brocq, an outstanding French biologist who was born with Saturn at its highest point in the sky. The outstanding neurologist Jean Martin Charcot, one of the teachers of Sigmund Freud, was born with Saturn just rising above the horizon at the moment of birth.

Two outstanding French 'men of letters', both with the moon at the highest point of the sky, were the poets Guillaume Apollinaire and André Berry.

Some interesting English examples exist where Gauquelin's findings seem to be borne out. Recently I came across a book entitled *British Entertainers – the astrological profiles* by Frank C. Clifford, which illustrates very well some of the points made by Gauquelin.

According to Gauquelin, great actors are also often associated with Jupiter when it is either rising, or is at the highest point in the sky at the moment of birth. Nigel Hawthorn, the distinguished actor of TV and film, was born with Jupiter about to rise, and he therefore fits this pattern. Another very well known British actor is Richard Briers, who was also born with Jupiter just about to rise. The American actress Diahann Carroll was born with Jupiter just past the highest point of the sky.

It was shown earlier how Gauquelin linked writers and poets to the moon. However, he had also noted that the moon seemed to be connected with the births of several comedians, and once again Clifford provides examples which illustrate this. Maureen Lipman, Julie Walters and Peter Sellers were all born with the moon very close to its highest point in the sky at their respective moments of birth.

Lord Nelson, the great English seaman, was born with Mars just about to rise. This may seem odd, because the examples above suggest that sportsmen, rather than sailors, are associated with Mars, and one of Gauquelin's examples specifically feels he would have made 'a poor sailor'. However, Horatio Nelson was an active seaman with a flair for naval strategy which served him well in important battles afloat. He could be said to exemplify the principles of action and martial feeling which are associated with this planet.

An interesting example of an outstanding scientist whose birth was *not* associated with Saturn was the theoretical physicist Albert Einstein. However, he *was* born with Jupiter at its highest point, which is associated with outstanding leaders. Albert Einstein was in fact an unusual kind of scientist in that his main contributions to physics stemmed more from the philosophy of his approach to problem solving rather than from technical or mathematical skill. Einstein certainly does not fit the usual categorisation of the 'king' or 'great leader' associated with Jupiter's position at birth and, therefore, does not really support Gauquelin's findings about the position of Jupiter. It *is* true, however, to say that Einstein excelled in his chosen field of enquiry, that he broke new ground and that he gave a (philosophical) guidance and leadership to development of twentieth-century physics.

The theory and the Magi

Readers may wonder what possible relevance such a complicated scientific theory really has to questions about the Star of Bethlehem, the Magi and the birth of Christ. In the first part of this book I have claimed that it is necessary to see the Star in terms of the world-view which existed at the time of Christ's birth. This approach shows what the Magi themselves would have considered significant in view of their search for a messiah, and it was therefore possible to restrict the investigation to those astronomical events which were most likely to be candidates for the Star. As a result, the most likely candidate is the Jupiter–Saturn conjunction of 15 September 7 BC. All this also contributed to explain several other symbols and beliefs associated with the birth of Christ and the beginnings of the Christian Church. My theory provides another means of seeing why the Jupiter–Saturn conjunction was so important for the Magi, and rules out the other suggestions.

As a consequence of working on a scientific theory for certain limited aspects of astrology, one comes to the conclusion that ancient astrologers made some basic discoveries which linked both their earthly environment and human activities to the universe. These original observations were then gradually handed down, systematised and extended far beyond the limits in which the original correlation discoveries were valid. This would fit in with other claims that have been made in this book about human beings' natural tendency to construct explanations for the world about us. One way is to mythologise, i.e. to explain the forces of nature in terms of the gods, while astrology perhaps offered a different explanation in terms of the stars and planets in the night sky. This can therefore be seen as a first tentative step towards a scientific way of looking at the cosmos.

To observe correlations and deduce a hypothesis from these observations is a scientific activity. Naturally, in pre-scientific ages, it was inevitable that astrology would be greatly influenced by mythologising and religious tendencies. However, as Otto Neugebauer pointed out in his article in *Astronomy and History: Selected Essays* (1983), astrology did form the first model of the cosmos which may be referred to as scientific:

> We must emphasize that the modern contempt for the *Tetrabiblos*, the 'Bible of the astrologer', is historically very much unjustified ... The overwhelming historic influence of the *Tetrabiblos* can only be fully understood when we realize that this work is methodically the highest development of the first naturally simple world picture of mankind, in which earth and universe still have a comparative order of magnitude.

Much of modern astrology is a highly developed belief system which does not claim to be scientific, and which for the most part cannot be explained in terms of science. This may not matter at all for the usefulness of astrology to its practitioners, but it is worth applying a scientific criterion (i.e. my theory) to the various astrological suggestions for the true identify of the Star of Bethlehem.

There is no evidence that comets influence the terrestrial environment in either material or physical terms. They are 'potato-shaped' lumps of ice, a few kilometres in size; their masses are extremely low and they cannot affect the earth by means of their gravitational pull. The orbit of the comets is affected by the gravitational fields of those planets which they pass close to as they enter into the inner parts of the solar system. Their low masses cannot, even via resonant effects, rival the effects of the planets on the magnetic activity of the sun as mentioned above.

Although it is not unknown for a comet to pass between the sun and the earth, and, for a short period, to be in conjunction with the sun, there are no measurable effects of this on earth's magnetic field. The solar radiation reflected from the comet, and the particles given off from its nucleus, have no measurable effects on earth. It is therefore very unlikely that the ancients would have been aware of any effects either, and their association with doom, death and disaster was purely symbolic.

Novae and supernovae are stars which increase in brightness over a few days and then diminish in brightness over several weeks or months. The scale of distances to these enormous energy events is phenomenal: hundreds of millions of millions of miles. Although such events can sometimes be seen with the naked eye, in terms of the amount of extra radiation reaching the earth, the effects are minuscule. They do not have any gravitational effects, nor do they have any effect on the magnetic field of earth. In 1987 particles, or neutrinos, did actually reach earth from a supernova explosion. These neutrinos were detected by a special telescope at the bottom of a mine. However, neutrinos are minute particles with very little mass and no electric charge, so they do not interact with matter very easily. Ancient sky watchers could not have experienced a physical effect from any such stream of particles from a supernova explosion.

It might be suggested that an occultation of the moon by Jupiter might affect the lunar daily magnetic variation mentioned before. However, despite the fact that an occultation is an alignment of the earth, Moon and Jupiter, it is an alignment as seen from earth; it is not necessarily an alignment as seen from the sun. In any case, the moon does not play a part in triggering violent magnetic activity on the sun, and it is highly unlikely, although not impossible, that the earth and Jupiter will be in alignment as seen from the sun at an occultation of Jupiter by the moon.

The Jupiter–Venus conjunction of 2 BC was a conjunction of these planets as seen from earth and not from the sun. As a result, there was no particularly spectacular alignment to trigger any violent magnetic storms on the sun. Also, on 17 July 2 BC, the date in question, Jupiter and Venus were seen in the east at sunset.

Jupiter was therefore not in one of the key sectors of the sky which Gauquelin found to be associated with the birth of great leaders. Consequently, the conjunction does not fit the suggested scenario for being a physical event which would have been noted as significant by the ancient astrologers.

On 15 September 7 BC, Jupiter was in opposition to the sun, and Saturn was conjunct with Jupiter. Conditions were therefore right for enhanced solar activity, which, as seen earlier, gives rise to increased geomagnetic activity. Furthermore, at sunset on this day the Jupiter–Saturn conjunction was rising just as the sun was setting. Jupiter was therefore in one of the key sectors for the birth of a great leader. These conditions and circumstances meet the scientific criteria for having a physical effect and are significant in two ways:

1. They fit Gauquelin's statistical claim that there is a correlation between the position of Jupiter in certain key sectors of the sky with the birth of a great leader.
2. They meet the criteria formulated in my theory for a physical explanation of the birth of a certain type of personality under specific, complex magnetic conditions.

Additional symbolic significance for this particular date in the minds of the Magi are:
(a) the fact that Jupiter and Saturn were both in the constellation of Pisces, and that this was the first time that a triple conjunction of these planets had shared this sign with the vernal equinox;
(b) that on this day the sun was in Virgo, the Virgin.

All the theories proposed up to now are naive single-link theories. I have constructed a theory involving a few links in the causal chain to account for some of the evidence indicating close associations between cosmic cycles, terrestrial periods and biological rhythms. This theory ties together most of the separate pieces of evidence discussed in chapter 8. It also shows that it is possible to account for some apparent anomalies in the present data, and instances where particular experiments have not been sucessfully replicated.

EIGHT

THE LEGACY OF THE MAGI: A CONCLUSION

*One aim of the physical sciences has been to give an
exact picture of the material world. One achievement
of physics of the twentieth century has been to prove
that the aim is unattainable.*
(Jacob Bronowski)

Approximately 2000 years ago, the Magi travelled to Bethlehem;
Christ was born, and his birth coincided with the dawning of the
Age of Pisces.

On 15 September 7 BC the skies offered confirmation of an
incredibly significant scenario to learned astrologers like the
Magi. Jupiter and Saturn, linked together in the sign of Pisces –
the fishes – rose above the horizon at sunset. In opposition to this,
the sun was setting in the sign of Virgo – the Virgin. This
Pisces–Virgo, ascendant-descendant polarity made a powerful
astrological statement about that particular date. All the planets
except for the moon (which astronomically counts as a planet)
were in the sky.

For astrologers of the time, a triple conjunction of Jupiter and
Saturn in Pisces would have held enormous significance. Jupiter
foretold the coming of a king or great leader, Saturn was seen as
the 'Protector of the Jews', while the constellation of Pisces was
associated with the area of Judea. This particular combination of
astrological factors made it an extremely rare event, which had
never taken place before in recorded history. It was the first time
that this triple conjunction had occurred in Pisces when the sun
was also in Pisces at the point of the vernal equinox.

Evidence suggests that ancient cultures did know about the
phenomenon of the precession of the equinoxes, whereby the sun
slowly crosses the constellations of the zodiac, remaining in each
constellation for an average span of about 2000 years. As
supremely learned astrologers, the Magi would have been in
possession of this knowledge, and would also have known about

the Pythagorean and Platonic notions of a Great Year. They knew that the 2000-year age of Aries was coming to an end, and that a new age of Pisces was about to dawn, and this enhanced the astrological significance of a predicted saviour. But even more than this, the sun's move out of Aries was the culmination of a span of twelve of these ages. The sun's entry into Pisces marked the beginning of a new Great Year – a whole new cycle of the sun's path through the zodiac. A new age of ages was about to begin, and all the signs pointed to the birth of an infant who would be the messiah and representative of this unique event.

The symbolism of the ancient world, which is linked to the astrology of the Magi, was looked at earlier in this book, as well as the church's discomfort with this pagan symbolism and its attempt to promote the interpretation of these symbols in terms of orthodox doctrine. The symbol traditionally associated with Christianity is the Fish. The letters of the Greek word for fish – I, Ch, Th, U, S – were said to stand for Jesus' name. The orthodox reason given for the rise of this symbol was that the early Christians used the sign of a fish to secretly identify each other and express Jesus' name when they were being persecuted by the Romans. However, the learning of the time could easily explain the use of the symbol of Pisces as a description of this great messiah, not only the saviour of the Jews, but a greater figure, saviour for all mankind, and representative of the new Piscean age and the new cosmic order.

The symbol of Virgo is the Virgin. Christ's mother was the Virgin Mary. At sunset on 15 September 7 BC the sun was in the sign of Virgo. Astrologically speaking, someone born at this moment could be said to have 'the sun in Virgo', or just as legitimately said to be 'a son of Virgo'. This kind of description is perfectly valid in a culture which accepts and uses symbolic language, and is a likely source of the description of Christ's mother as a virgin. This of course was not a possibility in the view of the orthodox doctrine of the Church, which stated that the birth of Jesus was miraculous, and that Mary his mother had received immaculate conception from God.

Strangely – or perhaps not – the development of Christianity and the development of scientific thought have shared the same period of time. As we have seen, this 2000-year period is called the Age of Pisces. Broadly speaking, this 2000-year period encompasses roughly the same amount of time as the period of

190

the sun's observed position (on the first day of spring) as it journeyed across the constellation of Pisces. As we have also seen, this Age of Pisces may be described as one of the Great Months of the Platonic Great Year – the time it takes for the sun's observed position on the first day of spring to travel once around the zodiac, through all the constellations (roughly 26,000 years). The period preceding the Age of Pisces was the Age of Aries, when the Egyptian civilisation grew and thrived; and before that the Age of Taurus, 4000 years before the birth of Christ, when the cultural ideas of the Sumerian civilisation influenced human thought and development in the Mediterranean, Near and Middle Eastern parts of the world.

Is it a coincidence of passing interest that Christianity and the development of scientific thought should have closely shared the same historical period? Is there any real meaning, apart from the pleasure of noticing coincidences or patterns, in correlating the sun's passage through the Great Year with human progress?

From a scientific point of view these Great Months, or the Great Year as a whole, do not possess any meaning or significance because there are no physical consequences which relate to these phases. The only factually measurable way in which the precession of the sun's position at the vernal equinox affects us, is that it affects our calendars: every so often over these long periods we are obliged to adjust our calendar systems. These extremely slow movements of the sun's position during the various 'Great Months' have not therefore had any particular physical effect on our world. They have not had any measurable effect in the kind of way that, for example, planetary alignments are being discovered to have.

But as we have seen, it appears that humans have noticed the precession of the sun's position on the first day of spring. Over the various ages, as they have adjusted their calendars, they have also adjusted their ideas about their gods. The effect of precession can therefore be said to have had a cultural or symbolic influence upon human intellectual thought. In this context it is interesting to see that human intellectual development, which of course is tied to cultural and religious ideas, can very broadly be linked to these Great Months, or Ages.

Important human developments do not fit neatly into exact spans of years. There are always events which precede and events which result from any measured phase. However, speaking generally we can define certain 'Ages' of human development. In *Relating*, Liz Greene speaks from the point of view of an astrologer.

> The correlation between the precession of the equinoxes and the changing eras of man's development appears to be symbolically valid, even if we do not yet know the laws governing the enigma. This correlation is inescapable if one studies history, and particularly the development of religion and myth throughout history ... At the close of an era, many old gods die or are subordinated, and new gods – gods who are symbolic of energies which have not emerged into human consciousness before – are born.

The past 2000 years – the Age of Pisces – has seen the rise and development of rational science and cosmology, and also the rise of Christianity. Each of these has had a profound impact upon western civilisation. Modern science coupled with human inventiveness has provided the technological framework of our society, but the ethical structure by which we live is basically of Christian origin. This is not a coincidence. The rise of rational science two thousand years ago set the scene for sweeping away the older style religions and their associated superstitions, and therefore cleared the way for a new style of religious belief.

Despite the mystical elements in the teachings of Pythagoras, he made one overriding contribution to our general approach to interpreting the physical world about us. Pythagoras and the later Greeks not only introduced new notions, they believed that logic and rational thought were necessary to recognise and express reality. They introduced the requirement of formal proofs in mathematics which expanded into science, and specifically into astronomy, cosmology and astrology. In basing their cosmology on astronomical observations, the Greeks departed from older methods based on mythology and polytheistic religious beliefs.

The seeds were therefore sown for a radical shift in human thinking. Cosmology and science would cease to be within the domain of religious authority, and gradually there would come to be a split between religious and scientific reality. Of course this did not happen immediately, but the Greeks did profoundly undermine the more ancient structures of thought. One thing they did was to 'democratise' astrology. Having been a subject applied only to countries, great events, and kingly leaders, with the Greeks it became something which could apply to any individual.

The positions of planets at the birth of an individual therefore set a unique stamp, or set of character traits, on that individual. The Greeks believed that in principle it lay within each man's own power to think and judge for himself: this was new. The split between religious authority and the authority of the individual meant that morality was no longer handed down or demanded from above by God or the gods. There was therefore a need for a human-based morality that could be much more personal and apply to any individual.

Christ might well be said to have spearheaded a new direction in religion. The Magi were not Greeks, but they would certainly have been influenced by the exciting and extraordinary new thinking of the time in which they lived. Christ perhaps did not set out to found a new kind of religion, yet his life on Earth did give birth to a new faith. The last 2000 years has therefore been a history of Christianity's struggle to come to terms with the notions of individual and personal authority, and with the development of science and technology.

We are now coming to the end of the twentieth century, and are also approaching the close of the Age of Pisces. Without question today, human intellectual development requires new ways of thinking and understanding. What can we say of the development of science throughout this period?

The Hellenistic world into which Christ was born was the seedbed from which our modern and scientific world-view developed, although much Greek knowledge and ways of thinking had been inherited from the Babylonians:

> Thus the astronomical tradition in the West is linked to Babylonian mathematical astronomy. Mathematical astronomy was, however, not only the principal carrier and generator of certain mathematical techniques, but it became the model for the new exact sciences which learned from it their principal goal: to give a mathematical description of a particular class of natural phenomena capable of yielding numerical predictions that can be tested against observations. It is in this sense that I claim that Babylonian mathematical astronomy was the origin of all subsequent serious endeavours in the exact sciences.
>
> (A. Aaboe, 'Scientific Astronomy in Antiquity',
> *The Place of Astronomy in the Ancient World*)

The approach to solar, lunar and planetary tables used by the astronomers of Babylon was quite modern in one specific sense: unlike the Greeks, at no time did they try to understand geometrically how the sun, moon and stars were arranged in space. However, even today, in many areas of physics, people find it impossible to describe mechanically exactly what is going on. Theoretical physicists therefore content themselves with mathematical formulae and procedures which provide them with numerical results that can then be tested against further observations and experiments. This is a very different activity from that of the Greeks.

Unfortunately, it is impossible to prove a scientific theory. All that can be done is to show that a theory is consistent with all the data available at a given time. As a result, in many ways the practice of science requires a humble attitude, and its task is a limited one. However, accepting these limitations and working within these constraints has given humanity a vast and very productive alternative way of looking at the world. This was the new approach given to us by the Greeks, and this new way of thinking affected everything: it changed the way people thought about the gods, about history and about themselves. In particular, the Greeks brought their powers of scientific reasoning to bear on the problems of astronomy and cosmology.

In *The Copernican Revolution*, Thomas Kuhn says:

> This close association of astronomy and cosmology is both temporally and geographically local. Every civilization and culture of which we have records has had an answer for the question, 'What is the structure of the universe?' But only the western civilizations which descend from Hellenic Greece have paid much attention to the appearance of the heavens in arriving at that answer. The drive to construct cosmologies is far older and more primitive than the urge to make systematic observations of the heavens.

Kuhn then draws attention to the importance of the dual role of a cosmological framework:

> The requirement that a cosmology supplies both a psychologically satisfying world-view and an explanation of observed phenomena like the daily change in the position of sunrise has vastly increased the power of cosmological thought. It has channeled the universal compulsion for at-homeness in the universe into an unprecedented drive for the discovery of scientific explanations.

The Greek cosmology, which was to hold sway for many centuries, was Aristotle's cosmology, although the actual mathematical model used for calculating future positions of the sun, moon and planets was a later modification by Ptolemy. The new astronomy and cosmology provided the basis for a much more comprehensive approach to astrology. Astrology therefore became the very first attempt at an overall 'theory of everything'.

But what is meant when a theory of everything is referred to today? It means an all-embracing explanation which, in principle, is able to incorporate all objects and all relationships between objects in the entire universe. Such a comprehensive theory should operate at all levels: from the behaviour of sub-atomic particles to the origin, past evolution, present structure and distant future of the universe. It should also explain everything in between: the evolution of intelligent life from the most primitive forms right up to explaining human behaviour in terms of bio-chemistry and biophysics of the brain. To require or anticipate the development of such a theory is reasonable and logical and is merely an extension of the 'scientific method'. For some scientists today this is the 'Holy Grail' of fundamental physics. As Professor Michio Kahu (of the City College of New York) said in a BBC TV *Horizon* programme about Einstein, 'Grand unification has become the name of the game.'

Other present-day thinkers feel that this belief – although understandable – is mistaken, and I agree. The scientific approach, which began with the Greeks, has enabled both the accumulation of an enormous amount of information as well as the construction of a great body of knowledge. If this had not happened, human beings would not be as highly developed as they are today. We can travel into space; we can cure disease, alleviate suffering and live longer; we can communicate in ways unthinkable to people like the Magi; and above all, we can look at ourselves and understand our own activities.

Humans have developed a capacity for self-reflection, a direct inheritance of the Greeks, and a modern human capacity. However, this very capacity shows us our limitations, which may be its most useful function. The scientific world at the end of the Piscean era is an extraordinary place, and some very difficult fundamental questons remain.

The Copernican revolution and its consequences
With the Renaissance in Europe came a crisis of intellectual confidence for all learned men and the Church of Rome. The

doctrine of St Thomas Aquinas, based as it was on the teachings of Aristotle, was about to be challenged by the work of Nicolas Copernicus (1473–1543). To quote Thomas Kuhn:

Initiated as a narrowly technical, highly mathematical revision of classical astronomy, the Copernican theory became one focus for the tremendous controversies in religion, in philosophy and in social theory which, during the two centuries following the discovery of America, set the tenor of the modern mind.

Copernicus' theory rocked Christian theological security for all time. The earth was *not* the centre of the universe; instead, the 'God-given' world of the human race was merely part of a large system, with the sun at its centre. It is interesting to discover that belief in a sun-centred universe already had ancient precedents: the followers of Pythagoras believed in a sun-centred universe, an idea which was taken further by Aristarchus of Samos in the third century BC. These ideas would not have been unknown to the Magi. However, this demotion of the earth's cosmological position was particularly threatening to Renaissance thinkers because it damaged beyond repair the belief in the Aristotelian scheme of perfection, circularity and timelessness, a foundation of perfection upon which the tenets of Christianity firmly rested.

The work of Copernicus was taken further by Tycho Brahe (1546–1601), Johann Kepler (1571–1630), Galileo (1564–1642) and Isaac Newton (1642–1727). Tycho Brahe was a meticulous, but conservative observer. His work challenged the authority of Aristotle, but it was left to Kepler to make the real break with ancient views on planetary motion. He calculated that planetary orbits were elliptical, not circular, a discovery which undermined even further the circularity and perfection of the heavens.

Galileo built a telescope and turned it on the night sky. This was a new way of collecting data, and was a giant technological leap forward. However, the most decisive contribution to astronomy was the theoretical work of Isaac Newton. With his universal law of gravitation and his laws of motion, he provided the important concept that the laws of physics should be universal, i.e. if true, they should apply not only to the earth's surface, but everywhere throughout the universe.

Initially formulated to explain planetary motion, Newton's laws were found to apply to all large-scale phenomena: the movements of ocean currents; the dynamics of atmospheres on earth and other planets; satellites orbiting earth, and space probes sent to study the far reaches of our solar system. It may be said that Newton reached the pinnacle of scientific method as it is normally understood. His laws work, and they are the basis upon which the modern technological world rests. In almost all normal scientific and technological practice, the laws which Newton formulated represent reality. He was successful, and most modern understanding stems from his work.

However, human understanding does not stand still, and Newton's theories cease to be successful or useful at a more fundamental level.

From Pisces to Aquarius – the end of Christianity?

Some great scientists have understood the limitations of our knowledge. Newton said:

> I do not know what I may appear to the world, but to myself I seem to have been only a boy playing on the seashore, and diverting myself in now and then finding a smoother pebble or a prettier shell than ordinary, whilst the great ocean of truth lay undiscovered before me.

According to Einstein, 'The only justification of our concepts and system of concepts is that they serve to represent the complex of our experiences; beyond this they have no legitimacy.'

There is a special kind of difficulty about the fundamental questions of science today. The systems of thought which have led civilisation through the Piscean era, which is also the Christian era, threaten to bring us up against a different kind of obstacle: the limitations of our own humanity, which affects not only *what* may be said about the world, but *whether* much can be said about it. The problem is not only that we don't have or can't obtain the type of data needed in order to find answers, as in some cases. For example, as the philosopher Naom Chomsky pointed out, in trying to understand exactly what language is, it is not possible to venture into someone's mind or brain and have a look at what is taking place there. For a number of reasons, it is impossible to directly observe ourselves in the activity of 'doing' language. Nor can distant areas of the universe be visited to see what is there. Whatever science fiction may suggest, there are problems of time and of technology which modern civilisation is nowhere near solving. It is recognised today that our original thoughts about the universe only apply to roughly 5% of it: a terrible shock to modern notions about the cosmos. However, because it is impossible to directly observe the universe, there is no way to go out there to see what it is really like, and how it differs from our original thoughts about it.

The more profound problem is that there are limitations to the ability to frame sensible questions about what is known and what is real. In attempting to explore what is taking place at the subatomic level, it becomes clear that such explorations cannot be done without affecting the data; in a sense, we get in our own way. When our knowledge about the universe is pushed to the limits, we discover that although our local situation is well-understood, at the galactic level and greater, our laws do not seem to apply, so little is actually known about the bigger picture. If answers to these kinds of problems are required, it is going to be necessary to find a different way of looking at them, or a different way of thinking, which is something we are not yet ready to attempt.

Based as it is upon scientific enquiry, it is almost as if the whole elaborate organisation of modern Western thought is a mirage. Our cosmos seems real and physical enough, and up to a point our 'laws' of reality prove themselves without doubt. But clearly there is more to it than that. An 'otherness' is glimpsed, which is not part of anything that is known or understood, and, as a result, scientific certitude is thrown into confusion. It might be no more than a mental construct, highly complex and very beautiful. The development of scientific thinking has perhaps been a human process, developed out of human minds and enabling us to achieve the fullest mental capacities available to a human being. This process has been accelerated, starting with Hellenistic Greece in the period which roughly corresponds to the Piscean era, and which further corresponds to the history of Christianity, starting with the Magi's journey to Bethlehem as they followed the guidance of the Star.

Einstein and Newton were great scientists who could not reject the importance of the history of science to human thought. But both men were also the kind of scientist who knew that the scope of science was limited, and that a fuller human understanding could not be constrained simply by scientific attitude. The behavioural scientist William N. Schoenfeld pointed out that it is in acknowledging the limitations of knowledge that people turn to religion: 'That realization is also the major bridge that a man uses when he crosses from naturalism to religion. Thus, for Aquinas, the imperfection of knowledge is at the heart of faith, and is assumed in the definition of faith.'

Perhaps the Magi shared the humility which is frequently a mark of human beings who recognise greatness when they meet it, whether in people or in ideas. The impression that we get is that little is known about them. They were among the wisest and most learned men of their time, yet they possessed the humility to pay homage to the infant Jesus. This was the Messiah, who had come both to save the people, and to develop the quest for knowledge and wisdom. The Magi did not show any element of Herod's envy, they came to welcome the one whom they believed to be the master of the wisdom they sought. Morton Smith says:

> People said that Tiridates and his magi initiated Nero in their mysteries and secret meals; the gospel story implies that Jesus needed no such initiation: he was the predestined ruler of the magi, as well as of the Jews; but unlike the ignorant Jews, the magi knew this. They understood the star that signaled his coming and came themselves to meet him, make their submission, and offer the gifts due to their ruler. Moral: all magicians to the same; Jesus is the supreme magus and master of the art.

The history of Christianity has occupied roughly the same period of time as the history of science. One special claim of Christianity is that it is a very personal, human religion, a religion for individuals. Whatever the doctrinal arguments of different sects within Christianity may be, all Christians who follow Christ are assured of their personal significance and value as human beings. This particular quality of Christianity gives a special kind of emphasis to the individual. Perhaps this emphasis allows for an attitude which the Greeks gave us: that in our own sphere of human activity (i.e. in science), we are the measure of all things. Whether or not this can be said to be so, Christianity was born with the Piscean Age, and, as a result, the person of Jesus is sometimes identified with the Piscean type of perfection: loving, gentle and sacrificial, with a human understanding that there is a spiritual world beyond the material level of reality, and representing as a god an example of spirituality and wholeness. Piscean symbols have a history of being used in connection with Christianity. It is true that this does not necessarily fit in with orthodox Christian doctrine. However, it is interesting to see that the notion of a personal, accessible godliness accompanies the development of scientific exploration of the world and of the cosmos.

Today, Christianity is at a crossroads where the Church can no longer confidently rely on its role at the heart of society. While for some there is a vibrant truth to be found within Christianity, for many others its teachings seem either rigidly limited or alienating. Our society is a secular society, where religion is often seen as irrelevant. The clergy seem woefully inadequate to answer spiritual or moral questions; the Church has lost its authority, and a study of its history further undermines any remaining trust in it as a viable spiritual institution. Have we come to the end of Christianity as we come to the end of the Piscean era?

The Western world is sometimes described as being in a post-modernist phase. This describes an attitude, and rather a world-weary one, where we aim to stop kidding ourselves about our values, our relationships and our illusions. As Liz Greene has put it:

> We are no longer psychological children. All the pomp and pageantry and mummery and glamour and violence of past ages has been our childhood, and we have passed through a childhood no better and no worse than the childhood of any individual . . . Adult Man is beginning . . . to exercise his gift of reflection at last.

It is not a comfortable place in which to be, but it may be useful to look forward from this standpoint. For Christianity, although there have been periods of crisis, there is no historical precedent for where humanity finds itself today. Nor have we previously encountered the same kinds of problem in terms of scientific knowledge. So, as we enter the Age of Aquarius, where do we go on to from here? In *The Sea of Faith*, Don Cupitt, theologian and philosopher, said:

> Human beings can never wholly lose touch with the forces of re-creation. When an order of meanings and values, a 'reality' that people have lived by, begins to fall into disrepair there are always a few prophetic spirits who sense what is happening and know as if instictively what they themselves are called upon to undergo. Through the inner turmoil that they enter, a new order begins to take shape.

Both Christianity and science seem to be demonstrating their limitations. If this is the case, a new way of looking at our world is genuinely needed. Perhaps ideas which are normally only found outside conventional religion or conventional science should be tolerated and actively encouraged? Astrology is offering ideas which need to be explored much further, and a readiness to look further afield is already taking place. The Scientific and Medical Network is a British, loosely organised group which makes it possible for people with a scientific background to explore ideas outside the boundaries of orthodox science, and other, similar groups exist all over the world. The need to find new understandings and relevant meanings is asserting itself, not only in religious thinking, but also in philosophy and art. And in science.

The Millennium

All over the world people are preparing for the millennium, and there is both excitement and apprehension about its arrival. For example, in the UK all sorts of parties and celebrations are being planned, and the Millennium Dome at Greenwich is due to be the focus of national attention. Although the calendar date of 1 January 2000 AD is not a particularly significant day in scientific terms, there is an emotional feeling that this day will be tremendously important. On the other hand, there is much concern about the 'millennium bug' which, it is said, is likely to cause extremely serious problems for computer systems and must be resolved urgently. Furthermore, insurance companies are assessing the predictions of certain astrologers that major disasters will occur in the year 2000.

While we congratulate ourselves on living in a highly rational and scientifically based culture, we are still capable of letting ourselves down in this respect. We have not really prepared in a rational and forward-looking manner for the year 2000, and we are capable of feeling as much apprehension as joy at its approach. The point is that in all this we share with our ancient predecessors the same range of emotional responses, hopes and fears about change. And like them, we choose to ascribe a significance and a value to the moment we move into a new era. It is therefore possible to appreciate the awe and fear that ancient civilisations experienced when they recognised the limitations of their old mythologies, and sought for new ways to explain the mysteries of their cosmos.

201

Richard Feynman, a great physicist who was also a great optimist, said:

> We are at the very beginning of time for the human race. It is not unreasonable that we grapple with problems. But there are tens of thousands of years in the future. Our responsibility is to do what we can, learn what we can, improve the solutions, and pass them on. It is our responsibility to leave the people of the future a free hand.

APPENDIX I
COSMIC INFLUENCES

The Shorter Oxford English Dictionary gives several definitions of the word 'influence', including: [Astrological] The supposed flowing from the stars of an ethereal fluid acting upon the character and destiny of men, and affecting sublunary things generally. In later times taken as an exercise of occult power.

In the medieval world people believed that diseases were the result of some form of astrological 'influence' and these ideas were later developed into a branch of the subject called 'astrological medicine'. In this discipline various signs of the zodiac were considered to have an influence upon different parts of the human body. For example, Aries was supposed to control the head, Leo the heart, Virgo the stomach, Aquarius the lower legs and Pisces the feet. Elements of this original ascription of signs to parts of the body remain today.

The astrological concept of influences finds its counterpart in modern times in the scientific concept of fields. Science claims that its use of the concept 'field' to describe a situation is fundamentally different from an astrologer's use of the concept 'influence'. At one level there may be surprisingly little difference between the concepts, even though astrologers use intuition and art to recognise influences and scientists use observations and scientific method to recognise fields. When we have looked at different types of cosmic fields, we can then relate this scientifically established information about fields to an area which is normally dismissed as being beyond the sense and scope of science. We will see how such fields can be used to explain – in a strictly limited sense – certain interesting claims which exist for astrological influences.

Johann Kepler introduced the idea of forces, or fields, to explain planetary motion. He introduced two concepts to explain observed movements of the planets around the sun, the first of which he called the *anima motrix*. This was a force, consisting of invisible rays radiating out from the sun, which pushed the planets around in their orbits. These rays, he believed, were restricted very closely to the plane in which most of the planets moved. He reasoned that the number of rays which impinged on a planet, and hence the corresponding force that drove the planet around the sun, would decrease with distance from the sun.

Kepler's second radical new concept was that of magnetism. From ancient times it had been known that the mineral called lodestone could attract iron and substances that contained substantial traces of iron. Not much use was made of this idea until the Chinese invented the diviner's board, a flat wooden board around the edge of which were marked Chinese zodiacal signs. On this board was placed a spoon made of lodestone. The heavy base rested on the board but the curved handle was well clear of the board. The spoon was set spinning and when it came to rest, it always pointed very nearly to the stars near the north pole of the sky. At this time it was believed that the spoon was responding to an (astrologically defined) influence of these stars. From this Chinese tool eventually developed the mariner's compass, which was used by seamen to find direction when they were out of sight of land.

In Elizabethan times great voyages of discovery were made. The experience of seamen on these long voyages led William Gilbert, physician to Elizabeth I, to formulate the notion that the earth was an enormous magnet. Kepler knew of Gilbert's work and he developed the idea, suggesting that the planets and the sun all had magnetic fields. He then reasoned that it was the attractions and repulsions between the poles of magnets within the planets and the sun which forced the planets to move in elliptical orbits rather than circular ones around the sun. This was extraordinarily insightful and creative thinking for the time.

By the time of Isaac Newton it was becoming clear that Kepler had not fully explained the movement of the planets. Newton introduced three laws of general motion, together with his law of gravitation.

Newton's law of gravitation says that every particle in the universe attracts every other particle. The greater the mass of any object, the stronger the force of attraction. But this force of attraction grows weaker the greater the distance between particles. So a massive body like the sun would have a much greater intrinsic force of attraction than, say, a far smaller body like the moon. But the earth can have a greater gravitational pull on, for example, a person standing upon earth than the sun, because although the sun is far more massive, it is also much further away. Newton's theory explained not only planetary movement but also tidal behaviour. He showed that tidal ebb and flow was due to the combined gravitational pull of the sun and moon upon the waters of earth, with the moon playing the more important role.

Later scientists extended Newton's ideas to show that precession of the vernal equinox was due to the gravitational pull of the moon on the equatorial bulge of the earth. It must be stressed that Newton did not consider gravitation to be a field. He thought of it merely as the 'ability' of one body to attract another without any intervening agency. His concept therefore came to be described as 'action at a distance'.

Scientists in Newton's time recognised this lack of a real explanation, and some of them labelled Newton's gravity as an 'occult' force.

As well as magnetic and gravitational fields we also have electric fields. The Greeks knew that if amber rubbed on fur, the amber would 'attract' pieces of straw. This of course is what we call 'static' electricity. The term 'electricity' was coined by William Gilbert. By the beginning of the eighteenth century it was obvious that there were two kinds of static electricity – some substances could be negatively charged and others could be positively charged. Two bodies having the same charges would repel each other, but opposite charges would attract. In modern language we would say that around a charged body or particle there exists an electric field. The real inventor of field theories, and the man who gave us a highly pictorial way of thinking about them, was Michael Faraday. Faraday made many important experimental contributions to our understanding of electricity, magnetism and chemistry, but in theoretical terms his major contribution was his 'lines of force'. He believed that electric lines of force start on positive charges and end on negative charges. He believed in the physical reality of these lines of force, and pictured them as having real physical properties. First, he considered that each line had a tension along its length, rather like an elastic band. Second, a bundle of these lines pointing in the same direction had a pressure at right angles to these lines, so they would tend to bulge outwards. It was the tension along the lengths of these lines, he said, which generated attraction between two oppositely charged particles.

Faraday said that magnetic lines of force had similar properties to electric lines of force, but started on the north poles of magnets and ended on the south poles. So the attraction between the north pole of one magnet and the south pole of another was similarly due to tension along their lengths. All bodies had mass, and gravitational attraction could also be pictured as tension along gravitational lines of force – these began and ended on all masses. But he said that gravitation was always attractive (unlike electricity and magnetism). This was because all particles were sources of gravitational lines of force. Electric lines of force, however, could only *diverge* from positive charges and *converge* on negative charges. Magnetic lines of force could only *begin* on magnetic north poles and *end* on magnetic south pole. Thus an electric or magnetic line of force might be either attractive or repulsive.

Using the concept of 'lines of force', Faraday went on to show that an electric current was the result of a whole series of electric charges in motion. Furthermore, a straight line of electric charges in motion would give rise to concentric magnetic rings of force centred on the line of moving charges.

Today, we still find Faraday's concept of lines of force extremely useful, although they have never been accepted as 'real' by physicists. Astronomers in particular use the notion of lines of force to talk about the universe. Electric, magnetic and gravitational lines of force do not interact directly, but can interact via particles. A stationary charge will not interact with a magnetic field, but a charge in motion becomes an electric current and so has a magnetic field, and as a result it will tend to spiral around magnetic lines of force.

These concepts are not particularly easy to understand, but are useful in understanding how the solar system can affect terrestrial life.

Let us now look at the important role which gravitational and magnetic fields play in the large-scale universe. Our terrestrial environment is linked to, and influenced by, the wider cosmic environment via these fields.

The force of gravitation keeps bodies in the solar system from flying apart into open space. It is as if they are 'tied' by gravitation. The moon thus appears to be tied into orbit around earth, and earth and the other planets appear to be tied to their orbits around the sun. The planets also attract each other by means of gravitation and cause slight mutual changes to their orbits around the sun. This was how two mathematical astronomers calculated the presence of the planet Neptune. They analysed small changes in the orbit of the planet Uranus, and could only explain them by the presence of another, as yet unknown, planet. Neptune was then discovered in 1846.

The force of gravitation also moulds and holds massive objects like planets and stars in their (almost) spherical shapes. Gravitation moulds and holds our sun, which is one of the hundred thousand million or so stars that make up our Milky Way galaxy: this vast system of stars is itself also kept together by the force of gravitation. Gravitation is the major force to consider when calculating the present structure, past evolution and possible origin of the whole universe.

Magnetism in the cosmos

Over the last fifty years it has become increasingly apparent that magnetism plays an important role in the general activity of the universe on a wide variety of levels. We need to look briefly at magnetism because it is relevant to the rest of the book. (For those interested, a fuller explanation can be found in my book *Cosmic Magnetism*.) Let us start by looking at the magnetism of planets.

We know that our earth behaves as if it had an enormous bar magnet at its centre. For the sake of mariners this field has been charted in great detail round the surface of earth and over the oceans. However, only recently, with the coming of the space age, have we mapped the earth's magnetic field high above the surface. One of the early triumphs of the American space programme was the detailed mapping of this field by orbiting earth satellites.

We now know that on the sunward side of earth the field is compressed, but on the other side it is drawn out into a long tail. This field is normally very large, at least fifteen to twenty times the diameter of earth, and on days when the field is disrupted by 'magnetospheric storms' it can be even larger. Trapped within the earth's field (the geomagnetic field) there are two collections of charged particles which are shaped like distorted doughnuts, which are called the Van Allen radiation belts. We also now know that the field is the result of electric currents flowing in the interior of earth. The geomagnetic field has an extraordinarily wide and complex range of fluctuations. One of these is called the 'lunar daily magnetic variation' – it is the result of the moon pulling on parts of the magnetosphere of earth, via the force of gravitation. When we observe this lunar daily magnetic version over a full lunar month, we notice that it has two maxima and two minima per lunar day (i.e. it achieves its strongest effect and its weakest effect twice in each day). This variation has most interesting biological consequences for life on earth.

Evidence that Jupiter has a magnetic field first came from the radio astronomical discovery that the planet was a powerful source of radio waves. These waves are generated by doughnuts of charged particles, similar to the earth's Van Allen radiation belts, spiralling in the very extensive and powerful magnetic field of the planet. The structure of this field was mapped in more detail when we sent space probes to this region of the solar system. We now also know that the following planets have magnetic fields: Mercury, Saturn, Uranus and Neptune. Our moon does not have a large-scale field, but it has substantial magnetic deposits on its surface. Venus definitely does not have a magnetic field, and we are not yet certain about Mars. Distant Pluto has not yet been visited by a space probe so we have no data on magnetic fields in its neighbourhood.

The sun's magnetic field was discovered through the colours of the rainbow. The sun and stars give off light, which can be passed through a prism. The light ray then appears as a band of colours interrupted by dark lines, so it looks something like a rainbow with a 'bar code' imposed on it. This bar code has also been used to show that our sun has a magnetic field. The number of lines in the bar code is increased when the body has a magnetic field.

The sun periodically seems to develop sunspots, which are magnetic storms on the surface of the sun. The bar code technique has been used to show that sunspots usually come in pairs, with a strong magnetic field coming out of one spot and going into the other. We now know that the number of spots increases every eleven years to what is called the 'solar maximum', but the polarity of the spots in the two hemispheres changes from one maximum to the next, so the full cycle has roughly a 22-year period. By studying the geometry of these sunspot groups, it has become clear that as the cycle increases towards the solar maximum, the magnetic field just below the surface must resemble canals parallel to the magnetic equator. We will soon discover that these canals are important.

Near the equatorial plane of the sun the magnetic field is in the form of four sectors. In alternative sectors the field radiates out in gentle spirals, but in two of them they point out from the sun while in the other two they point in towards the sun. These lines of force stretch out right to the outermost edges of the solar system, and they are carried out by the outflowing of the outer atmosphere of the sun called the 'solar wind' (this is composed of very fast-moving fragments of atoms). The field itself is called the 'interplanetary magnetic field'. It is the interaction between the solar wind, the interplanetary magnetic field and the magneto-spheres of the planets that causes them to be compressed on the sunward side and drawn out into long tails on the side facing away from the sun. Some of the particles in the solar wind are trapped in the magnetic field of earth. Many of them spiral, along the magnetic lines of force, down into the atmosphere of earth near the magnetic poles. As they collide with the molecules and atoms in these regions, they give rise to the aurora borealis (northern lights) and the aurora australis (southern lights).

Although the particles are dumped near the poles, the solar wind compresses the whole of the field on the noon side of earth and so the ground level field on this side is stronger than elsewhere. As the earth spins on its axis each meridian of longitude will pass through this strong field region, and it is this increase with time that we call the 'solar daily magnetic variation'. The amplitude of the solar daily magnetic variation varies with the time of year and this is linked with the earth's movement around the sun. The amplitude also varies with the sunspot cycle.

Not all fragments of atoms or subatomic particles which strike the surface of earth have come from the sun. Certain very fast-moving particles dive in from all directions of space – these are the galactic cosmic rays. Most scientists accept that these particles are generated in supernova explosions. But they move far too fast to be captured and held within the gravitational field of our galaxy. How could this be? Another explanation was needed. The particles could, however, be explained if the whole of the *galaxy* had a magnetic field. We now have evidence for the existence of this field, which has come from other techniques.

Light usually vibrates in all directions at right angles to the direction in which the beam of light is moving. We call this 'unpolarised light'. However, some substances are able to polarise light waves so that they vibrate only in one direction. If a transparent sheet of polarising material is placed between a light meter and the source of light, it will cause a slight weakening of the intensity of the light from the source. If a second sheet is placed between the first sheet and the light meter and then rotated, there is a point of orientation between the two sheets at which no light would reach the meter. This happens when axes of polarisation of the two sheets are at right angles to each other.

In the late 1940s astronomers did this with a telescope and discovered that for certain orientations of the filter, the light from distant stars was slightly reduced. This implied that somewhere in space there was another filter. We now know that this second filter is formed by tiny dust grains in space, which have become aligned in specific directions by the large-scale magnetic field of our galaxy.

Later on radio astronomers found that as some of the high-energy particles from supernova explosions spiralled around the lines of force of this field, they generated radio waves. This was my field of research in the 1960s. It was my task to analyse data from optical and radio astronomy observations in order to work out geometrical models of this large-scale field.

In recent years it has been found that certain of the highest-energy galactic cosmic ray particles can cause damage to electronic components of computers in aircraft control systems. At low altitudes our atmosphere offers some protection from these particles, but at very high altitudes the low density of the atmosphere offers much less protection. Here, these particles can cause the failure of certain components and this could affect the safety of the control systems. This is therefore an active field of further research. It is also known that the number of galactic cosmic ray particles reaching earth's surface decreases a few hours or days after a violent event on the sun. This is called the 'Forbush decrease', and is caused by the fact that a violent event, such as a solar flare, injects more particles into the solar wind, which also carries with it a strengthened magnetic field. This strengthened field combines with the earth's own further compressed field to provide a stronger shield against galactic cosmic ray particles.

Unseen rays from the universe
Electromagnetism explains why a changing magnetic field produces an electric current and how a current generates a

magnetic field. A single ray of light consists of a varying electric field and a varying magnetic field, and these two fields are not only at right angles to each other, but are also at right angles to the direction in which they were moving. This is why light is called an electro-magnetic form of radiation. Our eyes can respond to light, and until this century this was our only means of receiving information on the state of the extra-terrestrial universe. But there are other forms of electro-magnetic variation. Some types of this radiation have a wavelength shorter than light and others have wavelengths longer than light. Generally, our eyes can only respond to light waves, but our skin can 'feel' infra-red rays, which have a longer wavelength and are sometimes called heat waves. Much longer wavelengths are called 'radio waves', and these are used to transmit radio and television programmes over long distances. Ultraviolet 'light' has a shorter wavelength than light and it is the component of sunlight that causes sunburn. X-rays are a still shorter form of electro-magnetic radiation which can penetrate human tissue and can be used as a diagnostic tool in medicine.

Astronomers now use all these types of radiation to study the universe, because many celestial objects radiate the full range of these, although not to the same extent. Not all types of radiation emitted from extra-terrestrial bodies can penetrate our atmosphere (for example ultraviolet light and X-rays), and so these have to be studied using special detectors on board orbiting earth satellites. Radio waves can be transmitted through the atmosphere and can be picked up by radio telescopes, which are really highly directional aerials on the surface of earth. The different types of electro-magnetic radiation form another 'channel' by which we are connected to the wider universe. But how do the different channels that we have so far introduced affect life on earth?

Biological clocks in tune with cycles of light
The French astronomer, Jean Jacques d'Ortous de Mairan, made a discovery about the heliotrope plant, which was reported to the French Academy of Science by his friend Marchant:

> M. de Mairan observed that this phenomenon [of turning its leaves and branches in the direction of greatest light intensity] was not restricted to the open air; it is only a little less marked when one

maintains the plant continually enclosed in a dark place – it opens very appreciably during the day, and at evening folds up again for the night ... The sensitive plant senses the sun without being exposed to it in any way, and is reminiscent of that delicate perception by which invalids in their beds can tell the difference between day and night.

There are many examples in the plant world very similar to this one. These experiments seem to indicate that sunlight is the environmental agency for synchronising an internal clock. However, if left in the dark too long, the periodic activities of the various leaves and branches get out of step with each other, which shows that occasional checking against environmental cues is necessary to maintain synchronisation.

Light also seems to play a part in the seasonal migration of birds. Evidence suggested that seasonal variation in day length was the controlling factor for the pre-flight behaviour of birds. The greater yellowleg, which breeds in Canada, migrates to Patagonia in the autumn, and returns to Canada to breed again in the early spring. In spite of this long journey the breeding period is very precise, with eggs hatching between 26 and 29 May each year. It was concluded that increasing day length after 21 December was the only factor precise enough to play such a role of environmental synchroniser.

For a long time we were puzzled over how birds could navigate over the large distances of migratory flights. Besides using the magnetic field of earth, they can also use light. Diurnal migrators naturally use the sun, but there now exists substantial evidence that nocturnal migrators can use the stars.

As the earth spins on its own axis, so the sun will rise towards the east, be high in the south near midday and set in the west at night. How can a bird use such a variable object to find direction? It can do so if it has an internal clock which it combines with its observations of where the sun is at a given time. For about three or four hours on either side of midday, the sun is roughly moving parallel to the southern horizon (in the northern hemisphere) at about 15 degrees per hour. The bird seems to 'know' that in the morning the sun must be towards its left, at midday it must be directly ahead and in the afternoon it must be towards its right. Thus it knows, more or less, the direction in which it must fly with respect to the sun.

Bees can also find their way to and from their hives by using the sun. They, however, do so more indirectly. The light from the sky at the zenith during daytime is slightly polarised at right angles to the direction of the sun. Bees have complex eyes that are able to respond to this polarisation, so indirectly they can use this to find the direction of the sun. During the last war a sky compass was invented which allowed pilots flying near the North Pole (where magnetic compasses were rather sluggish, and hence did not work well) to find direction using polarisation of the sky. Essentially, it was the same method as that used by the bees.

A number of different types of experiments show quite clearly that birds can also use the stars for navigational purposes. On clear nights birds have been noted to generally fly in directions in which they will eventually migrate, whereas on cloudy nights they fly in random directions. When placed in cylindrically shaped cages with radial symmetry, the birds tend to hop in their migratory directions. When placed in such cages under the artificial sky of a planetarium, they do the same thing. This is important evidence which suggests that nocturnally migrating birds can respond to the very low light levels of starlight.

Biological clocks linked to tides

Several marine organisms are known to have biological clocks linked to the tides. Certain species of crab have two biological clocks. One is tied to the solar day and controls the migration of pigments in their shells, the other is tied to the lunar day and controls their general activity cycles. Some turtles have a more complex lunar clock, which is tied not only to the position of the moon in the sky, but also to phases of the moon. These turtles tend to lay their eggs near the top of high tide, when the moon is new or full and the tides will be spring tides.

There are even more complicated versions of biological tidal clocks. One such is the clock controlling the reproductive behaviour of the palolo worm, which lives in the oceans just off some of the Pacific Islands. The main sex cycle of these worms takes place once a year, during the last quarter of the moon in November, which corresponds to spring in the southern Pacific. The main rising is in November, although a smaller one can occur in October. At the main rising the worms swarm onto the beaches at dawn, just as the sun comes up, when it is also high tide.

A still more spectacular example of precision timing of a

lunar-annual rhythm is provided by a deep sea creature, of the biological family Echinoderms, which lives just off the coast of Japan. This creature liberates its sex cells just once a year in October at three o'clock in the afternoon at either the first or last quarter of the moon. In the years following the time of first release, the time of the lunar month at which the sex cells are released changes from one year to the next, but it always alternates between the first and last quarters of the moon. Hence it alternates between first-last-first, getting earlier in October each year, until about the first of the month, when it jumps abruptly to near the end of the month to start the same cycle again. The result is an eighteen year cycle, called the 'saros cycle', and this is caused by small changes in the orbit of the moon around the earth.

Eclipses and life
Eclipses of the sun, when the moon totally obscures the sun's bright disc, are the most spectacular of the visible interactions between these two bodies. For centuries these events have given rise to intense human emotions – those of fear, dread and awe – in many different parts of the world. Even today the next total eclipse to be seen in England on 11 August 1999 at eleven o'clock in the morning (BST) is already raising a lot of intense interest, not only in the parts of Devon and Cornwall (the only places in England where there will be a total eclipse), but many people from other parts of the UK have already booked their holidays, in appropriate areas, to coincide with the event.

Human beings are not the only species which respond to eclipses – some other life forms also react to the reduction in light associated with a total eclipse of the sun.

On 15 May 1836 there was a total eclipse of the sun visible in Chichester. George Newport, an English surgeon, kept two hives of bees, which he studied carefully before, during and after the eclipse. He reported his findings to the Royal Society in an 80-page paper. His findings showed that as the light diminished, the bees returned to their hives, so during totality there were no bees about. As the light returned to normal levels, the bees started to fly once again.

Just 100 years later Syuiti Mori, a Japanese biologist, carried out more detailed investigations on a species of fly, known to be active during the daytime, during the eclipse of 19 June 1936 which was visible in Hokkaido, Japan. He, too, noted that the activities of this species decreased considerably just before and during totality but recovered again as conditions returned to normal. He also made several observations on a variety of other species, and noted that the crowing of roosters, roosting of crows, croaking of tree frogs and swarming of midges all decreased during totality. However, he also spotted some anomalies to the general behaviour. For example, starlings, mynah birds and sandhoppers paid no attention at all to the eclipse.

Anomalies were also noted by another biologist, A. N. Weber, during an eclipse which took place in southern Iraq on 25 June 1952. He saw that most birds, moths and honey bees sought cover, while crickets and cockroaches exhibited normal nocturnal behaviour. However, there were exceptions to this general rule.

Much more research needs to be done to measure all the normal and anomalous behaviour which is displayed by different species during a total eclipse, although the subject of biological clocks in different species provides a basis for understanding some of the behaviour patterns of animals, birds, insects and other forms of life.

Cosmic influences on earth

There are other known cosmic influences on earth, of which meteors are the most numerous. These are normally very small particles – about the size of a grain of sand – that orbit the sun. They only become apparent when they plough into the earth's atmosphere. Since they are moving at between 40 and 50 miles per second, they are heated by friction with atmospheric particles, and most of them burn up in the upper atmosphere. The vapour trail of hot gases which they leave behind can be seen as a brief streak of light across the night sky which is sometimes, erroneously, called a shooting star. Just under one million of these particles penetrate our atmosphere every hour, but so far very little evidence exists that they have any large-scale effects on environmental factors or on terrestrial life.

It is now generally believed that meteors are cometary debris. Comets are lumps of water ice impregnated with gaseous impurities and covered in a dark sooty material. They orbit the sun in highly elliptical orbits, and thus spend most of their time in the far reaches of the solar system. When they do get close to the sun, the heat boils off the outer layers to form an atmosphere called the 'coma'. The solar wind drives this coma into a very long tail, which we can see as a result of reflected sunlight. On each encounter with the sun bits of the comet can break off, as pockets of gas within the nucleus of the comet expand and blow off some of the overlying material. These are the fragments which eventually become meteors.

It is possible for earth to pass through the tail of a comet but since the density of the material in the tail is so low, it is extremely unlikely to have any noticeable effect on earth. However, when it was predicted that earth would pass through the tail of Halley's comet on 18–19 May 1910, some people prepared for the end of the world.

Over the last few decades Professor Fred Hoyle and his close collaborator, Professor Chandra Wickramasinghe, put forward the theory that microscopic forms of life are being formed all the time in the vast spaces between the stars, and that the dust grains in interstellar space, which block out light from the distant parts of our Milky Way, are really viruses. They further claim that some of these life forms came to our earth many millions of years ago and evolved into the present life forms that inhabit our planet. Some of the viruses spawned in interstellar space are still coming to earth on the tails of comets, and in the past they brought epidemics and death on a large scale. This, they argue, gives scientific justification to the idea that comets were the bringers of disaster and death. However, these views have not been generally accepted by the scientific community.

Prediction and uncertainty in modern science
The scientific age has in many ways been typified by taking older concepts, collecting new information, and combining it with improvements in mathematical techniques to produce a new unified theory which incorporates some of the older ideas. This is a very good way in which intellectual knowledge can make real progress. However, there are scientists today who believe that this process has come to an end. Some people believe that we have explored all possible areas of physical knowledge – we can, in principle, explain everything. We already have the intellectual tools we need, and any slowness or failure to give a satisfactory explanation is therefore a result of inadequate practice or simply a (temporary) lack of detailed information.

There are scientists who believe not so much that we already know everything as that we *nearly* have every tool we need – we are not there yet, but with one more theory, or one more profound insight, we will arrive at a stage where we can make scientific statements to explain fully the nature of life, the universe and everything.

To other people (scientists and non-scientists) today, both these approaches sound astonishingly arrogant and strangely naive. In both cases there seems to be an ignorance, or denial, of what human 'knowledge' really is.

In its history of exploring the cosmos, science has largely been a process of constructing models to predict the outcome of experiments. For example, we have learnt how to predict eclipses accurately, and we were even able to predict the existence of the planet Neptune before it was actually observed. Chemists can design new compounds and accurately predict their effects. But in other areas the success rate has not been so high. Although weather forecasting has improved considerably, we are still a long way from a 100% success rate. It is even harder to predict earthquakes. In biology the study of genetics is well developed and highly mathematical, yet predictability is not as accurate as in the physical sciences.

Professor Aaboe claimed that the Babylonians gave science its principal goal: 'to give a mathematical model of a particular class of natural phenomena capable of yielding numerical predictions that can be tested against observations.'

The quest for predictability has been, and still is, one of the basic aims of scientific method. However, the twentieth century has seen a new discovery in the most fundamental aspects of the physical sciences. This discovery is that there are limitations to what we can know in certain circumstances. It is also becoming evident that there is an apparent conflict between two of the basic theories of modern theoretical physics. Those who believe that certainty is just around the corner have not learnt the lessons of history. A similar euphoric situation existed at the end of the last century.

Let me give an example of how pride can go before a fall. At the end of the last century certain eminent scientists believed that the most important laws of physics had been discovered and that the twentieth century would merely see a tidying up of loose ends. One such scientist was William Thomson (later Lord Kelvin). He believed that there were just two major problems left to solve in physics.

The first involved calculating the range of colours emitted by bodies at different temperatures. It is well known that when a metal bar is just below melting point, it has a bluish white colour, at lower temperatures it is yellowish and at still lower temperature it is reddish. This principle can be used to find the temperatures of the stars. To be able to calculate the relationship between colour and temperature was a crucial test of the theory that linked the subjects of light, electricity and magnetism – Maxwell's electro-magnetic theory of light. Unfortunatly, the 'laws of physics', as understood at that time, did not give the right answer.

The second problem concerned the negative result of attempts to measure the speed of earth with respect to the universe. Lord Kelvin predicted that a successful solution to these problems would be provided in terms of nineteenth-century physics – and he was wrong.

These problems required two completely new approaches to fundamental theoretical physics. A successful solution to the first problem was indeed provided by the German physicist Max Planck. However, in the process of seeking a solution, Planck initiated a totally new approach to physics (which we now call 'quantum theory'). Lord Kelvin's second problem, too, was eventually solved by Albert Einstein. Again, in so doing Einstein had to create the special theory of relativity. The laws of physics are now fundamentally different from those of Kelvin's day. Far from merely having some loose ends to tie up, we are faced with looking at the universe in a completely different way which stretches our mental capacities to the utmost and presents a whole new range of problems.

A shocking discovery of twentieth-century science is that at the very basis of our knowledge there is a fundamental and unavoidable element of uncertainty and unpredictability. It is there, and there is nothing we can do about it. It occurs at two different levels of science.

Quantum mechanics deals mainly with the mechanics of matter at the very smallest level of science, i.e. the subatomic level. In the first three decades of this century, it became unavoidably clear that quantum mechanics involves a basic element of uncertainty, which is now called 'Heisenberg's uncertainty principle'. This principle shows that if we try to make an accurate measurement of one property of a subatomic system, then we have to be content with great uncertainty in our knowledge of another related property of the same system. For example, if we wish to measure the position of an electron accurately, the way we do this is to bounce a certain type of radiation off it. Yet in doing so we alter the motion of the electron. Therefore, we are unable to know its velocity accurately. Let me use an analogy as an example. In order to find the speed of a moving car, the police may point a radar detector at it. This bounces radio waves off the car, and then measures properties of the waves on their return to the detector. However, the radio beam has its own energy and when the beam is returned to the detecting device, this energy will have been changed (if the car is travelling towards the detecting device, the energy will have been increased, but if the car is travelling away from the device, the energy is decreased). This energy will have been taken from the motion of the car, so in principle this means the speed of the car will actually have been changed (slowed) by the operation of the device. In practice this change of speed is so minute that it is far below any measureable limit. So the use of the device is not invalidated by this principle! But for an electron the energy in the radiation beam focused on it is much more equal to that of the electron itself. This means that the effect upon the electron is great. The beam affects the behaviour of the electron and so affects that which we are trying to measure. If we are measuring position, we can get an accurate answer, but estimates of the velocity are inaccurate. If we are measuring velocity, we can get an accurate answer, but the position of the electron is modified and so we cannot know its position accurately. We simply do not have a method of observing the behaviour of an electron which avoids this kind of uncertainty. This has fundamental implications for what we really can or cannot say about matter.

The developers of quantum mechanics, Niels Bohr, Edwin Schrödinger, Maurice Dirac and Werner Heisenberg, were quick to realise that this was an essential part of the subject they had created. But Albert Einstein was very unhappy with this situation. In a letter to Max Born, written in 1926, Einstein said: 'At any rate, I am convinced the He [God] does not play dice.'

Jacob Bronowski, the mathematician and scientist who wrote *The Ascent of Man*, acknowledges the limitations of fundamental science in the quote at the start of chapter 8. He also said:

But what physics has now done is to show that that is the only method of knowledge. There is no absolute knowledge. And those who claim it, whether they are scientists or religious dogmatists, open the door to tragedy. All information is imperfect. We have to treat it with humility. That is the human condition; and that is what quantum physics says. I mean that literally.

Uncertainty in quantum mechanics has been around for 70 years, but in recent decades the appreciation of a new kind of uncertainy has been emerging. This has led to a new branch of mathematical physics called 'chaos theory'. In essence this says that the belief, inherent in many applications of Newtonian mechanics, that cause is directly related to effect, is in fact wrong. In most cases in the real world, the relationship between cause and effect is not a simple and direct one. This means that there are limits on how far into the future we can predict the outcome of a given set of present circumstances and past events. The mathematician Sir James Lighthill drew attention to this kind of unpredictability at a Royal Society meeting and introduced the concept of a 'predictability horizon':

> Systems [which are] subject to the laws of Newtonian dynamics include a substantial proportion of systems that are chaotic; and . . . for these latter systems, there is no predictability beyond a finite predictability horizon. We are able to come to this conclusion without ever having to mention quantum mechanics or Heisenberg's uncertainty principle.
>
> A fundamental uncertainty about the future is there, indeed, even on the supposedly solid basis of the good old laws of motion of Newton, which effectively are the laws of motion satisfied by all macroscopic systems.

This kind of uncertainty arises because in many systems in the real world the relationship between cause and effect is not always straightforward. The fact that the results of a force can be greater than one would normally expect, means that in certain cases it is only possible to predict the outcome of a given situation over a certain time period, after which the predictions become unreliable. This period of time is the 'predictability horizon'. It varies considerably from one system to another. For example, with weather systems it is only possible to do reliable predictions over a few days, or at most a week or two. Even the very highly stable dynamics of our solar system has a predictability horizon. Using modern computers it is possible to predict eclipses of the sun and moon, as well as conjunctions and other configurations of the planets well into the next millennium. However, after about 100,000,000 years into the future, predictions become unreliable. This is called 'chaos', and it is believed that the cause of chaos is most likely to be resonances between the periods of the innermost planets.

As we have seen, some scientists ignored problems that existed at the end of the last century, and there are scientists at present who want to believe we have almost come to the end of our quest for basic physical laws which will give us all the answers we need. For these people, presently unsolved problems in physics and cosmology present no challenge to an otherwise highly successful structure of thought. Perhaps they should consider the lesson of Lord Kelvin's misplaced confidence. There are two problems which exist at the moment which have profound implications for science. Some thinkers feel these problems will only be solved by some, as yet unexpressed, novel approach to what we call knowledge.

Einstein's theories of relativity tell us that generally nothing can travel faster than the speed of light. In recent decades this concept has been challenged by a new theorem in quantum mechanics, which has been experimentally verified. This theorem is called Bell's theorem, after John Stuart Bell, who first demonstrated it mathematically. Basically it shows that if quantum mechanics is valid, then measurements made on two particles will always be correlated, no matter how far apart they are. This can be demonstrated using two subatomic particles. These particles spin on their own axes rather like toy tops or planets. In the simplest possible system – a two-particle system – the two particles spin in opposite directions. This is usually referred to as 'spin UP' and 'spin DOWN'. Bell's theorem tells us that this situation will apply in all possible circumstances, and regardless of whether the two particles of the system are close together or extremely far apart. So if we measure the spins of these particles when they are separated by a very large distance, one will always be spin UP and one spin DOWN. This is an all-too-brief explanation of a complex theorem, but the implication is that somehow or other the two particles of any system are 'communicating' with each other, and that this communication necessarily occurs instantaneously, which is to say faster than the speed of light. This prediction has been verified on at least two separate occasions. According to physicist Henry Stapp, 'the theorem of this paper [Bell's paper] supports this view of nature by showing that superluminal [faster than light] transfer of information is necessary.'

In his book *Quantum Reality*, another physicist, Nick Herbert, said:

> Religions assure us that we are all bothers and sisters, children of the same deity; biologists say that we are all entwined with all forms of life-forms on this planet ... Now physicists have discovered that the very atoms of our bodies are woven out of a common superluminal fabric.

In *Speakable and Unspeakable in Quantum Mechanics*, John Bell said of his own work:

> For me then this is the real problem with quantum theory: the apparent essential conflict between any sharp formulation and fundamental relativity. This is to say, we have an apparent incompatibilty, at the deepest level, beween the two pillars of contemporary theory ... It may well be that a real synthesis of quantum and relativity theory requires not just technical developments but a radical conceptual renewal.

The second major unsolved problem in modern cosmology, which is concerned with the large-scale structure of the universe, is the principal constituent of the universe. What is the universe really made of? The question arises because our calculations about the universe imply it should have certain mass, or density – yet when we look at what is in it there does not seem to be enough matter. There just is not enough 'stuff' out there to explain our calculations.

Astronomers can use the seemingly slow movement of the stars in galaxies to find total masses of galaxies. These measurements indicate that the sum total of all stars and other detectable material does not account for the total masses of galaxies. If, as most now believe, the universe started with a big bang some ten to twenty thousand million years ago, the density of the universe would have fallen very rapidly. Yet if this is so, how could galaxies form out of such a rapidly decreasing density? What 'pushed' the remaining material together to form clusters of matter out of which the galaxies, and subsequently the stars, were formed? We need a higher density of matter than we do in fact find in galaxies. All indications are that there is a 'hidden' component of matter in the universe. However, it cannot be the normal forms of matter that we know from directly observable or detectable parts of the universe. Normal matter, by definition, either emits or absorbs radiation, but this 'hidden' component of the universe does neither. What could the nature of this component be? We simply do not know, because whatever it is, if it exists, does not fit in any sense with our definitions of matter. Why should we bother about some undetectable aspect of our universe (which has been given the name 'cold dark matter')? Because our calculations about the size of the universe, which are based on our otherwise sound physical principles, suggest that the hidden component comprises 90–95% of the total mass of the universe! In other words, the physical environment of the universe, which scientists have been studying for centuries, accounts for only 5% of something massive – something which is completely unknown and totally undetectable to our investigations. This discovery is so extraordinary that it is almost impossible to take it seriously. Yet it is a rigorously worked-out result, a consequence of precise application of the very laws of physics which we hold dear as the most basic scientific realities.

Faced with such mind-boggling logical consequences at the outer reaches of fundamental physics, it is perhaps not surprising if many scientists turn away from the chaos and the uncertainty, and allow themselves to believe that answers can and will be found within the scientific framework of knowledge that has until recently been so productive.

Paradigms and paradigm shifts

At any given point in history the scientists of the time will make use of the knowledge of their time. This will comprise a particular set of methods, techniques, mathematical formulae and models. Thomas Kuhn was the person to label this 'set' of ideas as being a 'paradigm'. As he pointed out, paradigms represent the security of a certain body of knowledge, or a certain way of looking at things. It is not only scientists who operate within a given paradigm. We all have collections of opinions or sets of values, and these too are found to be within a current paradigm of understanding. What Kuhn showed was that generally the shift from one paradigm to another will be firmly resisted. In science new theories are often hastily rejected by the orthodox practitioners of that discipline. Challenges to the accepted doctrine are frequently ignored for as long as possible. When they can no longer be ignored, the status quo will be protected, usually in terms disparaging to the proposer of the radical new idea. This is not very surprising. Science works by a reductionist approach which excludes information which has not been previously tested and explained in order to preserve the rigour of scientific method. As far as that goes, it is the correct way to do science. However, when new theories eventually break down the old prejudices, even the most reluctant of sceptics come to accept the new evidence. And this forms part of the process which is called a 'paradigm shift'.

The reluctance to accept new evidence is even greater if it comes from another discipline. A good example of this is given by the arguments concerning the age of the earth at the end of the nineteenth century. Physicists and astronomers had calculated that the earth was no more than 100,000,000 years old. However, geologists and biologists (including Darwin) at the turn of the century needed a longer timescale for the evolution of the earth and life on it. They could only explain their findings if the world was really at least 300,000,000 years old. Some scientists agreed that there was a problem, but the physicists, led by Lord Kelvin, were unmoved. The problem was eventually resolved by the discovery that atoms had very dense central nuclei and that the energy locked up in nuclei could be released in the radioactive decay of certain substances in the interiors of planets and in the very hot centres of stars, where heavier elements are built up from lighter ones. We now call this 'nuclear energy'. This branch of science is called 'nuclear physics' and it shows us that stars similar to our own sun, in their present form, have a lifetime of 10,000,000,000 years. Our own sun is halfway through its lifespan. Thus the world was indeed much older than had previously been thought. Darwin and his contemporaries were vindicated, and scientific knowledge in all sorts of areas continued to grow.

The point of this excursion into the history of science is to demonstrate the reluctance of established experts to alter the boundaries of their opinions about scientific knowledge. Evidence did exist for this subatomic type of energy in timescales inherent in the evolution of earth and life on earth. However, this evidence was ignored by most people working in the physical sciences because it was awkward and did not fit the current paradigm. Only when the weight of evidence began to build up in favour of subatomic energy from physics itself, were physicists prepared to consider, and finally accept, the evidence for an older universe. Why was this so?

It is very much to do with the 'currency' of evidence in different branches of science. Just as the currency of one country is not readily accepted in another, so what is seen as acceptable evidence in one scientific discipline is not necessarily accepted as evidence in another. Scientists often think that their own discipline is the 'best' one, and that people in other fields are likely to misunderstand the true nature of science. This is to some extent a valid assumption. Science today is highly complex in every discipline, and there is so much to learn that it is much harder for a scientist to be a generalist. To be expert in, say, genetics generally takes so much time and effort, and uses such specific experimental procedures, that it is not possible to also be expert in a quite different field like fundamental astrophysics. So there is no generally accepted 'scientific currency', and scientists today sometimes find it difficult to talk to people outside their own specific field of expertise. But history shows that conservatism of thinking is a human trait, rather than a specifically scientific one. As Kuhn pointed out, historically it has frequently been the case that radical thinkers are despised and rejected by their peers. Often it is only after the death of the individual that the radical ideas are taken seriously.

These difficulties of incorporating new ideas or new evidence in science are even greater when the challenge comes from outside science. A good example of this is the challenge posed to the scientific paradigm by astrology. The current scientific paradigm accepts that astrology is nonsense without a doubt. It is regarded as so obviously unscientific that the very word invokes notions of objectionable mumbo-jumbo. Therefore, any scientist who wants to be accepted by his colleagues runs an enormous risk in even suggesting the possibility that there might be a truth to be sought in astrology. This explains the hostility that the scientific community has generally shown to the work of Michel Gauquelin. Astrology, because it is not a scientific discipline, has been quite far removed from the paradigm boundaries of science. Therefore, the 'paradigm attitude' of science has been to ignore it. Now, however, Gauquelin and others have suggested ways of testing certain points within the prescribed limits of scientific method. This poses a closer threat, and therefore the paradigm attitude has moved towards denial and disparagement of the idea and the man who suggested the idea. Gauquelin is no longer with us, but times move on and perhaps his evidence will come to be explored and tested properly in scientific terms.

Resisting questions about astrology is an extreme case of resistance to any paradigm shift, but this kind of resistance is also occurring within the physics community itself. In *Physics Today* (September 1990), the Nobel prizewinner, Professor Philip Anderson, drew attention to this problem. Some experimental physicists, working in solid state physics, were encountering difficulties in getting their very puzzling results published in scientific journals. Anderson wrote:

> This example appears to me to reveal a major weakness in our approach as scientists, a collective unwillingness to welcome new or anomalous results ... We don't want to lose sight of the fundamental fact that the most important experimental results are precisely those that do not have a theoretical interpretation.

In an article in *Speculations in Science and Technology* (No. 4, 1989), another scientist, Professor Thomas Gold, a cosmologist and astrophysicist, said:

> Whenever the established ideas are accepted uncritically, but conflicting new evidence is brushed aside and not reported because it does not fit, then that particular science is in deep trouble – and it has happened quite often in the historic past. If we look over the history of science, there are very long periods when the uncritical acceptance of the established ideas was a real hindrance to the pursuit of the new. Our period is not going to be all that different in that respect, I regret to say.

Many scientists, even those well-versed in technical aspects of modern physics, have still not appreciated the seminal lesson of twentieth-century theoretical physics; that is, that a mathematical theory capable of explaining a set of observations or experimental results should not be immediately rejected just because it is contrary to common sense or because it goes beyond what is valid in terms of the logical methods invented by the Greeks and now known as 'classical logic'. In fact, in order to cope with some of the more unusual results of quantum mechanics, quantum logic had to be invented. Einstein's general theory of relativity could not have been formulated in terms of ordinary geometry – known as 'Euclidean geometry' – so Einstein had to use a different form of geometry – called 'non-Euclidean Geometry'.

APPENDIX II
NUMBERING THE UNIVERSE

Number plays a variety of important roles in all branches of science. It is used very simply to quantify measurement; it is used in statistical analysis; and it is used in quantum mechanics to express the essence of our understanding of the behaviour of matter at its most fundamental level.

Measuring time and shape
All cultures need workable calendars. The real problem in the ancient world was to find useful relationships between natural cycles of the day, the lunar month and the solar year. Since these are not simply related to each other by convenient whole numbers, people had to manipulate the basic cycles to end up with a calendar which could predict, fairly precisely, when the cycle of the seasons would repeat. This in many ways laid the foundations of all methods and systems of physical measurement, that is, by representing larger quantities of time, length and mass in terms of smaller, more accessible units. It was necessary to define these smaller units accurately. The natural divisions could not of course be changed in any way, but there is complete freedom of choice to subdivide the large natural units into smaller, humanly defined ones.

Division of the day into twenty-four hours was dictated by the Egyptian way of measuring time in daylight and during the night, but it was to a large extent an arbitrary division which had its basis in astronomy. The Egyptian division of the year into 36 weeks, each one consisting of ten days, was not entirely arbitrary, but followed from their star clock. The later adoption of a seven-day week was a decision dictated partly by astronomy, partly by cosmology and largely by astrology. So longer natural periods of time were given in terms of shorter arbitrary intervals, which were themselves dictated by other factors. This became the standard for constructing systems of measurements.

It is less clear how people went about constructing units of length and mass, but it is apparent that such units did exist long before they were systematised in any formal way. Professor Alexander Thom tried to find the basic unit of length used by the builders of megalithic monuments, such as Stonehenge, by analysing all reasonable length measurements associated with these monuments and then trying to see if they were simple whole-number multiples of some smaller unit. Thom came up with what he called the megalithic 'yard', which is 5.44 feet or 1.66 metres. However, not everyone accepts Thom's work in this respect, and it now turns out that the statistical analysis of data of this type has more pitfalls than was at first realised.

Neugebauer, in *The Exact Science in Antiquity*, tells us that Egyptian theoretical geometry and arithmetic was not as highly developed as that of their neighbours. Even so, they produced the most sensible calendar of the ancient world. And they also managed to build the pyramids, which meant that they must have known about important geometrical principles. It is even possible that they were aware of properties of rectangles, squares, triangles and three-dimensional extensions of these shapes. This is normally considered to be the later discovery of the Greeks, but the Egyptians might even have had a working knowledge of the theorem which is ascribed to Pythagoras, long before he and his school gave us formal proof.

The use of number for measurement is a basic and rudimentary utilisation of numerical concepts. However, there also arose in the ancient world an appreciation of properties of numbers in a more abstract sense, and the realisation that particular properties of special numbers could be used to represent fundamental aspects of the world. Much of this is today dismissed as meaningless numerology, but it was in fact the beginning of theoretical science, in much the same way that astrology acted as a stimulus to mathematical astronomy.

Pythagorean numbers

In *Islamic Cosmological Doctrines* Seyyed Hassein Nasr describes exactly what number meant to the Pythagoreans:

> The Pythagorean numbers, being a qualitative rather than just a quantitative entity, cannot be identified simply with division and multiplicity as can modern numbers. They are not identical with

quantity, that is, their nature is not exhausted by their quantitative aspect alone.

Another scholar who specialised in Pythagorean philosophy was F. Schuon, who explains the idea of number in *Gnosis – Divine Wisdom*:

> This is number in the Pythagorean sense, of which the universal rather than the quantitative import is already to be divined in geometrical figures; the triangle and the square are 'personalities' and not quantities, they are essential and not accidentals . . . Geometrical figures are so many images of unity . . . they denote different principial quantities . . . the triangle is harmony, the square stability; these are 'concentric', not 'serial' numbers.

The Pythagorean concept of number as being the essence of things became part of the idea that the distance of the planets from earth could be related to the diameters of spheres fitted between the corners of the regulars solids, nestling one within the other. This was a Platonic concept that had a great influence on the work of Johannes Kepler. Although this notion led Kepler to his third law of planetary motion, which relates the distances of the planets from the sun to the periods of the orbits around the sun, his work showed that the Platonic concept did not give the right distance of the planets or, what was more, the distance of the planets when around the sun in elliptical orbits.

In 1772 J. D. Titius discovered that there was an approximate relationship between the terms of a numerical sequence and the average distances of some of the planets from the sun. This approximate relationship was popularised by J. E. Bode, thus it is also called the Titius–Bode law or Bode's law. The sequence is generated in the following way.

The first term is 0.
The next term is 3.
Thereafter, each term is double the term before, thus:
0, 3, 6, 12, 24, 48, 96, 192, 384.
Moreover, if 4 is added to each term and then the terms are divided by 10, we end up with the following sequence:
0.4, 0.7, 1, 1.6, 2.8, 5.2, 10, 19.6, 38.8.

Compare these figures with actual distances of planets from the sun:

Planet	Term	Distance
Mercury	0.40	0.39
Venus	0.70	0.72
Earth	1.00	1.00
Mars	1.60	1.52
Asteroids	2.80	—
Jupiter	5.20	5.20
Saturn	10.00	9.54
Uranus	19.60	19.18
Neptune	38.80	30.10

TABLE 2: THE TITIUS–BODE LAW

We can see that the law works reasonably well for most of the planets, with the exception of Neptune. It now appears that there is no scientific basis for this law and the correlation is purely coincidental.

Whole numbers in subatomic physics

The twentieth century was to see a twist in the fundamental structure of matter and the nature of whole numbers. We know that hot objects emit colours related to their temperatures. Relatively cool objects give off a reddish colour, warmer objects have a yellow colour and very hot objects have a bluish white colour. Max Planck came to the conclusion that radiation could not come in amounts, but that it came in the form of lumps (quanta), but the minimum size of the lump depended on the colour of the radiation. These lumps are now called 'photons' and they represent a 'quantum' of energy. When a photon strikes the surface of specific metals in a vacuum, an electron (a subatomic particle) can be emitted. This is called the 'photo-electric effect', and until Albert Einstein put his mind to the problem, no explanation for it could be given, at least in terms of physics of the nineteenth century. Einstein applied the concept of quanta of energy, or photons, to the problem to explain the photo-electric effect. From this came the quantum theory of radiation, and the start of a whole new approach to subatomic physics. Essentially this new subject was to show that certain physical quantities, including energy, could only come in whole-number multiples of one or two fundamental constants. Other scientists were to apply the concept of 'quantum numbers' to the structure of the atom itself.

Until 1911, no one understood the structure of the atom, then Ernest Rutherford carried out some experiments at Manchester University which established the basic idea of what was to become known as the Rutherford–Bohr atom. An analogy can be used to describe this in simple terms. Think of the atom as a miniature solar system. Most of the mass of the atom is concentrated in its nucleus, just as most of the mass of the solar system is concentrated in the sun. Electrons orbit the central nucleus in a similar fashion to the way in which planets orbit the sun. However, this analogy was too simple to be taken very far. Scientists knew that electrons in an atom were moving very fast, and that fast-moving charged particles give off radiation. According to the then known principles, the radiation should have caused the electrons to spiral into the central nucleus. But they did not do this – why?

The problem was solved by Niels Bohr, a Danish physicist who went to work with Rutherford in Manchester. He applied the radical new ideas of quantum theory to this simple and basic model of the atom. He suggested that electrons would not give off radiation and therefore would not spiral into the nucleus if they were in a stable orbit. But since they were observed to be giving off radiation, this could happen when they moved from a bigger orbit to a smaller one. Bohr also stated that the stable orbits must have certain radii which related to a sequence generated by whole numbers – the principal quantum numbers.

The great significance of Bohr's work was that he realised that the 'laws' of physics as understood in the nineteenth century did not necessarily apply at the extremely small scale of the atom. This was as true of Newton's laws of gravity and motion as it was of laws governing electricity, magnetism and light. This was an enormous challenge to orthodox science and many scientists had great difficulty in accepting Bohr's radical conclusions.

Bohr's new approach took into account the work of another great German physicist who had proposed that radiation could only be emitted in certain minimum 'packets' (or quanta) of energy, but the size of the minimum packet depended on the wavelength of the radiation being emitted. Bohr first applied his theory to the hydrogen atom, and showed that the stable orbits in this atom were given by squares of whole numbers multiplied by a constant that involved some of the basic numerical constants of physics. This result is shown in the table below, where the radii of the first five orbits are given in units of the above-mentioned constant.

Number	1	2	3	4	5
Size of Orbit	1	4	9	16	25

TABLE 3: STABLE BOHR ORBITS IN THE HYDROGEN ATOM

Thus we end up with something akin to Bode's law for the solar system, but unlike this law, 'Bohr's law' for the hydrogen atom does have a scientific explanation in terms of quantum physics.

Atomic structure has another link with the work of Pythagoras, who showed that there was a restriction on the number of ways in which a string fixed at two ends could vibrate. The first mode had just one maximum of vibrational movement in the middle, the second had two maxima, the third had three, the fourth four and so on. A full wavelength consists of two such maxima and one can say that all the allowed modes must have a whole number of *half wavelengths* just fitting into the total length of the string. The French physicist, Louis de Broglie, was to further clarify the stability of the Bohr orbits using a modified form of the vibrating strings concept.

De Broglie reasoned that if vibrations of radiation (such as light and radio waves) could only come in lumps or quanta of energy, which gave them some of the properties of particles, then particles could have some of the attributes of waves. The 'wavelength' of an electron is related to its energy and the stable Bohr orbits are those into which one can fit a whole number of half wavelengths along the circumference of an orbit. This was eventually developed by other great physicists, such as Edwin Schrödinger, Werner Heisenberg and Paul Dirac into the vast edifice of modern theoretical physics that we now call 'quantum mechanics'.

There is an amazing variety and diversity at all levels in the universe. On the largest cosmic scale there are many different types of galaxies, and many of these consist of thousands of millions of stars that can be grouped into several different classes and types of star. There are now clear indications that some of the stars in our own Milky Way galaxy are like our sun – i.e. they support planetary systems similar to our own solar system. On the surface of earth there exists a wide variety of substances made up of many different chemicals. In the biological world we have a large variety of different living organisms. However, this vast diversity is built up from a much smaller range of basic chemicals, which is called the 'elements'.

There are more than 90 naturally occurring chemical elements, and if we add those which are artificially produced for short periods in special laboratories, then there are just about 100 elements in all. All these elements are made up of just three different types of particles, called electrons, protons and neutrons. The protons and neutrons are almost 2000 times more massive than the electron. The proton has a positive charge, while the electron has a negative charge (of equal magnitude), and the neutron has no charge at all. Protons and neutrons reside in the nucleus of atoms, whereas electrons orbit the nucleus. In an ordinary atom there is no overall electric charge because the number of electrons orbiting the nucleus is equal to the number of protons in the nucleus. This number is called the 'atomic number of the atom' and it is this number which characterises any particular element, because it is the number of electrons orbiting the nucleus that determines the chemical properties of an element. In other words, the ability of the atoms of an element to interact with atoms of any other element is entirely determined by the number of electrons orbiting its nucleus. It was largely Rutherford's work which gave us this picture of atomic structure.

Geometry and the shape of the universe
The two-dimensional geometry we learn at school is based on the work of Pythagoras and Euclid. Euclid had considerably extended the work of Pythagoras, and others were to extend this to three dimensions, so all geometry to which we can apply Euclid's theorems and the theorem of Pythagoras is called 'Euclidean geometry'. This lasted for centuries, but eventually René Déscartes changed everything in the seventeenth century. This French philosopher and mathematician invented a new approach to geometry called 'coordinate' or 'Cartesian geometry'.

Essentially this consisted of applying algebraic methods to geometry. In three dimensions this consists of giving each point in space three numbers, or coordinates, which uniquely specify the position of any point. Algebraic methods can thus be used to solve problems in geometry, and geometry can be used to visualise purely algebraic problems. This approach was to transform mathematical astronomy and physics. The orbit of a planet or the motion of a particle could be described in terms of an algebraic expression linking together sequential positions of the orbit or path. In a very real sense the work of Déscartes laid the foundations of the work on calculus which was to follow with Newton and others.

Since this geometry still makes use of straight lines and Pythagoras' theorem can still be used to find the distances between any pair of points in space, it is classed as 'Euclidean geometry'. For over two hundred years the Euclidean space together with the Cartesian coordinate system was the arena in which planets, satellites and particles would move, and they could interact via the various fields of influence that could exist within this space. However, space itself did not partake in the movements or in the interactions of the particles, any more than the backdrop in a theatre partakes in the acting taking place on the stage. Einstein's work on the general theory of relativity was to change all that in a decisive way.

In order to discuss the movement of a particle it is necessary to specify its position in space at a consecutive set of moments in time. It was realised that instead of describing particles' positions in space at a sequence of times, it was better to use a four-dimensional space, consisting of three spatial dimensions and one dimension of time. This four-dimensional version of space is called 'space–time', and this idea was of central importance to the development of general relativity.

Einstein's general theory of relativity shows that the shape of this space–time is determined by the distribution of matter. Close to massive bodies like the sun, the shape of space–time is distorted from its 'flat' Euclidean form. In such a region of space–time, a straight line is no longer the shortest distance between points. Gravitation is no longer described as a force, and the orbit of a planet is recognised as the natural path of an object in curved space–time. Normally, in space which is very nearly empty and far from massive bodies, light will travel in straight lines. But a ray of light passing close to the surface of the sun will be bent by the curved space–time in this region. This means that stars that are actually behind the sun could be seen because the rays of light just grazing its surface would be bent towards the earth. So an experiment could be done to check Einstein's theory. At the time of a total eclipse of the sun on earth, the moon would blot out the sun. If photographs were taken in the vicinity of the sun, those stars that should really be behind the sun ought to be visible near the sun's edge. During the eclipse of 1919 this prediction of Einstein's theory of general relativity was tested and the measurements were in keeping with his predictions.

Mathematics and number

The study of the nature and properties of numbers is one of the most difficult areas of mathematics. This branch of the subject was also initiated by the Pythagoreans. They introduced the concept of formal and logical proofs for theorems of mathematics. The Egyptians, and perhaps the Babylonians, were probably aware of ratios of the sides of particular right-angled triangles, such as the one with sides in the ratio 3:4:5, which is considered a Pythagorean concept. But what the Pythagoreans did was to generalise this finding, and prove that this would be the case for any right-angled triangle. They produced the first formal proof of this theorem, which now bears the name of Pythagoras. Thus they made a general contribution to mathematical methodology which forever altered the nature of mathematical research.

Mathematics and logic are the only two subjects where it is possible to prove conclusively the consequences of a set of assumptions. (In all other areas we tend to avoid words like 'proof'). A proof in mathematics or logic means that, provided a given number of statements are true, it will necessarily follow that certain consequences of these statements are also true. A proof is the formal demonstration that the second set of statements is a consequence of the validity of the first set of statements. This is very different from the situation in science. It is impossible in science to establish conclusive and absolute proof for a given theory. All that can ever be said in science is that a given set of observational data is consistent with the predictions of a theory. The knowledge or discovery of even one set of data which contradicts the theory is sufficient grounds for distrusting the very foundations of the theory.

The continuing influence of Pythagorean concepts in mathematics has been demonstrated very recently. De Fermat's last theorem is in essence a generalisation of the theorem of Pythagoras. De Fermat stated his last theorem in the margin of a book, adding that 'I have discovered a truly marvellous proof, which this margin is too narrow to contain.'

For over three and a half centuries mathematicians have been trying to prove this theorem. In 1995 Andrew Wiles, an English mathematician working at Princeton University, provided a formal mathematical proof, in grand Pythagorean style. The full story can be found in *Fermat's Last Theorem* by Simon Singh.

Pythagoras' theorem states that if we square (multiply by itself) each of the shorter sides of a right-angle triangle and add the results together, then this will be equal to the square of the longer side. This can be illustrated by using the 3, 4, 5 triangle: $(3 \times 3) + (4 \times 4) = 5 \times 5$ or $9 + 16 = 25$. Fermat's last theorem tells us that this cannot be done with whole numbers, if one is using the cubes of the sides. For example, for the following expression: $(3 \times 3 \times 3) + (4 \times 4 \times 4) = z \times z \times z$, z cannot be a whole number whatever numbers are used on the left-hand side. In fact the theorem says that it is impossible to solve this type of equation in whole numbers by multiplying the individual numbers by themselves more than twice. In other words, this type of expression can only be solved in whole numbers for Pythagoras' original version.

The 'square' aspect and right angles

We have seen that violent events on the sun correlate with certain planetary alignments as seen from the sun, including conjunctions, opposition and squares. We also saw that astrologers have, for centuries, claimed that such alignments, as seen from earth, increased cosmic influences of the sun, moon and planets on terrestrial events. We further saw that if any two of the planets Mars, Jupiter and Saturn were in conjunction with each other, and in opposition to the sun, then earth and the two planets in question would be in conjunction as seen from the sun. This means that, in certain cases, the circumstances that give rise to violent events on the sun are also those considered important by astrologers. It is difficult to see why ancient astrological teachings should have considered squares to be important, especially since when the sun and moon are square as seen from earth, we have weaker tides than normal. In most cases of the five naked-eye planets, squares, as seen from the sun, would not be the same as squares as seen from earth. However, there is evidence that heliocentric squares do give rise to violent solar events that have terrestrial consequences.

Let us consider a particular alignment of sun, earth, Jupiter and Saturn. If earth and Jupiter are in conjunction as seen from the sun, but Saturn is square to these two, then the terrestrial point of view will be as follows: Jupiter and the sun would be in opposition and the angle between Jupiter and Saturn would be 96 degrees, not 90 degrees. I think it is possible that, because the Greeks were so committed to the special properties of right-angled triangles, they incorporated the square aspect into their astrology. But because they were somehow aware that it was the 96-degree configuration that gave the stronger influence, they introduced the idea of 'orb', orb being the 'tolerance' allowed for a given aspect to still retain its effect.

Cosmology, large numbers and numerical coincidences

An interest in very large numbers and numerical coincidences was another topic from arithmetic which intrigued ancient astronomers, and it is a topic that still concerns some eminent modern scientists with an interest in cosmology. Joseph Campbell mentions numbers connected with the Great Year in *Occiental Mythology*. Here, he points out that Saint Patrick was supposed to have come to Ireland in AD 432, but cautions that this date is suspect, because it might have been 'chosen' to create a link with the Platonic Great Year, since 432×60 (the basis of the Babylonian number system) gives us 25,920, which is very close to the Great Year. Campbell continues:

> I have remarked that in Genesis, between the creation of Adam and the time of Noah's deluge, there are ten Patriarchs and a span of 1656 years. But in 1656 years there are 86 400 seven day (i.e., Hellenistic–Hebrew) weeks . . . And, finally, 86 400 divided by 2 gives 43 200: all of which points to a long-standing relationship of the number 432 to the idea of the renewal of the eon; and such a renewal, from the pagan to the Christian eon is exactly what the date of Patrick's arrival in Ireland represents.

Should we take these interesting numerical coincidences seriously? My own feeling is that, unless there is good experimental evidence or a well-tried theory to support or underpin these coincidences between numbers from different sources, they should always be treated with great caution. However, it is worth pointing out that in almost every age we find individuals who are fascinated by such problems connected with numbers.

Sir Arthur Stanley Eddington (1882–1944) was not only an outstanding astrophysicist, he was also a great populariser of science. His work on the internal constitution of stars set the standard for further research on stellar structure, and he did much to introduce Einstein's general theory of relativity to the British scientific community. In fact Eddington was in charge of one of the expeditions that tested the theory on the occasion of the total eclipse of 1919. However, in later life he formulated his own fundamental theory, which tried to link theories of relativity with quantum theory. He tried to calculate fundamental constants of physics which were just pure numbers, on purely mathematical grounds, without using observational data. This aspect of his work is no longer taken very seriously, and even at the time, few scientists felt it had any real merit.

Paul Adrien Maurice Dirac (1902–1984) was another outstanding British physicist who was interested in cosmological consequences of large numbers. He won the Nobel prize for Physics for successfully formulating relativistic quantum mechanics, by blending the special theory of relativity with quantum theory. One consequence of this theory was that the electron should have an antiparticle equivalent, which should have a positive electric charge rather than a negative charge. This particle was discovered a short while later and it is now called the 'positron'. Dirac noted that the number representing the ratio of the electrical to gravitational forces between the electron and proton was a very large one – 10 with 39 further noughts. He further noted that this was the age of the universe expressed in atomic units of time. He reasoned that if there were a meaningful relationship between the two quantities, there must be some relationship between the age of the universe and the gravitational constant. He tried to construct a cosmology in which the gravitational force decreases with the age of the universe. The theory never had a wide following and seems, at the moment, to be in conflict with observational data.

SELECT BIBLIOGRAPHY

The following books have been mentioned in the text and may be of particular interest.

Introduction
Cupitt, Don, *The Sea of Faith*, BBC Publications, 1984
Hughes, David, *The Star of Bethlehem Mystery*, Dent, 1979
Strachan, Gordon, *Christ and the Cosmos*, Baborum, 1985

Chapter 1: Lights in the Heavens
Seymour, Percy, *Astrology: The Evidence of Science*, Penguin, 1990

Chapter 2: The Abode of the Gods
Bauval, R. and Gilbert, A., *The Orion Mystery*, Mandarin, 1995
Campbell, Joseph, *The Masks of God*, Penguin, 1985
Hogben, L., *Science for the Citizen*, Allen and Unwin, 1942
Pannekoek, A., *A History of Astronomy*, Interscience, 1961
de Santillana, G. and von Dechend, H., *Hamlet's Mill*, David R. Godine, 1961
Sellers, Jane B., *The Death of Gods in Ancient Egypt*, Penguin, 1992

Chapter 3: The Celestial Mirror
Hughes, David, *The Star of Bethlehem Mystery*, Dent, 1979
North, J. D., *Horoscopes and History*, Warburg Institute, 1986
Schonfield, Hugh, *The Passover Plot*, Element, 1993
Seymour, Percy, *Astrology: The Evidence of Science*, Penguin, 1992
Tester, Jim, *A History of Western Astrology*, Boydell, 1990
Thorndike, L., *History of Magic and Experimental Science*, Macmillan, 1934

Chapter 4: Signs in the Sky

Addey, John, *Selected Writings*, American Federation of Astrologers, 1976

Gilbert, Adrian, *Magi – The Quest for a Secret Tradition*, Bloomsbury, 1997

Jung, Carl, *Aion, Collected Works*, part 2, vol. 9, Routledge and Kegan Paul, 1981

Martin, E. L., *The Star that Astonished the World*, ASK Publications, 1991

d'Occhieppo, K. F., *Der Stern von Bethlehem*, Franckh-Kosmos, 1991

Seymour, Percy, *The Scientific Basis of Astrology*, Foulsham, 1997

Chapter 5: How the Magi Found Jesus

Addey, John, *Selected Writings*, American Federation of Astrologers, 1976

von Beckerath, Erich, *Secret Messages in Pictures*, Belcsak, Iberaverlag, 1987

Sandauer, Hans, *History Controlled by the Stars*, Prisma/VVA, 1979

Smith, Morton, *Jesus the Magician*, Aquarius, 1975

Chapter 6: Cosmic Biology

Baker, R., *Human Navigation and the Sixth Sense*, Hodder and Stoughton, 1981

Baker, R., *Human Navigation and Magneto-reception*, Manchester University Press, 1989

Ertel, S. and Irving, K., *The Tenacious Mars Effect*, Urania Trust, 1996

Gauquelin, Michel, *Cosmic Influences on Human Behaviour*, Futura, 1976

Gauquelin, Michel, *The Truth About Astrology*, Hutchinson, 1984

Roberts, Peter, *The Message of Astrology*, Aquarian Press, 1990

Seymour, Percy, *Cosmic Magnetism*, Adam Hilger, 1986

Wiltschko, R. and W., *Magnetic Orientation in Animals*, Springer, 1995

Chapter 7: Written in the Stars?

Seymour, Percy, *Astrology: The Evidence of Science*, Penguin, 1990

Seymour, Percy, *The Scientific Basis of Astrology*, Foulsham, 1997

Seymour, Percy, *Cosmic Magnetism*, Adam Hilger, 1986

Seymour, Percy, *A Causal Mechanism for Gauquelin's Planetary Heredity Effect*, ISBN 0 9508616 1 8

Chapter 8: The Legacy of the Magi: A Conclusion

Bronowski, Jacob, *The Ascent of Man*, Futura, 1987

Herbert, N., *Quantum Reality*, Rider, 1985

Kuhn, T. S., *The Copernican Revolution*, Harvard, 1979

Singh, Simon, *Fermat's Last Theorem*, Fourth Estate, 1997

Appendix I: Cosmic Influences

Seymour, Percy, *Cosmic Magnetism*, Adam Hilger, 1986

Seymour, Percy, *Astrology: The Evidence of Science*, Penguin 1990

Seymour, Percy, *The Paranormal: Beyond Sensory Science*, Penguin, 1992

Appendix II: Numbering the Universe

Nasr, S. H., *Islamic Cosmological Doctrines*, Thames and Hudson, 1978

Neugebauer, O., *The Exact Sciences in Antiquity*, Harper, 1962

Seymour, Percy, *The Paranormal: Beyond Sensory Science*, Penguin, 1992

Singh, Simon, *Fermat's Last Theorem*, Fourth Estate, 1997

INDEX